T0096640

View and Meditation
Essential Teachings
by some of the Shamarpas

View and Meditation

Essential Teachings
by some of the Shamarpas

translated, annotated and introduced
by Tina Draszczyk

with a preface by Gyalwa Karmapa
Trinley Thaye Dorje

RABSEL
PUBLICATIONS

RABSEL PUBLICATIONS
16, rue de Babylone
76430 La Remuée, France
www.rabsel.com
contact@rabsel.com

© Rabsel Publications, La Remuée, France, 2021
ISBN 978-2-36017-031-9

Note: For the sake of simplicity, in most cases where I thought that it would be easier to retain terms in either Tibetan or Sanskrit, the Sanskrit terms have been used (for example, Sanskrit *dharmakāya* instead of Tibetan *chos sku*). Unlike the Sanskrit transliteration, the exact transliteration of the Tibetan is difficult to read for all those who are not familiar with the Wylie transliteration system. For this reason, within the text a simple phonetic version of the Tibetan words and names is used, while in the notes the precise transliteration is provided. Because Sanskrit and Tibetan terms appear frequently throughout this book, they are rendered in italics only when emphasized or defined. In the translations, square brackets indicate insertions that are intended to facilitate an understanding of the text, parentheses are used for the insertion of technical terms in Sanskrit and/or Tibetan, and braces are used in part 6 for interlinear notes contained in the original Tibetan. Titles of books are always italicized regardless whether this concerns original Sanskrit or Tibetan titles, the translation of these titles into English or publications in English. The notes were compiled by the translator. All dates are in the Common Era unless otherwise stated.

Table of Contents

Preface by Gyalwa Karmapa Trinley Thaye Dorje

The teachings called *Concept Dharmakāya* by the great Gampopa (1079-1153) are a unique guide to realising Buddhahood, which, for Buddhists, is the goal.

The precious commentaries on this subject of *Concept Dharmakāya* by the late Mipham Chokyi Lodro, His Holiness the 14th Künzig Shamar Rinpoche (1952-2014), and Chodrag Yeshe, the 4th Shamarpa (1453-1524), serve as a guide for those who wish to journey with certainty. The same goes for the other instructions by the 2nd, 4th, and 14th Shamarpas contained in this collection of treasures, on the vast and profound topics of Mahamudra and meditation.

The Buddhist measure of authenticity is based on both scripture and logic. Within these writings, both scriptural sources and logical reasonings are present. The essence of the journey toward awakening is compassionately and skilfully presented in the most precise and concentrated manner for our learning, contemplation and meditation. This is Their Holinesses the Shamarpas' presence through their living words.

May we be able to cherish these teachings with undivided devotion.

In this day and age, the tendency to follow new trends constantly takes a heavy toll on us. We are always on the lookout for possible futures. While there is nothing intrinsically wrong with that, this habit continuously wastes the invaluable quality of being in the present.

In the context of cherishing teachings such as those that are presented here, or in other words, timeless wisdom, I cannot stress enough that the so-called old-school ways have apt means to be in the present, to develop undivided devotion.

In other words, the classical means and methods of any culture had a certain excellence in which there was a lack of choices. Not that this was always a good thing, but at least it presented less distraction.

Nowadays, there are seemingly limitless choices. Information of immense proportions is available and on top of that, all of this information is labelled with advertisements of the 'ideal' life.

Therefore, ironically, the abundance of choices often hinders us from making use of the little time that we have, or from investing time at all. We feel that we need to do this and that. We feel rushed all of the time.

The olden days were somehow lacking in freedom, I suppose – the freedom of expression in various ways. However, even if we are presented with an option, we often do not know what to do with it. Of course, we could reflect later and say we didn't even have a chance to choose. But dwelling on missed chances of what could have been or should have been is more for amusement when we have enough time to spare.

Not that we have to go back in time, but if we could at least understand that a lack of choices is not equivalent to restriction and suffocation, then we could find the means to dedicate ourselves to what we truly yearn for.

A real change. Not the kind of change where we feel the constant pressure of making ends of peer and social expectations meet.

But a change where the alive and vibrant freshness of the present is allowed to take its place. When that change is not allowed, we become worried and anxious. We feel that we need to make a choice between 'to be' or 'not to be'. 'To be conceptual' or 'not to be conceptual'. Anxiety arises.

Not that allowing changes truly changes the present. The present is not 'to be' or 'not to be'. The present is not bound by choices or the opposite of choices. It just flows.

Like water: If cupped it abides. If boiled it steams. If gravitated it pools. If cold it solidifies. If hot it evaporates. If blown upon it waves. If allowed it flows.

The present doesn't make choices. It simply complements the conditions. When experienced through the human mindset, it 'conceptualises', or rather, 'he' or 'she' conceptualises.

Being and not being go together interdependently, without offending each other.

Form and emptiness go together interdependently, without offending each other.

Anxiety is then cared for and not exiled. Insanity will not overtake sanity and vice-versa.

With humility, I feel that we will be able to devote our time to cherishing the precious wisdom presented in the Shamarpas' works.

Dr. Tina Draszczyk, one of the most fervent devotees of His Holiness the late 14th Shamar Rinpoche, who served him as an interpreter for many years, has carefully compiled these rare commentaries and made them available to all readers and practitioners. It is indeed a pleasure to offer my gratitude to her for translating these writings.

May these perfect words of Their Holinesses the Shamarpas reach our hearts that yearn for timeless wisdom.

The 17th Karmapa Trinley Thaye Dorje

Preface by the translator

The first seed of what eventually unfolded as this compilation was planted, I assume, many years ago when Künzig Shamar Rinpoche showed me the booklet of a text he had written in Tibetan: *The Ornament of Gampopa's Intent. Dispelling Doubts Regarding Concept-Dharmakāya*. It had just been published by Shri Diwakar Publication in India. After Rinpoche passed away in 2014, when I was preparing his book *Boundless Wisdom. A Manual for Mahāmudrā Practice* for publication, I felt that a translation of this pithy treatise on the topic of concept-dharmakāya—the heart of the view cultivated in the Dagpo Kagyü tradition—would complement his most valuable meditation teachings presented in *Boundless Wisdom*, all the more so as he mentions the issue therein in a few short words. As will become clear in the Introduction, in the course of my research I have added a number of other texts relating to this topic. Suffice it to say here that immersing myself in these writings was a great source of joy and inspiration.

At this point I would like to express some words of gratitude. I wish to thank everyone who supported me in preparing this publication. The translations of parts two, three, five, and six were all done with the help of my dear and respected colleague at the University of Vienna, Khenpo Könchog Tenpel. I am extremely grateful for his most professional support. As for part four, the *Sixty Verses on Mahāmudrā*, I prepared a first draft translation in 2012 in collaboration with my colleague Dr. David Higgins whom I would like to thank for his very helpful contribution. In the fall of the same year I had the good fortune to discuss this text with Künzig Shamar Rinpoche himself. This took place in Kalimpong, India, where Rinpoche, despite his busy schedule, patiently took the time to go through these verses with me. I would also like to thank Dr. Timothy Riese, Christoph von Pohl, Jim Baston, Chris Fang, and Paul Catty for their efforts in correcting and improving my English. Without their help I would not have been able to produce these translations in English.

My deepest gratitude, however, goes to Künzig Shamar Rinpoche. I cannot find words to describe his great kindness. His teachings as well as those of two of his predecessors are an expression of their spiritual mastery.

I hope that the translation of these teachings and texts will serve as a helpful inspiration in support of meditation practice. If this publication enables some readers to access the treasury of the Shamarpas' instructions, the translations will have fulfilled their purpose. Of course, with this kind of work errors and misunderstandings may occur. It goes without saying that any such mistakes are solely mine, and I welcome any suggestions and corrections, which could hopefully be worked into a revised future edition. I therefore request everyone who finds errors to kindly contact either the publisher or me directly.

May what is wholesome and virtuous increase.

Introduction by the translator

To facilitate navigation through the different parts of this book, particularly for readers who may not be familiar with this kind of teaching, I would like to provide an introduction to: (1) the reasons for the selection of the texts translated here, (2) their common theme, (3) a short summary of each of the six texts, (4) brief information on the three authors, (5) the term "concept-dharmakāya" (Tib. *namtog chöku*[1]) in the teaching system of Dagpo[2] Kagyü Mahāmudrā, and (6) the context of the spiritual practice of concept-dharmakāya.

(1) The reasons for the selection of the texts translated here

Having completed the translation of *The Ornament of Gampopa's Intent. Dispelling Doubts Regarding Concept-Dharmakāya* (part two) by the 14th Shamarpa (1952–2014), I checked the extant writings of previous Shamarpas to see whether there is any material that would supplement this short text. The first choice fell on *A Treasury of Immaculate Teaching. The Practice-Method of Concept-Dharmakāya* (part three) by the Fourth Shamarpa (1453–1524). As the title indicates, it deals with exactly the same topic as *The Ornament of Gampopa's Intent.*

Next, as concept-dharmakāya concerns the gist of Dagpo Mahāmudrā, the subsequent choice fell on the Fourth Shamarpa's

Sixty Verses on Mahāmudrā (part four) for two reasons. On the one hand, there is a personal reason, in that I had worked on this text with the late Shamarpa who encouraged me to publish my translation at some point in the future. On the other hand, there is a contextual reason, in that these verses place the teachings on concept-dharmakāya in a broader context.

Finally, knowing that the late Shamarpa highly esteemed the writings of the Second Shamarpa (1350–1405), I selected two short texts by this author: *The Point of Meditation, a Summary* (part five) because it is such a direct, encompassing, and poetic instruction on the practice of meditation; and *The Stages of a Meditation Practice of Unity* (part six) because in this text the meditation, which consists in the unity of calm abiding and deep insight, is elucidated in greater detail. The 14th Shamarpa also recommended this treatise, as an opportunity to deepen one's understanding of Buddhist meditation.

The Tibetan texts of these five treatises are provided at the end of the book.

Having finalized the translations of these texts, which are all written in a classical Tibetan style, I thought that it might be helpful to start with a particular teaching given orally by the 14th Shamarpa. His lively and direct manner of conveying the core of the practice of Dagpo Mahāmudrā is like a key instruction that opens the pathway for the rest.

Finally, I would like to mention that the texts in this book are arranged according to when the authors lived in reverse chronological order. They are not arranged with regard to their content.

(2) The common theme of these six texts

The theme common to all of these teachings might best be summarized in a short instruction on view, meditation, and conduct, which the 14th Shamar Rinpoche gave in the Karma Kagyü center in Vienna in 1993:

> (…) The method to free oneself from saṃsāra is to free one's own mind from its delusion. For that purpose, mind must know itself. The mind must come to recognize its true nature

and familiarize itself with it. Then delusion comes to an end. For this to happen, view, meditation, and conduct are to be combined. (…) Mind is emptiness. Understanding this is the *view*. Yet, even if one knows that mind is emptiness, one cannot experience it right away. For that one has to meditate on mind's nature or its mode of abiding. When the right view leads the *meditation*, it will be successful because one is able to recognize and deal with obstacles. In the process of meditation, one will eventually experience mind's mode of abiding. This experience should be continuously sustained, because without stability it will vanish again. Moreover, if one truly understands emptiness, one also knows that appearances and emptiness are inseparable from each other, and that appearances manifest by virtue of emptiness. (…) Therefore, knowing emptiness means that one also understands the principle of cause and effect. The certainty that corresponding effects will always follow the particular causes will bring about great care as to what types of causes one produces. This leads to pure *conduct*. View, meditation, and conduct are thus interrelated and support each other. (…)[3]

Accordingly, and throughout part one to part six, this view, the associated meditation, and conduct as taught in the Dagpo Kagyü tradition is presented here by the 14th, Fourth, and Second Shamarpas. By virtue of the great care taken by masters of the Kagyü tradition in safeguarding these texts, these written words of pre-eminent holders of the Karma Kagyü school[4] are still accessible today. Readers are invited to appreciate this heritage of spiritual instructions, to read these texts carefully and to reflect upon them. Such writings are meant as guidelines and inspiration to support practitioners on the Buddhist path in their endeavor to unite view, meditation, and conduct in order to approach the awakened state.

(3) A short summary of the six texts
Part 1: *Mahāmudrā, a Brief Introduction*

This part consists of an edited transcript of excerpts from public teachings given by the 14th Shamarpa on April 23–24, 1990, in the Kamalashila Institute in Germany, which was founded at his instigation. At the time I had the honor of interpreting his teachings as they were given, and I am very happy to be able to provide an emended version of the translation here. In this teaching, Künzig Shamar Rinpoche first contextualizes Mahāmudrā. He then points out how precious its transmission is and appeals urgently to the responsibility of every practitioner to make sure that he or she truly understands the instructions and applies them without misunderstanding. He also points out how unfortunate it is when these teachings are misused. Künzig Shamar Rinpoche continues summarizing the meaning of "Mahāmudrā, the Practice of the Connate"[5], by delineating mind's genuine mode of abiding, that is, its essential emptiness and its character of knowing or clarity. He introduces the topic of concept-dharmakāya without going into detail and points out that the samsaric or distracted mind "turns into" or appears as the entire range of outer and inner perceptions while the awakened mind abides in its peaceful nature of wisdom and compassion. Finally, Rinpoche emphasizes the need for a proper view in support of meditation and the requirement to gradually develop through the respective processes of practice by way of continuous and stable meditation.

Part 2: *The Ornament of Gampopa's Intent. Dispelling Doubts Regarding Concept-Dharmakāya*[6]
The text itself is preceded by a preface by Karmapa Thaye Dorje and an introduction by Prof. Sempa Dorje, in which the 14th Shamarpa's text is pre-eminently introduced and contextualized. I need add no more than a few words. In his text, written in prose, the Shamarpa explains the topic "concept-dharmakāya" by describing how Gampopa made use of this term to introduce his students to "Mahāmudrā, the Practice of the Connate". After a brief reference to criticism raised against the term concept-dharmakāya by various scholars, the Shamarpa emphasizes that both the term concept-dharmakāya as well as the meaning communicated there-

by fully accord with the prajñāpāramitā teachings of the Buddha, that is, the teachings on the perfection of wisdom. He also quotes a number of sūtras and tantras, which form the background for this view and practice, as well as quoting some Indian Mahāsiddhas and various Tibetan masters. By means of these references, he shows that through this *one practice*, the objective of *all trainings* will be achieved; that is, "by knowing one, all is liberated."

Part 3: *A Treasury of Immaculate Teachings. The Practice-Method of Concept-Dharmakāya*[7]
In this prose text the Fourth Shamarpa also makes a brief reference to criticism leveled against the term concept-dharmakāya. He then proceeds to state that, in addition to followers of other traditions, some proponents within the Kagyü school also misunderstand this term, thinking that concepts are simply identical with the dharmakāya and that therefore buddhas and sentient beings are equal. He clarifies this misinterpretation by pointing out that concepts *by nature* are the dharmakāya, but not their conditioned and conditioning samsaric manifestation. By quoting a number of sūtras and tantras, the Fourth Shamarpa continues to argue that buddha nature imbued with qualities is just another term for the dharmakāya and that therefore even ordinary sentient beings *by nature* are never separate from the qualities of the awakened state. He thus reveals that concept-dharmakāya, and therefore "Mahāmudrā, the Practice of the Connate", is to be understood and practiced on the understanding that mind-itself is fully endowed with buddha qualities and that the practice consists in letting adventitious defilements dissipate so that mind's true nature, i.e. the qualities of wisdom and compassion, can unfold unobstructed.

Part 4: *The Sixty Verses on Mahāmudrā. Illuminating the Kagyüs' Intent, a Short Presentation of Mahāmudrā*[8]
In these verses, the Fourth Shamarpa gives an overview of Dagpo Mahāmudrā. In the first six verses (1–6) he presents his intent and the main points. He then sets out to deal with mistaken views which he considers detrimental for the realization of suchness, and

presents his own view in short (verses 7–13). In the twenty-five verses that follow (14–38), he describes his view of a correct path leading toward the realization of suchness. In that regard, verses 14 through 16 provide a description of the spiritual teacher and the student involved in the process of actualizing reality. In verse 17 he presents the basic structure of the instructions concerning preliminaries, the actual meditation practice, and the subsequent attainment, i.e. how, by virtue of formal meditation and the insight developed thereby, one is able to sustain wisdom and compassion outside of formal meditation. Verses 18 through 22 describe the four conditions that ripen the student so that he or she will be able to continue successfully on this path. Verses 23 through 34 describe the meditative phases—the Mahāmudrā level of śamatha and vipaśyanā—culminating in a yogi's capacity to accommodate whatever arises. Verse 35 describes the subsequent steps, i.e. the practice outside of formal meditation. Verse 36 explains how this meditation can be combined with the tantric practice of power-fulness (*tummo*[9]). Verses 37 and 38 elucidate the final realization of the all-ground, the fruition of Mahāmudrā meditation. In the following nineteen verses (39–57), the author refutes various additional objections to the Dagpo Kagyü exposition and practice of Mahāmudrā. Finally, in verse 58, he sums up the core of Dagpo Mahāmudrā, the so-called connate grounded in the view of the inseparability of saṃsāra and nirvāṇa. Verses 59 and 60 constitute the conclusion, in which he apologizes for any possible mistakes in his exposition and dedicates the merit to the awakening of all sentient beings. As for the literary style, even though the verses are arranged in quatrains, after verse sixteen the subject matter of the quatrains often continues from one to the next.

As this overview shows, *The Sixty Verses on Mahāmudrā* touches on the entire teaching corpus of Dagpo Mahāmudrā in terms of view, meditation, and conduct. Here it becomes especially evident that key instructions on Mahāmudrā, which are often brief and succinct, draw on a tremendously rich background. In the translation, I have endeavored to reflect this by means of detailed notes.

Part 5: *The Point of Meditation, a Summary*[10]

In these inspiring verses, the Second Shamarpa begins by draw-
ing the reader's attention to the preciousness of a human life. He
speaks not just about a human life endowed with the general opportunity for spiritual practice—which in itself is already of immense value—but about a life in which one has gained access to
key instructions that inspire practitioners so deeply that they can
actually succeed in their spiritual practice. He continues with the
topic of the urgency of one's spiritual training because death can
come at any time. On this basis he goes through the different aspects of practice in both sutric and tantric methods and does so in
the context of both the formal meditation sessions and the subsequent attainment, strongly emphasizing the key point of practice,
which is to look at the very essence of one's mind.

Part 6: *The Stages of a Meditation Practice of Unity*[11]

This prose text by the Second Shamarpa is a summary of the *The
Meaning of the Gradual Approach in Meditation* (*Kramaprāveśikabhāvanārtha*[12]), attributed to the Indian master Vimalamitra;[13] it is
an instruction on the unity of calm abiding and deep insight meditation. In his summary, the Second Shamarpa begins by describing
the need to take the bodhisattva vow and engage in the practice
of the pāramitās with a focus on the pāramitā of meditation. He
emphasizes that meditation is to be practiced in a gradual way by
first stabilizing the mind with the method of calm abiding. On this
ground, deep insight is to be integrated by way of first exploring
the workings of mind and its nature and finally by abiding stably
in the insight into its true nature. The Second Shamarpa quotes
a number of sūtras as scriptural references for these instructions
and guides the readers through the various steps of the practice.
As the process of meditation depends greatly on the inner and outer conditions of one's life, he describes all those factors that are
conducive to meditation. And, as progress in practice depends on
the meditator's skills in dealing effectively with experiences and
challenges, he discusses the classical obstacles to the meditative
absorptions and the remedial measures to be taken. All in all, the

emphasis is on how to combine calm abiding and deep insight so that a stable realization of reality can be achieved and sustained.

(4) Short information on the three authors

Künzig Shamarpa, Mipham Chökyi Lodrö (1952–2014),[14] was the fourteenth incarnation of the so-called "Red Hat Karmapas", who together with the "Black Hat Karmapas" are the main holders of the Karma Kagyü transmission. He underwent his training in Buddhist philosophy and meditation under the guidance of the 16th Gyalwa Karmapa, Rangjung Rigpe Dorje (1924–1981),[15] and studied for many years with him as well as with a great number of other teachers of different schools of Tibetan Buddhism. After the Karmapa's demise, Künzig Shamar Rinpoche assumed responsibility for completing a number of projects initiated by the 16th Karmapa. One of these numerous projects was establishing the Karmapa International Buddhist Institute (KIBI) in New Delhi. In 1994 he recognized the 17th Gyalwa Karmapa, Trinley Thaye Dorje (born 1983) and, from then on, supervised his spiritual training. Moreover, Shamar Rinpoche taught all over the world and set up his worldwide network of Bodhi Path centers with the intention of providing opportunities for authentic Buddhist practice free from any form of sectarianism. He also set up a monastery and retreat center in Nepal, established various schools and teaching institutes for Buddhist monks, and founded several non-profit organizations engaged in charitable activities. Along with a number of books in English,[16] most of which have also been translated into other languages, he left behind some publications in Tibetan. He edited, for example, a collection of the most important Mahāmudrā texts by Indian and Tibetan authors,[17] wrote short recitation texts for meditations, including for the practice of Buddha Śākyamuni, for the Foundational Practice of Mahāmudrā, for a Chenresig Yidam Practice, as well as for a Guru Yoga, and authored a number of other short texts.[18]

The Fourth Shamarpa, Chödrag Yeshe Pal Sangpo (1453–1524),[19] received his name from the Seventh Karmapa, Chödrag Gyamtso (1454–1506),[20] and was trained extensively under him and various other teachers such as Jampal Sangpo (15th c.)[21] and Gö Lotsawa (1392–1481).[22] His close connections with the Pagdru rulers led to a situation in which he performed the function of the ruler at the Pagdru court in Central Tibet for a period of eleven years, bearing the title Chen Nga Chökyi Dragpa.[23] During this time he founded the monasteries Lhündrub Chöde and Yangpachen.[24] The Fourth Shamarpa left behind a collection of works on a wide variety of subjects.[25] Among his main students were Pawo Tsuglag Drengwa (1504–1566)[26] and Karma Trinle Chogle Namgyal (1456–1539)[27], who both contributed significantly to upholding the Karma Kagyü lineage.

The Second Shamarpa, Khachö Wangpo (1350–1405),[28] was trained by the Fourth Karmapa, Rölpe Dorje (1340–1383).[29] According to the hagiography written by the Fourth Shamarpa, he extensively studied all fields of Buddhist philosophy and meditative training, on the basis of both the sūtras and the tantras, with teachers from different traditions and spent much time in various hermitages. He is considered an adept whose teachings had a major impact on the Mahāmudrā transmission of the Karma Kagyü school. Of his *Collected Works*, which originally comprised seven volumes and in which a broad range of subjects relating to philosophical and meditative training as transmitted in this tradition are covered, four volumes have come down to us.[30] He passed on the instructions of the Karma Kagyü tradition to the 5th Karmapa, Deshin Shegpa (1384–1415).[31]

(5) The term "concept-dharmakāya" (Tib. namtog chöku) in the teaching system of Dagpo Kagyü Mahāmudrā

As mentioned earlier, the starting point for the compilation of these texts was the treatise written by the 14th Shamarpa on concept-dharmakāya, a key term in the Dagpo Kagyü tradition. In Buddhism, concepts are usually regarded as that which is to be relinquished and—in the Mahāyāna—the dharmakāya as that which is to be achieved. Therefore, the combination of the terms "concept" and "dharmakāya" might at first sight look somewhat contradictory, and this holds true not just for the use of the English terminology. Details of the view and practice which underly this term will become clear in the translated texts. At this point it should therefore be sufficient simply to analyze the term concept-dharmakāya.

In the context of Dagpo Kagyü Mahāmudrā, the first word, *concept* (Sanskrit: *vikalpa*; Tib.: *namtog*;[32] Engl.: also *thought*), designates samsaric states of mind. Thus, the term "concept" signifies the dualistic, conceptual, conditioned and conditioning consciousness; in other words, it denotes all thoughts, emotions, memories and ideas regarding one's self, as well as all perceptions of what seems to be an outer world.[33] According to the Buddhist view that underlies this notion, all concepts are mental representations or images that appear in the dualistic consciousness and are known by it. Whatever the dualistic mind knows is therefore nothing other than inner concepts. These dualistic processes of consciousness are conditioned by deeply rooted habitual tendencies and, in turn, condition the mostly automatic emotional and cognitive reactions. These, in turn, trigger physical, verbal, and mental deeds with their corresponding consequences. As the term "concept" designates inner images or thoughts, one could also render it in English as "representational concepts" or "conceptual thoughts or modes of knowing". It is important to bear in mind that in this view, the perceiving consciousness, i.e. the "subject", and the perceived, i.e. the "object", are considered as not being different from one another, but simply as processes of consciousness manifestating as perceiver and perceived. By this token, both are understood as conditioned and conditioning processes of consciousness occurring in the dualistic mind (Tib.: *sem*[34]) and, being naturally empty, as lacking any substance.

In the context of Dagpo Kagyü Mahāmudrā, the second part of the word, *dharmakāya* stands for the nature of mind, for mind-itself (Tib.: *sem nyi*[35]) being both empty and unobstructed as well as self-aware wisdom. Mind-itself is never affected by all those concepts mentioned above. Mind-itself is therefore comparable to the sky, which as such is neither affected by all the cloud formations—the adventitious processes of consciousness—gathering and dissipating, nor is it essentially different from them: the true nature of the adventitious processes of consciousness is not different from mind-itself.

(6) "Concept-dharmakāya" as a spiritual practice

The goal of this practice: The spiritual practice underlying the term concept-dharmakāya aims at letting go of all clinging to concepts or samsaric states of mind and to realize them as dharmakāya. Thereby, the state of unawareness becomes the state of full awareness or the wisdom of the connate. The latter signifies the realization of the nature of reality with all its perspectives, the inseparable unity of appearance and emptiness, of clarity and emptiness, and last but not least of compassion and emptiness. In this way, concepts are realized as dharmakāya. Gampopa explains in his *Elegant Teachings to the Assembly*:

> The outer [world] appearing as a variety of manifestations and the inner [world] arising as a variety of thoughts, i.e. memories and cognitions, all of these are but the luminous dharmakāya. (…) These phenomena of memories and manifestations appearing as a variety of happiness and suffering—all that [which is postulated] as that which is to be relinquished and remedies, as flaws and qualities etc., is by nature the luminous dharmakāya. Therefore, there is nothing to modify, increase or decrease, refute and establish, relinquish and to be adopted. As it is said in the *Ultimate Continuum,* "therein there is not the slightest to remove and not the slightest to add."[36]

The foundation and basic principle of this practice: The instructions contained in the translated texts treat this theme comprehensively both in terms of the related view and in terms of meditation. Thus, they are concerned with the heart of the teaching system of Dagpo Mahāmudrā as it has been and still is transmitted in the Kagyü schools of Tibetan Buddhism. However, this specific approach to Buddhist practice requires a stable foundation on the part of the practitioners. The translated texts also address this essential aspect repeatedly.

As a basic principle, the spiritual path in Buddhism relies on a solid understanding of the starting-point, of the path to be travelled, and of the goal that is strived for. In this regard, the Buddha taught on these lines already in his first famous teaching, the *Sūtra of the Turning of the Wheel of Dharma*,[37] in which he expounded the Four Noble Truths. First, he emphasized the need to comprehend the principle of suffering. The first truth regarding suffering pursues this purpose. Next, the causes of suffering should be relinquished, which is elucidated in the second truth regarding the origin of suffering. Both of these perspectives naturally require a process of development, which the Buddha described in the fourth truth concerning the path to be practiced. The result of this process is in turn what he taught in the third truth regarding the cessation of suffering.

The Buddha referred to this spiritual training as the "Middle Path", a path which avoids extremes in terms of view and conduct. An essential aspect of this Middle Path is presented through the template of what is termed "dependent arising",[38] which focuses on letting go of any type of extreme view. On the one hand, this relates to clinging to the supposed constancy of outer and inner phenomena, literally the "view of permanence". On the other hand, it pertains to clinging to negation where the existence of things is simply denied, literally "the view of extinction". Such descriptions may sound rather abstract or purely philosophical; however, they are meant as very concrete indications as to how practitioners are supposed to shape their path of spiritual development in a way that can actually lead toward the state of awakening.

In any case—and this is also frequently addressed in the translated texts—the different perspectives of reality need to be acknowledged and understood. Step by step the practitioners are then supposed to arrive at inner experiences, which eventually allow a liberating realization of reality in all of its facets to arise. Nāgārjuna[39], who is highly esteemed in virtually all Buddhist traditions, writes about this in his famous *Root Verses of the Middle Path*:[40] "The teaching of the Buddha is based on the two realities, the conventional reality of the world and reality in an absolute sense" (XXIV.8). A little further he adds: "Without relying on the conventional, the absolute cannot be taught. Without realizing the absolute, nirvāṇa cannot be attained" (XXIV.10).[41]

In concrete terms this entails practitioners first turning toward the conventional, i.e. relative reality. On the one hand, this means nothing other than becoming more and more aware of one's own mental processes as they occur here and now as well as of their causes and effects. On the other hand, spiritual development essentially depends on wholesome actions and the practice of fundamental spiritual training[42] in order to gain access to deeper levels of meditation. In any case it is necessary to develop differentiating and reflective introspection by means of which one is able to perceive one's own conditioned impulses and to learn how to deal with them appropriately, that is, in a wholesome and constructive manner. Since childhood, not to mention earlier lifetimes, in the different frames of reference that occurred in our lives and continue to occur, habitual patterns have been and are being stored in our mind streams. Whether in the context of our family, partnerships or other social communities; whether in a religious, political, or job context; or in terms of mental or physical skills that we have acquired etc.—all of these habitual patterns contribute directly or indirectly to our thinking, feeling, and acting, and they also do so when we are not aware of them. Unwholesome tendencies which produce suffering, even when they are concealed or latent, are eventually able to subside when one becomes aware of them. Wholesome habits, which lead to more and more well-being, can be enhanced to the maximum when one becomes aware of the power of wholesome attitudes and deeds. As one's introspection becomes subtler and clearer, one's understanding and positive actions can unfold accordingly. And as one's being in the relative or conventional world becomes clearer and more constructive, it eventually becomes easier also to integrate the perspective of absolute reality, because conventional and absolute reality are essentially not different from one another. In the context of Buddhist Mahāyāna practice, this process requires an explicit orientation toward the path to awakening, the clear and altruistic intention of bodhicitta, a high degree of mindfulness and continuous meditation practice, which, as the 14th Shamar Rinpoche frequently used to say, should be led by the right view. And just as the right view needs to be developed and cultivated, the same holds true for ethically appropriate conduct.

The course of this practice: As the inner stability that develops through the meditation of calm abiding increasingly combines with those experiences that arise through the meditation of deep insight, emotional and cognitive obscurations, which cloud the mind, and their deeply rooted tendencies can eventually dispel. According to the teachings of the Kagyü tradition, this entire process of spiritual maturing is intended to enable the practioner to directly realize the inseparability of the two perspectives of reality, i.e. the true nature of all outer and inner phenomena, and their ways of manifesting. Thus, practitioners become able to let go of false assumptions about themselves, others, and reality in general, to gradually resolve the causes of suffering, and to support others in an ever growing, encompassing, and deep way by means of a bodhisattva's open-minded and compassionate attitude.

The wording of this practice: In different Buddhist traditions we find specific terms for the process of practice and the required view. In this regard, the Fourth Shamarpa explains for example in one of his works:

> The [view of the] Dagpo Kagyü [tradition] corresponds to the Madhyamaka of Unity.[43] In this sense "connate" signifies the original nature of any phenomenon whatsoever, the simultaneity of emptiness and clarity [i.e. manifestation].[44]

The specific terminology of the Dagpo Kagyü tradition that he is using is the practice of "the connate". The connate or simultaneity meant here is that of the inseparability of emptiness and manifestation or appearance, i.e. of absolute and conventional reality. The "connate" is therefore closely associated with the term concept-dharmakāya: any concept that appears in consciousness is simultaneously empty by nature *and* manifests unobstructedly. Thus, also in its manifestation it is essentially never anything other than the nature of mind. In the tradition of Dagpo Mahāmudrā, a state of mind that truly experiences and realizes this is referred to as "natural awareness",[45] the wisdom of the connate.

I would like to conclude this part of the introduction with a quotation from Gampopa who—in the context of the wisdom of the connate—emphasizes in his *The Great Teaching to the Assembly* this further key term of the Kagyü tradition, i.e. natural awareness:

> (…) If one now wishes to liberate oneself from saṃsāra, it is necessary to realize natural awareness because this is the root of all qualities. So, what is referred to as natural awareness is one's mind abiding in itself, not diluted by any phenomenon whatsoever, not polluted by any worldly consciousness whatsoever, not obscured by any drowsiness, torpor and concepts whatsoever. When this is realized, it is self-aware wisdom. When it is not realized, it is connate unawareness. When realized it is referred to as awareness, essence, connate wisdom, natural awareness, the innate, freedom from elaborations, luminosity (…) Natural awareness is the ultimate truth. (…) Natural awareness makes the ultimate directly the path; it is direct [cognition]. The realization of natural awareness is the king of insight. (…) This is the king of all wisdoms, the king of all qualities.[46]

Translations

Part 1: Mahāmudrā, a Brief Introduction

Oral teachings given by the 14th Shamarpa, Mipham Chökyi Lodrö[47]

in the Kamalashila Institute, Germany, April 23–24, 1990

Mahāmudrā is not a simple matter, and it cannot by explained in just one hour. However, as requested I am going to provide some basic explanations on this practice.

(…)[48] In Buddhist traditions, general meditation methods were written down, while precise details regarding meditation practice were and are rather given orally. The respective holders of the teaching lineages gave these instructions only directly to actual practitioners. They did so in order to prevent possible misuse of these methods. Meditation instructions must be given with great care, and this is not a matter of a cultural differences between East and West. In fact, the human condition is the same everywhere in that, irrespective of the particular cultural background, human beings are under the sway of emotional defilements such as desire, anger, ignorance, pride, envy, etc. It is for precisely this reason that Dharma teachings are easily used in distorted ways. Whether in the East or in the West, the existence of defilements means that there is always vast scope for such misuse. To preserve the tradition accurately, then, it needs to be protected. Because this has been and is being done by authentic Buddhist masters, the Buddha's teachings have to this day been preserved without impairment.

Such misuse can be brought about by ignorance; someone who does not truly understand the teachings might, merely by his or her ignorance, think that he or she understands everything. Misuse can also be caused by envy; one person might want to compete with someone else. Misuse can come about through the desire for popularity, which might lead a person to invent a new -ism, a new religion. Misuse can be caused by anger, and so on. This is what I meant by saying that there exists a vast scope for misuse. On the other hand, there is also a vast scope for using the instructions on Buddhist meditation properly, provided that one applies them with the intention to attain enlightenment and with a genuine concern for the benefit of sentient beings. In this way, as there is both—the potential for perfect use and for misuse—Buddhist masters teach these methods on the one hand and protect them on the other hand. (…)[49]

Regarding the practice of Mahāmudrā, I would like to draw your attention to Dagpo Tashi Namgyal's *Mahāmudrā Moon Beam*.[50] Its English translation is entitled *Mahāmudrā: The Quintessence of Mind and Meditation*.[51] This is a very scholarly and meticulous translation. However, it is not easy to read and understand and, in fact, this is so on purpose. Lobsang Lhalungpa[52] was asked to translate this text by the 16th Gyalwa Karmapa and by the great Sakya scholar Dezhung Rinpoche,[53] who assisted him in his translation. In his concern that future readers might misuse the instructions given in this text, Dezhung Rinpoche effectively protected the teachings by ensuring that it is not possible to put them into practice merely by reading the book without having received the key instructions for the practice from a qualified teacher. On the other hand, a practitioner who has already received instructions from an authentic

Mahāmudrā teacher will find this book very helpful. So, without instructions by a qualified and experienced Mahāmudrā teacher it is not possible to understand the book properly by just reading it.

The Mahāmudrā teachings in Tibet were given in an extraordinarily skillful way by masters such as Milarepa, Gampopa, Pagmo Drupa, and Karmapa Düsum Khyenpa.[54] Three approaches were taught:

The first approach to Mahāmudrā practice was taught for practitioners who do not want to commit themselves to the maintenance of Vajrayāna samayas and commitments.[55] Of course, these practitioners first take the vows for individual liberation, which can either be the full ordination as a monk or nun, the novice ordinations, or the upāsaka vows for lay practitioners. Next, they take the bodhisattva vow as required, followed by the practice of the six pāramitās. On this basis, by practicing Mahāmudrā in the sense of the so-called "path of liberation", the awakened state can be attained in one lifetime. It just takes a little longer than with the Vajrayāna approach.

The second approach to Mahāmudrā practice is based on the tantric methods of the creation and perfection processes of, for example, Hevajra or Cakrasamvara.[56] This practice involves the Six Dharmas of Nāropa,[57] which are Powerfulness, Illusory Body, Dream Yoga, Luminosity, Intermediate State, and Transference.[58] These Six Dharmas belong to the so-called perfection process with characteristics.[59] On that path, the practitioner carefully maintains both the bodhisattva vow and the Vajrayāna samayas and commitments that go with the respective empowerments. Through this approach one can also attain the realization of Mahāmudrā, the awakened state, and can do so more quickly. This practice corresponds to the "break-through" and the "leap over"[60] stages in the Nyingma Mahā Ati tradition. The methods are different, but the level of practice and the results are the same.

The third and ultimate Mahāmudrā practice requires neither an empowerment nor the creation and perfection processes. It consists in a direct introduction to mind's true nature by means of which the awakened state is attained. However, this only works

with highly advanced students. One example of this type of practitioner was Gampopa, who needed just eighteen days to realize
the awakened state. This level of Mahāmudrā, this method, is
even more profound than the "break-through" and the "leap over"
teachings of Mahā Ati. Nowadays, however, nobody or almost nobody can practice this highest level of Mahāmudrā, especially no
one in the West—at least so far nobody has succeeded in doing
so. I have never seen a person of this kind. I spent very much time
with His Holiness the 16th Gyalwa Karmapa. He was the "king of
Mahāmudrā", and none of his disciples had this qualification. So
even for a teacher such as the Gyalwa Karmapa, who was like a
buddha, it was difficult to have such highly advanced disciples. But
don't be discouraged. It depends on the time, on the personality,
and on the relevant background. At all events, today I'm not going
to teach on this highest level. But (jokingly) if your past deeds
qualify you, it may be that, while I am giving the brief instruction
on Mahāmudrā, you suddenly become a buddha on the spot. I will
keep an eye open. (…)

The term "Mahāmudrā" is a poetic expression. In Sanskrit,
words often have various levels of meaning. In our context, the
first part "mahā", which usually means "great", pertains to the
"great state of buddhahood". "Mudrā", which among other things
means "hand", indicates that "you have the Buddha's guarantee"
that there is nothing which would be better than this, nothing beyond this. Moreover, "Mahāmudrā" is connected with the so-called
"Practice of the Connate",[61] which refers to "connate wisdom",[62]
also called the "wisdom of the ground",[63] and this in turn means
that our mind-itself is wisdom, innately.

Human beings, and of course this holds true for all living beings, are born, live, and die. However, what dies is just the body,
not the mind. These cycles of birth, physical death, and being born
again have persisted since beginningless time. However, the continuity of mind-itself is never interrupted by this. Mind-itself never
stops, it never comes to an end, it never disappears or dies, because
mind-itself is buddha, is wisdom. For this reason, it does not become nonexistent. Yet, even though one's mind in itself is buddha,

as long as one is not aware of this, one is in a state of delusion, because of which illusory manifestations continuously appear. As long as this delusion persists, illusory manifestations will never end of their own accord.

In simple words, mind and wisdom are connate. To understand "Mahāmudrā, the Practice of the Connate", one must understand mind's nature or, phrased differently, "mind's mode of abiding".[64] Then it will become clear that not recognizing mind's mode of abiding is the state of samsaric delusion, and recognizing it is the state of a buddha. If one knows this, then one understands how to practice the Mahāmudrā method of the connate in order to actualize the non-deluded state, the wisdom of a buddha.

Therefore, our first subject is going to be mind's nature. Generally, when we talk about "mind" most people's tendency is to consider it to be somewhat physical or as having a somewhat substantial nature that is connected with the brain, blood, nerves etc. For example, when the eyes see a visual object, the mind takes in this information and apprehends a physical form. When our hand touches a hot or cold object, the information of this hot or cold sensation is transmitted to the mind. In this sense, many people relate to the mind in a somewhat concrete way. To be sure, in the course of perceptual processes the mind does take up or acquire information by focusing on sense objects. However, the mind that relates to these data is in itself by no means physical, not at all. Rather, mind's nature or mind-itself consists in being "the knower", it simply knows. Mind is that which knows, whatever that may be; it is just knowing. This knowing is mind's character. On the other hand, mind's essence is empty in that it has no physical form—it does not have any concrete self-nature.

Mind's essence is emptiness; mind's character is knowing. This is why the mind can know and think of anything, whatever it may be. Given its empty essence, there is no obstruction in this knowing, it is completely unhindered. If the mind had a substantial or physical existence, there would always be certain obstructions or limits, yet this is not the case. So, given mind's empty essence and its quality of knowing, concepts[65] of anything, of whichever type, can occur in the mind; it is very spacious.

All living beings have the mind that we have. This is precisely what the Tibetan term for "living beings" means; it literally translates as "endowed with mind". This holds true not just for humans but for any sentient being, even if it is as tiny as a mosquito. In fact, in this regard there is not the slightest difference. Any sentient being's mind is like that. That is mind-itself, empty and knowing.

However, the mode of mind of ordinary sentient beings is that the mind does not abide in its actual nature but is distracted. As soon as some sound reaches our ears, for example, the mind wanders to this sound; when the eyes see a visual form, the mind wanders to these forms and is thus distracted from itself. As the mind wanders and is distracted, it turns into all kinds of concepts. The meaning of "nam tog", the Tibetan term for what in English is rendered as concepts or thoughts, is that the mind appears as concepts. This is what happens in moments of distraction; when the mind is not distracted from itself it does not appear as concepts.

This brings us to the mode of mind free of concepts. In this mode the mind abides in its own nature, its own mode of abiding, which means its empty essence. Knowing itself, it is self-aware, self-illuminating, and unhindered. This is not a kind of coma or some unconscious state. It is not as if one has fainted, it is not sleep-like or a total absorption into oneself. Rather, in its true mode of abiding, the mind is experienced as empty, knowing, and unhindered. If one is able to sustain this—when one has gained such control over one's mind that it abides in this state—this is what we call *realization*, the mind recognizing its true nature. By abiding therein, one is able to maintain this recognition and to perfect the realization of it. Ultimately, the full maturation of this realization culminates in attaining the state of a buddha.

When the mind is distracted, it turns into concepts. So "concept" is the way in which the conditioned mind connects to certain objects. It connects, for example, to this noise right now; [66] our mind connecting to this, i.e. hearing it, has turned into concepts. But, these particular concepts also have the entire nature of mind: they do not truly exist, they have no substantial form, and are therefore empty in essence. Moreover, the concept concerned is clear in that there is knowing. Because mind-itself is knowing, when relating to something like a sound, it can also know the sound, independently of whether it is pleasant or unpleasant. When the mind knows something,[67] the mind actually knows itself. Otherwise, nothing could be known; we cannot get anything from the outside. Therefore, when the mind is connected with objects, "acquiring information" means that the mind actually knows itself; it does not, in fact, directly apprehend *outer* objects. This natural ability to know is mind's clarity. If mind-itself were not clear, that is, knowing, then one would not be able to know anything. So, liberate yourself from this connecting with objects! A state of mind not controlled by a fixation on objects is clear, and this also applies to any concept. Being free from fixation on objects means that the objects do not control the mind.[68] And that state of mind, that particular concept or inner representation of an object, also has the nature of mind. It is just like with bubbles and water both being water by nature.

Once you arrive at a direct understanding of this, it (Rinpoche snaps his fingers) is "instant buddha". You become enlightened instantly. So, is there anybody who can do this? If so, there will be a buddha today (laughs).

When we look back into the history of the Kagyü lineage, you might have heard of how Tilopa helped Nāropa to arrive at this realization. Prior to that, Nāropa had to go through a great deal of practice. But in the end, he became enlightened, when Tilopa exposed him to a sudden shock. Nāropa was just sitting there and Tilopa came up to him and slapped him. This shock enabled Nāropa to fully realize mind's true nature. But of course, he had his background to help him. Nāropa had already developed precise insight into mind's mode of abiding, and Tilopa was a highly qualified teacher. He saw that his student Nāropa had come to the state where he was ready to attain realization. He knew that such a shock would help Nāropa to gain full control in his direct realization of mind's essence and mode of abiding. In this case, such a shock can be a good support, but not every shock will make you understand. All in all, the Mahāmudrā practice consists of those methods which can get you there—and then (jokingly) you may not need a shock on top of it.

We talked before about connate wisdom, which means that from beginningless time mind-itself has not been separate from wisdom. Thus, when mind's inherent nature is realized and one attains the awakened state, this person who now has become enlightened, whoever it may be, is most surprised and wonders "Why did I not realize this before? Why did I not get this earlier? This nature was always there; it's the true one! This wisdom is, in fact, always present. It is mind's nature. This is what the mind has always been, so why did I not understand this earlier?" By now we all know why we did not achieve realization so far. And, when you attain it, then you will think "Why I did not realize it before?" So, you should realize it!

To sum up the main point again: "The Practice of the Connate" refers to mind-itself being connate wisdom; that is, wisdom and mind-itself are of *one* essence. Just as wisdom and mind-itself are of *one* essence, concepts and mind-itself are also of *one* essence. Thus, concepts as such are wisdom. Wisdom refers to the natural quality of the mind. The term "wisdom" in Western languages has other connotations than this specific Buddhist perspective, where wisdom means a "mind not under the influence of its illusion" or "mind fully aware of itself, fully matured as to its natural qualities, and completely pure". This is meant with wisdom or mind-itself, whereas a mind which is distracted becomes thought processes. But still, every concept is also mind's actual nature, because it occurs in the mind. And this refers not just to our concepts in the sense of our general thinking. In fact, everything evinces that nature, that wisdom. However, it is very difficult to realize that whatever we see, hear, smell, taste, and feel—everything—bears that quality of mind's actual nature. This is difficult. Compared to that, it is relatively easy to realize that all our thoughts are not different from the mind.

Having discussed the nature of mind, that is, the "ground of purification",[69] we will now briefly examine the approach to realizing this: the so-called "method of purification".[70] This term does not refer to the widely familiar purification practices which help us to purify ourselves of karma. Of course, this is extremely important. In the context of Mahāmudrā, however, the "method of purification" refers to the actual Mahāmudrā meditation, which in itself is also a purification practice: on the basis of mind-itself, it purifies us of the habits of delusion. This is why it is said that mind-itself is both the "ground of purification" and the "method of purification". Both are the mind which comes to know itself. The Mahāmudrā method of purification is thus that mind recognizes itself and thereby frees itself of its delusion.

One might wonder why we then have to do so many other purification practices to purify ourselves of karma, like Dorje Sempa practice. Why do we have to do this? Why do we have to do so many merit accumulations known as the maṇḍala practice? Why do we have to do that? These questions may arise. Whether prostrations, maṇḍala offerings, 100-syllable mantra recitations etc., all of these have to be done, but why? Well, the answer is: until one has arrived at the point where one's mind is able to enlighten itself, the power of illusory manifestations continues to operate, and the intensity of these illusions depends on one's karma. Karma is therefore a main factor which obscures one's capacity to realize the awakened state. And the way to overcome negative karma and its obscuring power is through accumulating wholesome karma. What we need at present, then, is positive karma to counteract the negative karma, so that we can finally engage in the Mahāmudrā level of purification where mind realizes itself and progresses from the process of purification to a purified state.

As long as the causes of illusions have not been eliminated, we cannot rid ourselves of illusions. We cannot just dismiss them, and so we should simply accept them for what they are. What is more, illusions can be both "black" and "white", and the "white" one is always helpful. It is what we call the support of "merit-power", and it is this merit that we need. It is necessary to engage in wholesome deeds because we need "white" illusions. Right now, for example, we are in a tent. We all concentrate on the teachings. A "big mouth" is sitting here on the throne (laughs), and you are listening to these Dharma teachings. We all concentrate on that. It is an illusion, but a good one. At the same time, it is a little bit noisy here, which is a bit of a "black" illusion.

The different stages of wholesome illusions are what are called the "five paths" of spiritual development and the "ten levels" of a realized bodhisattva.[71] The "five paths" are also subdivided into eighteen stages, which are partly still within saṃsāra but which are good illusions; they are the so-called worldly stages. (...) All of these stages involve illusions, yet wholesome ones. When the majority of one's perception is under the sway of negative illusions, it is called saṃsāra. As these illusions become lighter and as the negative illusions dissipate more and more, one finally arrives at a level where there are only positive illusions, and one develops this further and further. This is the difference between the bhūmis, i.e. the ten bodhisattva levels. Otherwise, as the first and the second bhūmi are both enlightened states, for example, what other difference would there be? These bhūmis are distinguished with respect to the types of illusion. The English word "illusion" is quite negative, isn't it? But Buddha did not use this English word (laughs). So, maybe we can find another word for that, instead of illusion. Often people get confused just because of the words that are used. Yet, we have to translate, right! And as you don't have the precisely matching terms in Western languages, the listeners always have to make up their own mind in figuring out what it might mean. The term "illusion" may not be very apt for communicating the point here. (...)[72] So, what might work is to say pure manifestations or appearances versus impure manifestations. Pure manifestations arise by virtue of pure karma, by virtue of wholesome deeds, while impure manifestations are brought about by nonvirtuous deeds. An example of the former is Dewachen, the pure land of Buddha Amitābha, which consists of entirely pure appearances. But do they truly exist or not? Dewachen, does it really exist? No, it is just the same as with impure appearances, which also do not truly exist. Yet, as long as the karma is there, they manifest. The Madhyamaka[73] states that nothing truly exists. It also says that the qualities of the pure lands do not truly exist. From the point of view of absolute truth none of the appearances truly exists. So the only truth, we can say, is the dharmakāya, while everything else, including pure lands with beautiful lakes, beautiful lotus flowers etc., manifests but is not truly existent.

When you attain the bodhisattva level which is called "first bhūmi", you will, on the strength of your realization, be able to control your illusions, your own appearances. Once you have become able to control your own illusions, you will also be able to produce illusions or appearances; you can manifest them. You can change things here and there. It is similar to what is practiced in the so-called dream yoga: When you are able to control your dream, you can do all kinds of things in the dream and use it. That means your dream is an illusion. But at present, when you cannot control your dream, the dream controls you. Not until you are able to control your dream can you use it. Similarly, once you have attained the level of the first bhūmi, you can more or less control all of your illusions—although not to the extent that a buddha can. Still, these bodhisattvas can manifest many forms, help sentient beings, manifest even pure lands, support sentient beings to take birth therein, and help them to attain liberation.

To conclude, I would like to emphasize the main point: Once you can fully realize the true nature of your mind, you will no longer be under the influence of your illusions. The illusions will no longer control you—you can control the illusions. Someone who has as much background as Gampopa can go directly into that realization. That is the highest Mahāmudrā method. However, as you cannot claim that you are already qualified for that, you must go step by step, starting with the basic practices.[74] In the event that you already have Gampopa's highly qualified background, realization will come by itself. If not, you will improve through the ordinary practice. This is why we always emphasize that practitioners systematically go through the four foundations and similar practices. Then there is no risk. If one is ready to become a buddha now, it will happen by itself anyway. Starting with the foundational practices will not get in the way of this. All in all, it is very important that you try to find a qualified teacher and that you practice in a stable and steady way. Practice continuously. The results of meditation will depend very much on your familiarity with the practice. (…)[75]

Part 2: The Ornament of Gampopa's Intent. Dispelling Doubts Regarding Concept-Dharmakāya

By the 14th Shamarpa, Mipham Chökyi Lodrö[76]

Preface by the 17th Gyalwa Karmapa, Trinley Thaye Dorje[77]

> Having fully relinquished the dark forces of fourfold māra,[78] the nectar of instructions has been given correctly and excellently.
> May this sun of the Sage, which is free from all bias, shine and allow the lotus of wisdom to blossom.

In this world, sentient beings, whoever they may be, act in the context of their individual merit and then enjoy the fortune of delighting in the resultant happiness. Yet all joyful results such as these depend—whether directly or indirectly—on the teachings of the Sugata[79] and on the activities of the awakened state and are connected exclusively with these. As the *Introduction to the Bodhisattva's Way of Life* says (I.5):

> Just as a flash of lightning for an instant
> illuminates a dark and cloudy night,
> likewise, because of the power of the Buddha
> in the mind of the world, delight in merit occurs rarely and briefly.[80]

All happiness and well-being in the world depend exclusively on the authentic Dharma of the Sugata's teachings, which shows the ways to adopt virtue and relinquish negativity. The supreme access to this teaching system is the word of the Buddha himself, along with the works that comment on their intent, and the general and specific treatises associated with them. Furthermore, whether considering the words of the Buddha or the particular commentarial treatises, one engages with them through the ten Dharma activities, which include studying, reflecting, meditating, and accomplishing. The principle factor of these grounds of engaging is that scriptural systems are put into writing in accordance with the path of intellectual reasoning. Unfortunately, however, this has long been neglected.

Nevertheless, even [now] in the time of the fivefold degeneration[81] and a phase in which the Buddha's teachings are in a very precarious state, the Shri Diwakar Institute has started with its own *Series of Treatises of the Black and Red Crown Gyalwa Karmapa*.[82] The hope and aspiration in publishing these scriptural systems on inner science is that they will significantly contribute to the survival of the Buddha's teachings. Through modern technology and printing, many students have access to [these texts] regardless of their background in terms of traditions. This is an unending Dharma generosity, which is comparable with the continuous flow of a river. Such good and virtuous actions are extremely praiseworthy and a reason to rejoice. I pray that the outcome of this will be the attainment of perfect awakening.

> When the brilliant light of teachings shines from the
> celestial vessel,
> the ocean of the intelligent ones right away expands in all
> directions;
> this text has been printed for this to happen. Through this virtue
> may there be auspiciousness in the world with the joy of
> Dharma activities.

These words of aspiration were written by Thaye Dorje, the seventeenth holder of the blessed title of the Gyalwa Karmapa, in the year 2549 of the Buddha, on the full moon of the tenth month or, according to the western calendar, on Oct. 28th, 2004. May auspiciousness expand!

Introduction by Prof. Sempa Dorje

The Ornament of Gampopa's Intent. Dispelling Doubts Regarding Concept-Dharmakāya was recently written by Künzig Shamar Rinpoche, the glorious principal lineage holder. It is a treatise on the sequence of the secret core points and the hidden meaning of the specific view, meditation, and conduct of the incomparable Dagpo Kagyü[83] and possesses many special features. One such feature is that it reveals the entire meaning in just a few words. Still, as it might be difficult for people who are in the process of development to comprehend a wise person's understanding, I am delighted to write a brief introduction to this text. Marpa Lotsawa of Lhodrag, the king of translators, after surmounting hundreds of difficulties, found the essential meaning of all the sūtras and tantras, referred to as "Mahāmudrā". He became convinced that this is the ultimate intent of the great Sage, [the Buddha]. Moreover, as [is evident] from Marpa's own words, it was the path through which he himself attained realization: "The essential meaning of the ultimate vehicle is mental nonengagement[84] free from extremes. This Dharma, Mahāmudrā, was expounded to me so that I understood it."

Since Marpa's day, this flawless, long-standing tradition referred to as Mahāmudrā, which is one of the eight great carriages of practice lineages,[85] has been renowned far and wide all over the Land of Snows. Since then, this Mahāmudrā tradition has continued without interruption. Through the practice of its key instructions, a large number of noble (Sanskrit: ārya) Mahāyāna practitioners or accomplished individuals (Sanskrit: *siddha*) has emerged in Tibet.

In particular, the incomparable Dagpo Rinpoche [Gampopa] fostered this teaching tradition of Mahāmudrā in which the unity of mind, concepts, and dharmakāya forms the essential point. This

49

is an unsurpassable method appropriate for everyone, enabling [practitioners] to attain the level of irreversibility, regardless of whether they are of supreme or humble capacity. Therefore, even among those of Gampopa's students who were of basic proficiency, there were many who attained levels of great wisdom. Later, those who did not understand the secret core of this view and [practice for] realization denigrated it as a "meditation of fools",[86] and so on. They engaged in all sorts of refutations and expressed doubts. So I think that from time to time, when doubts as to one's own view and [practice for] realization etc. arise, it is the praiseworthy activity of the owners of the teachings to dispel these doubts.

Thus, at the beginning of this precious treatise *Dispelling Doubts*, [the Shamarpa] voices his homage to Buddha Śākyamuni in one stanza which starts with "You have overcome the abyss of painful existence ..." The next stanza, which starts with "As for Nāro's and Maitrī's ...", shows the succession of the lineage of instructions in general. In particular, the last verse ["Gampopa was his regent, whose subject I have become"] shows how the writer himself has had the good fortune to receive these instructions; implicitly it discloses that he is the holder of this lineage. Thereafter, with one stanza that starts with "The eloquent teachings ...", he uses metaphorical images to explicitly show his commitment to this text. He refers by implication to the four aspects of such treatises, such as the purpose, etc.[87]

At the beginning of the actual treatise, [the Shamarpa first] expounds the views of some opponents. He then makes use of the three[fold] system of dispelling doubts, i.e. refuting, establishing [one's own view], and dispelling [the opponents' arguments]. He thereby demonstrates the way in which the term concept-dharmakāya, which is a specific Dharma term for Mahāmudrā, the definitive meaning, taught in his own [i.e. the Dagpo Kagyü] system, is flawless in terms of both wording and meaning. He explains this in detail by scriptural citation and by applying reasoning.

At the end, the two stanzas starting with "From the ground consciousness which is holding all seeds ..." present a synopsis of the entire body of the treatise. This concise statement makes clear that, according to the writer [i.e. the Shamarpa], in the context of Mahāmudrā in Gampopa's system, the view—in terms of conventional [truth]—is that of the Madhyamaka propounding false representations.[88] After that the first three lines of the stanza [starting with] "The incomparable Gampopa who was predicted by the Victor ..." etc. reveals clearly Gampopa's innermost intent, the key factors of the three—saṃsāra, nirvāṇa, and the path. With the last verse, he dedicates the merit of the work for the benefit of sentient beings and the teachings and thereby perfectly seals [the treatise]. The colophon with its four parts is also given in a perfect way, and thus the purpose [of this treatise] is fully accomplished.

Upon reading this text, devotion and trust towards the writer's wisdom as a scholar and practitioner arose in my mind. For this reason, I think that the present treatise will be very helpful to the teachings of the Buddha in general and to the inheritors of the practice lineage in particular. At the same time [I want to mention that] Shri Diwakar Publications requested me to write an introduction and that in response to this, I, Sempa Dorje from Kunu, wrote this on Oct. 5th, 2011, in my own room at the Buddhist Temple of the Gyalwa Karmapa [KIBI, New Delhi]. May there be well-being.

The Text

The Ornament of Gampopa's Intent.
Dispelling Doubts Regarding Concept-Dharmakāya

By the 14th Shamarpa, Mipham Chökyi Lodrö

You have overcome the abyss of painful existence,
and so you have found the space[89] of indestructible
liberation.
You have relinquished the night[90] with its sleep in the
extreme of peace,[91]
and so the sun[92] of your wisdom shines everywhere.
You have cleared away the net of clouds of distracted
idleness,
and so the light-rays of benefit and joy radiate
unobstructed.
I pay homage to you the sun, the Buddha,[93] the only
ultimate refuge for all beings.

It was Marpa from Lhodrag who had the power to receive
the unceasing treasury of Nāro's and Maitrī's instructions.

Milarepa[94] was skilled in seizing all the most valued jewels
therefrom, and
Gampopa was his regent, whose subject I have become.

[These] masters' splendid teachings are [like] a necklace of
jewels
for minister[like] meditators in all directions.
[Beautifully] arranged [are these teachings, like] earrings,
signs of mastery.
With pure faith I delight in dusting them.

The oral tradition of the lineage of disciples of the Dharma master
Gampopa,[95] refers to what is known as concept-dharmakāya.[96]

In this connection, the all-knowing Jigme Lingpa[97] said that,
even though in terms of meaning [this teaching] is flawless, from
the point of view of the wording "concept" is the name for the
impure mind and "dharmakāya" is the name for freedom from delusion. It is thus a mistake to combine these two into one term;
this would be as if one would position a black and a white dzo
such that their heads face each other directly.[98] Moreover, Thu'u
ken Chökyi Dorje[99] is known for having said "If concepts were the
dharmakāya, then [ordinary sentient beings] would be more realized than the Buddha, and this makes no sense." Thus [to him], it
is also mistaken in terms of meaning.

On the grounds of such statements, some Tibetan and Western
teachers are today engaging in arbitrary speculation as to the ways
in which the Mahāmudrā instructions of the Kagyüpas are in error.
With a view to preventing damage to these teachings [founded on]
scriptural transmission and realization, Drupön Tenzin and Lama
Tsonyi from France thus asked me to write a clear explanation why
the assertion of such errors is wrong. Responding to their request,
I felt called upon to provide a brief treatment of the issue as it is
given to me to understand it.

First, an explanation of how Gampopa's concept-dharmakāya is
flawless in terms of the wording:

The literal meaning of [the Tibetan abbreviation] *namtog*[100] [i.e.
"representational concept"] is as follows. [The Tibetan term] *tog-*

pa[101] [i.e. "concept"]—in the epistemological systems of the Sautrāntikas and above[102]—pertains to consciousness apprehending an object. That is, consciousness holds the representation [Tib. *nampa*[103]] of the object that appears in the dualistic mind. This process is therefore called *nampar togpa* [i.e. "representational concept"]. Moreover, [it should be mentioned that] according to the *Thirty Verses on Grammar*[104], a sub-function of the second grammatical case[105] is [to indicate] that the object of an act and the agent are not different from one other. It is on the basis of the explanation of this function of the particle for the second case that earlier scholars coined the Tibetan term *nampar togpa* [i.e. "(objects being) sheer representational concepts"]. As an abbreviation of this, *namtog* [i.e. "representational concept"] emerged as an established term.

When Gampopa instructed his disciples, he used exactly this Tibetan term *namtog* [hereafter abbreviated to "concept" in the translation] and taught by means of logical reasoning the abiding mode [of concepts] as being beyond the four extremes: neither existent as being one, as being many, as being both, or then again being neither of the two.

Moreover, it is not the case that all concepts should be discarded like garbage and a completely pure nature of mind should be sought and extracted from the midst of them. Instead, the point is to look at the very nature of the present concept, [in a way which is] uncontrived, undiluted, without refuting or establishing etc. [When Gampopa with this] system of instructions [on concept-dharmakāya], known as the settling meditation of a kuśali [yogi], gave the introduction [to mind's nature]—where mind's mode of abiding is [experienced] as being not different from the mode of abiding of the concepts as such—his direct disciples and their followers realized the truth as it is. Thus, the wording is flawless. If most people had understood [from this wording] that there is no need to be diligent in studying, reflecting, and meditating because whatever arises as concepts is the dharmakāya, then the wording would certainly be mistaken. This is not the case, however, as is evident from the works and hagiographies of Gampopa's disciples.

Let us apply another method of analysis. In all the sūtras and tantras, "emptiness" and "dharmakāya" are said to be identical in meaning and different merely in name. If this were not the case, then emptiness as taught in the sūtras and tantras would be understood as a nihilistic void or as a void that is posited as the counterpart [of an existent] such as saying, "an empty vessel". This would make no sense at all.

In the Mother, [i.e. the *Perfection of Wisdom Sūtras*,[106]] with the four cycles of emptiness, such as "form is empty", all phenomena are established as emptiness. The text then continues as follows:

> Therefore, since the bodhisattvas have no attainment, they abide by means of the perfection of wisdom. As there is no obscuration of mind, there is no contamination. They go beyond any falsity and attain complete nirvāṇa. All the buddhas of the three times, by means of the perfection of wisdom, fully awaken to unsurpassable, true, complete buddhahood.[107]

With an incomplete [realization of] emptiness, buddhahood would not be possible.

The *King of Meditation Sūtra* says regarding this point:

> It is not taught that the nature of consciousness is other
> [than emptiness] and
> that emptiness is other [than consciousness].
> Thus, the one who perfectly knows consciousness
> perfectly knows emptiness.[108]

[Here, consciousness is explicitly mentioned, yet] it is applied to all of the five skandhas.[109]

The *Perfection of Wisdom Sūtra* says:

> Form is empty.
> Emptiness is form.
> Emptiness is not other than form.
> Form is also not other than emptiness.[110]

In these teachings regarding the two, form and emptiness, there is no terminological conflict as if two Dzos were positioned such that their heads face each other directly.[111] Likewise, I do not think it would be a mistake, either in the wording or in the meaning, to say:

> Concepts are the dharmakāya.
> The dharmakāya is concepts.
> The dharmakāya is not other than concepts.
> Concepts are not other than the dharmakāya.

Gampopa says:

> These concepts, which arise as [if they were something] concrete,[112]
> take them firmly to be the dharmakāya.
> That is meditation; only then one understands.
> When this becomes an experience, the nature [of mind] is seen.[113]

The proponents of the Madhyamaka's path of reasoning would certainly have found it more expedient had they heard "these concepts which arise as [if they were something] concrete, know them to be empty."

However, for the yogis the teaching "take them firmly to be the dharmakāya" and the following two lines were simply more apposite in terms of their understanding and experience. It seems to me that, apart from this [difference], both of these styles of explanation are flawless in wording and in meaning.

According to the Madhyamaka path of reasoning, the syllogism would be: On the subject of concepts, *ultimately, they are* the dharmakāya because their nature is free from the four extremes. By this, I believe, it is possible to convey the nominal ultimate, while the genuine ultimate[114] [is expressed] by saying "[on the subject of] concepts, *they are* the dharmakāya because they are free from the four extremes."[115]

All in all Gampopa explained to his disciples the essence of concepts and the meaning of the dharmakāya in a very skillful manner and gave them a profound and extensive direct introduction to [the understanding that] concepts are the dharmakāya. Then, as a term that summarizes [this entire] meaning, he referred to this view as concept-dharmakāya. Thus, "concept-dharmakāya" is a specific term that points to [experiences in] deep meditation. Otherwise, if it were an informal term in common parlance, then for instance parents who tell their children "don't think so mistrustfully" should instead say "don't be so mistrustful in your concept-dharmakāya." As this is certainly never the case, it is [evident] that it is not [everyday language].

Now I shall discuss the statement that [Gampopa's teaching on] concept-dharmakāya is also flawless in terms of meaning.

From among the various profound instructions of the Dagpo Kagyü tradition that are known as "Mahāmudrā, the Practice of the Connate"[116] [here] is a quotation from the venerable Master Gomchung[117]:

> Connate mind-itself is the dharmakāya as such.
> Connate appearances are the dharmakāya's light.
> Connate concepts are the dharmakāya's waves.
> Connate inseparability is the dharmakāya's actuality.[118]

If the meaning of [these verses] is explained in accordance with the intent of the sūtras, they cover in general terms the following. The two [words] "empty" and "dharmakāya" are terms used only when the three—ground, path, and result—are presented separately. Apart from that, they are of the same meaning. Based on that [understanding, we shall now examine the following]:

The [first] verse "connate mind-itself is the dharmakāya as such" *explicitly* shows, "Mind is empty. Emptiness is mind. Emptiness is not other than mind. Mind is also not other than emptiness." *Implicitly*, it indicates that—when [it is] not realized—the mind is the root of saṃsāra.

[The second verse] "connate appearances are the dharmakāya's light" *explicitly* shows, "Appearances are empty. Emptiness is appearances. Emptiness is not other than appearances. Appearances are also not other than emptiness." *Implicitly*, it indicates with the analogy of light that—when [it] is not realized—mind-itself appears as objects such as forms.

[The third verse] "connate concepts are the dharmakāya's waves" *explicitly* shows, "Concept is empty. Emptiness is concept. Emptiness is not other than concept. Concept is also not other than emptiness." *Implicitly*, it indicates with the analogy of waves that all concepts of dualistic fixations are mind-itself manifesting as representations of subject and object.

[The fourth verse] "connate inseparability is the dharmakāya's actuality" *explicitly* shows that the three—mind, appearances, and concepts—are present as connate essence and inherent emptiness being inseparable from each other. [This] is due to the meaning of the inseparability of the two truths [shown] in the first verse, the inseparability of appearances and emptiness in the second, and the inseparability of awareness and emptiness in the third. *Implicitly*, [this fourth verse indicates something comparable] to the example of the three—water, reflections in the water, and waves in the water: while *conventionally* they share the same composition of water, *ultimately*, in terms of their mode of abiding, which is emptiness, they are not different in nature but inseparable and connate. Likewise, also as to the three—mind, appearances, and concepts—"three" [does not imply] differences [as to their] essence. Rather, the inseparability of [their] essence from the expanse that is beyond the four extremes is there connately. That is referred to as dharmakāya. Thus, I think this conveys the resultant dharmakāya or the svabhāvikakāya.[119]

Nāropa also explains something similar to this:

> Appearance, liberated in itself, *is* the expanse of
> phenomena.
> Concept, liberated in itself, *is* great wisdom.
> Nondual sameness *is* the dharmakāya.[120]

Moreover, the first verse, "connate mind-itself is the dharmakāya as such", alludes to the dharmakāya at the ground [level]. *Implicitly*, this indicates the key point that both—appearances and concepts—are the self-expression of the dharmakāya, which does not exist separately from the mind, and thus reveals the way to settle in equipoise accordingly. In this way it points to the dharmakāya [at the time] of the path, which is meditation.

First, as for appearances,

Mahāsiddha Maitrīpa says:

> The variety of appearances, the nature of mind,
> —just by directly encountering it—
> is [seen to be] nonexistent, Mahāmudrā.[121]

Master Marpa:

> This magical wheel of confusion of outer appearances
> is realized to be nonarisen Mahāmudrā.[122]

Master Milarepa:

> Whatever outer appearances manifest,
> not realized, they are saṃsāra.
> Attachment to outer things fetters one.
> Realized ones perceive them as magical illusions.
> Objects and appearances arise as mind's allies.[123]

Master Gampopa:

> These appearances and sounds,
> [manifesting due to] tendencies of imputations,
> take them firmly to be the ultimate.[124]

These and other [quotations] show appearances to be the dharmakāya of the path.

Secondly, as for concepts it is furthermore said by Maitrīpa:

> From the nonarisen, adventitious concepts [are manifesting].
> The concepts as such abide as the nature of the expanse.
> I teach that these two [concepts and the expanse] are of one flavor.[125]

Master Marpa:

> The movement of mentation, [i.e.] the two, perceived and
> perceiver,
> dissolves into the dharmakāya, which is free from
> elaborations.[126]

Master Mila[repa]:

> These concepts of inner fleeting mentation,
> as long as [one is] not realized, they are [the state of]
> unawareness,
> the ground and root for all karma and defilements.
> When realized, they are [the state of] wisdom of self-
> awareness,
> complete in terms of all virtuous qualities.[127]

Master Gampopa:

> Concepts, which arise as [if they were something] concrete,
> take them firmly to be the dharmakāya.
> That is meditation; only then one understands.
> When this becomes an experience, the nature [of mind] is
> seen.[128]

These and other [quotations] show concepts to be the dharmakāya
of the path.

As to the resultant dharmakāya: [the verse] "the connate inseparability is the dharmakāya's actuality," shows the indivisibility of
ground, path, and result.

Moreover, the glorious Dignāga says:

> Besides concepts,
> a so-called saṃsāra is nowhere.
> Having become free from those concepts,
> you are thus forever in nirvāṇa.[129]

Query: Does the statement "concepts are the dharmakāya" [not
mean that even] the Buddha is [just] on the path of training?

Reply: This flaw does not apply. With deep meditation that
unites common śamatha and vipaśyanā, one relinquishes concepts.

With the illusion-like deep meditation that is combined with wishing prayers, concepts are transformed into an ally, and, with the deep meditation of the "Practice of the Connate", concepts appear as the dharmakāya. Thus, they are made the path, and there are specific stages of practice. In general, it is taught in all tantras that at the stage where the fruit is made the path,[130] it is necessary to realize defilements as wisdom. Basically, defilements are merely specific [types of concepts]; actually they are concepts. Primordially, the mode of abiding of all of them is emptiness. Without realizing that, the śrāvakas and pratyekabuddhas are also unable to relinquish them.

The *Sūtra Clearing Away the Remorse of Ajātaśatru*,[131] teaches that the method of purifying negativity is none other than looking at the nonperceptible mode of abiding of the negativity. Nothing other than this is what Dignāga [meant] when he described nirvāṇa as freedom from concept. [He did not imply] that there are so-called concepts that the Buddha had removed from his mind at the banks of the Nirañjana River, as if peeling an egg.

Therefore, Candrakīrti, who was skilled in expounding the noble Nāgārjuna's intent, enumerated various logical arguments demonstrating that no phenomena have a valid existence, even in conventional terms. In accordance with this intent, the glorious Gampopa also pointed out that the three—mind, appearances, and concepts—do not exist even conventionally. At the same time, he explained them to be the dharmakāya[132] in order to prevent future practitioners, such as the Tibetan community of meditators and others, from loosing their way in emptiness. I consider this a marvelous method.

Likewise, in the context of meditation too, corresponding with that view [i.e. that concepts do not validly exist even conventionally], he spoke about *concept*, [and thus used a word] known by ordinary people, thereby introducing that which is to be purified. Instead of considering the conventional and ultimate as two, [concepts] are understood as precisely the mode of abiding, the dharmakāya as such. By virtue of this—without needing to forsake one and then understand the other—by knowing one, all is known. The special key instruction endowed with this crucial point is known as "taking the result that is the purifier as the path."[133]

Therefore, Master Marpa says:

> When any perception that arises is experienced to be nonarisen,
> the six assemblages [of sense perceptions] arise as wisdom.
> Thereby the faculties undo themselves.[134]

The *Ornament of Sūtras* also says:

> The wise ones with the power of nonconceptual wisdom
> go in tune with it everywhere, at all times.
> By that the wilderness of faults is conquered
> just like poison through the strong antidote for poison.[135]

Nāgārjuna says:

> Knowledge [of it] not dependent on something else, peaceful,
> not elaborated through elaborations,
> without concepts, without distinctions—
> these are the characteristics of the ultimate.[136]

The victorious Maitreya says:

> Here is nothing to be removed,
> and nothing to be added.
> The actual is to be seen as it is,
> and when one sees the actual, one is free.[137]

And Maitrīpa says:

> Defilements are great wisdom,
> supportive for the yogis like a forest for fire.[138]

By the same token, there are very many vajra statements [like these].

Furthermore, as Maitrīpa says, one will not attain liberation easily by means of the explanations deriving from negating reasoning alone:

When not ornamented by the words of a teacher,
Madhyamaka as well is just mediocre.[139]

In a similar vein, the great noble Master Rendawa[140] says:

The primordial actuality is devoid of clarifying, obscuring,
drowsiness, and agitation.
Let it be in its own place; don't dilute it with an intellectual
yearning for meditation.
Let go and assign the guard of mindfulness.
Like a bird that flies from a boat in the expanse of the
ocean,
circling in all directions and landing there again
—however many hosts of concepts may manifest—
in the end, they land in their own abode, the expanse of
reality.
Thus, there is no need to stop concepts deliberately.
Let go and pay attention with mindfulness.
Similar to poison treated with mantras,
concepts and unawareness arise as great wisdom.[141]

In short, this instruction system of "Mahāmudrā, the Practice of the Connate" consists of four root stages of yoga: "one-pointedness", "freedom from elaborations", "one flavor", and "nonmeditation". Moreover, each of these has three levels—the basic, intermediate, and advanced levels. Consequently one distinguishes twelve steps of practice.

Where all of them are concerned, there are first the methods for settling [in meditation] and sustaining [it], and the methods for passing through the dangerous areas of hindrances, erring, and straying.[142]

In the middle there are the stages of the ways [of meditation] to make concepts the path, which [eventually leads to the experiences outside of formal meditation, in the practice of] subsequent attainment,[143] arising like a magical illusion. Thereby—in the conventional [context]—karmic actions and consequences are fully comprehended, and one investigates whether or not the seeds of the form kāyas have been planted.

Finally one is able to perfectly accomplish the ultimate state of the three buddhakāyas. This process begins with the way in which equipoise and subsequent attainment become one and, gradually, with countless key instructions such as transcendent certainty regarding the unhindered unborn, merging [equipoise and subsequent attainment] throughout day and night, training one's skills by the conduct of integrating [everything] in the path etc.[144]

Moreover, one might wonder whether—just as in the system of the unsurpassable Mahā Ati, where it is taught that the "breakthrough"[145] alone does not enable one to attain buddhahood, and thus one has to engage in the "leap-over"[146]—here as well one would have to ultimately engage in another path; and [the answer is as follows.]

In this system of instruction [i.e. of "Mahāmudrā, the Practice of the Connate"] the three—ground, path, and fruition—are completely [elucidated]. Therefore, this alone is sufficient to attain buddhahood. As it is also said in the *Tantra of Inconceivable Mystery*:

> [First,] through the samādhi of the majestic lion,
> shines one-pointedness, the unwavering lucid mind,
> awakening the wisdom of self-awareness from within.
> Warmth is obtained and thereby the power over birth.
>
> Second, through the illusion-like samādhi,
> by way of the great equipoise free from elaborations,
> inconceivable deep meditation arises as a dynamic power.
> The peak is attained and uninterruptedly further
> development takes place.
>
> Third, through the hero-like samādhi,
> multitude becomes one flavor and the realization of the ten
> bhūmis arises.
> The descendants of the victors of the three times accomplish
> the benefit of others.
> The acceptance is firm, and thus the suffering of the lower
> realms is dispelled.

Fourth, with the vajra-like samādhi,
by engaging in the practice of nonmeditation,
omniscient buddhahood and limitless pure worlds are attained.
It is the great supreme dharma, spontaneous and without
any searching.[147]

The speed [of development] depends on the strength of the person's individual capacity. He who had the supreme of the best capacities, i.e. the unsurpassable, incomparable king of the Śākyas, [the Buddha,] attained the state of the three buddhakāyas based on these samādhis after six years. That Jamgön Lodrö Thaye[148] made this instruction "Mahāmudrā, the Practice of the Connate" known as the "essence yāna" is also attributable to this point.

As for the "path of method" which is taught as "leap-over" in Mahā Ati, the difference concerns only the manner of teaching. In fact, it [i.e. the Mahā Ati path of method] is included in the path of method of the perfection process with characteristics, i.e. powerfulness, illusory body, dream, luminosity, intermediate state, transference [according to the Six Dharmas of Nāropa], and the six practices [according to the Kālacakra system] etc. taught in the tantras of the secret mantra. When one relies on the path of method of the perfection processes with characteristics in the Kagyü system, one receives—according to the style of the paṇḍitas and siddhas of Nālandā and Vikramaśīla[149]—step by step the four empowerments[150] based on a maṇḍala, which is either made from colored powder or painted. Or, in the event that one is of excellent ability, one receives the empowerment of the vajra wisdom. Then one has to practice, starting from the samayas of the five buddha types[151], guarding in great detail the root and the branch samayas, just like one's life or one's eyesight.

In the "leap-over" in Mahā Ati, it is also like that. In the *Wisdom Lama Instruction*[152] the key points of the three gates are shown. Then it is explained that one supplicates the lama three times as the method to enter the great wisdom maṇḍala of self-manifestations. One then continues to meditate that there is a dark blue syllable *A* in the lama's heart. The lama, along with the sound of his ḍamaru, bestows blessing and utters the powerful sound *Pé*[153]. Thereby he [or she] causes the wisdom-being to descend [and continues with the next steps of the initiation] up to bestowing the empowerment of the dynamic energy of awareness based on the fundamental nature [of mind]. Therefore, the "leap-over" Mahā Ati is a path of the secret mantras.

One might wonder for which reason this instruction system of the "Practice of the Connate" was named Mahāmudrā. In general, in India the term Mahāmudrā was given to the inherent wisdom, which arises in the course of an empowerment and becomes fully developed through the samādhi of the two processes.[154] Gampopa held both the Kadampa tradition, which was transmitted through Atiśa,[155] and the entire key instructions of mental nonengagement[156] from Maitrīpa, which Maitrīpa had given to Marpa from Lhodrag. Gampopa combined these two into one stream and gave his instructions accordingly. He thus taught a path by means of which one can easily attain the wisdom as taught in the mantras. It is for this reason that [later on, this teaching system] was given the title of a treatise ["Mahāmudrā, the Practice of the Connate"][157] and that the name of the result [i.e. Mahāmudrā] was given to the cause [i.e. the Practice of the Connate]. Moreover, I think that at that time people valued [a teaching] more when it involved the terms of the secret mantras. Therefore, this language was used in order to inspire all kinds of trainees to engage in this profound authentic Dharma.

As for the sūtra and tantra vehicles, and whether one is higher or lower than the other—the assessment depends on [a particular aspect] of Dharma being suitable during a phase of good or bad times [i.e. in good times the sūtra-aspect and in bad times the tantra-aspect]. Thus, either vehicle can be labeled as the greater one. Actually, I don't think that anyone who has not attained buddhahood has the capacity to see and realize whether one of them is higher or lower.

> From the ground consciousness, which holds all seeds,
> countless [moments of] appropriating consciousness[158] arise
> as illusions.

When one comes to ripeness, the reflection of the world—
appearances and objects,
that is the [particular] realm, the body, etc.—unfolds and
solidifies.

Again, the consciousness endowed with the representations
of objects
is clarity and awareness as such. Primordially, these
representational concepts have not arisen
but are empty in themselves—the key point of the
dharmakāya.
[This is] praised as the harmonious path, which enables
one, by knowing one, to liberate all.

The incomparable Gampopa who was predicted by the
Victor
taught this entire profound path, which shows the cause for
saṃsāra and nirvāṇa
[for those, who are] not [yet] able to abide
in [their] natural awareness,[159] to become able to do so.
May these [teachings] never disappear because [they are]
what] liberates sentient beings.

I, called Mipham Chökyi Lodrö, the Shamar-throne holder, wrote this in the time between the 14th and 24th July 2001 according to the western calendar in Kündröl Ling, the retreat center of the Karma Kagyü tradition in France, Europe, in the intervals between the empowerments and teachings which I gave to one hundred members of the sangha community on the occasion of their entering a new retreat. I completed this work on the 24th of July 2001, on the fourth day of the sixth month according to the Mongolian calendar, the special day, on which the Victor has set the wheel of dharma into motion.

Part 3: A Treasury of Immaculate Teachings. The Practice-Method of Concept-Dharmakāya

By the Fourth Shamarpa, Chödrag Yeshe[160]

Homage to the deva maṇḍala.

> With unalterable faith, I pay homage to
> the brilliant, primordial purity resembling a jewel,
> which, even when stained by the obscuration of
> defilements,
> is the unchanging essence, the dharmakāya with its display
> [of qualities].

> The power of the unobstructed insights' bright light-rays,
> of the sun[-like Kagyüs'] minds perfectly filled with
> numerous qualities
> shines on the snowy mountain of teachings of the
> omniscient peerless teacher [the Buddha]
> and makes the nectar-stream of the noble Dharma flow—
> victorious Kagyüs!

> I respectfully bow down to the teachers who guided [me],
> who have eliminated the net of doubts in my mind,

With the precious tool of precision as to canonical
scriptures and logical reasoning,
you are experts in engaging in the struggle with the Māra of
unawareness.

Faithful ones with one-pointed devotion to
the teaching of [this] lineage asked,
"What is its view as to the dharmakāya?"
Thus, to make their question fruitful,
I am writing this here, short but clear.

In this context, "concept-dharmakāya" has been taught by early
Kagyü teachers. There is actually no need to say much about this
because [concept-dharmakāya] does not constitute any flaw of
negativity[161] and because this [topic is already] clear from the authentic words of the Buddha.

However, some whose eye of intelligence is blinded assert, without knowing what they are saying, that [concept-dharmakāya] is
nonsensical. Right[162] [this is understandable], yet this is due only
to their not having studied the [relevant] scriptures.

In this context, the king of Dharma, [Gampopa,] the Healer from
Dagpo,[163] taught:

[...] because the dharmakāya's emptiness pervades all
sentient beings.[164]

And:

These concepts which arise as [if they were something]
concrete,
take them firmly to be the dharmakāya.
When this becomes an experience, the nature [of mind] is
seen.[165]

As far as the meaning of this statement is concerned, some of the
propounders of this tenet say, "all arising concepts are the dharmakāya and so there is no [difference in] quality between buddhas
and sentient beings." However, this is only a sign of their scant
knowledge of the Dharma. It is not like that. Rather, the *essence* of

concepts is the dharmakāya as such, not [simply] all the concepts that arise.

In the *Sūtra of Śrīmālādevī* it is said:

> Śāriputra, "the element[166] of a sentient being", is an expression for a tathāgata. Śāriputra, "tathāgatagarbha" is an expression for the dharmakāya. Therefore, Śāriputra, a sentient being's element, and the dharmakāya are not different from one another. Rather, a sentient being's element itself is the dharmakāya, and the dharmakāya itself is a sentient being's element. In terms of their meanings they are not two; there is only a semantic difference.[167]

In the *Sūtra of the Inconceivable Mystery* it is said:

> Śāntimati, it is like that: For example, space is present in all physical appearances. Likewise, Śāntimati, the kāya of the tathāgata is present in all who appear as sentient beings. Śāntimati, it is like this: For example, all that appears as form is contained in space. Likewise, Śāntimati, all that appears as sentient beings is also contained in the kāya of the tathāgata.[168]

Thus, the primordial emptiness of mind-itself is established as the dharmakāya, and [terms] such as "sugatagarbha"[169] or "element" were simply taught as synonyms. By the same token, Paṇḍita Abhayākara teaches this in detail in his *Ornament of the Sage's Intent* [saying]: "'Basis', 'seed', 'element', and 'nature' are synonyms."[170]

The tantras also speak about "the all-pervading dharmakāya". In the *Hevajra* it is [, for example,] said: "Sentient beings are buddhas as such."[171] And in the *Cakrasamvara* it is said:

> In whichever surrounding one is—it is the palace.
> In whichever company one is—it is Heruka.[172]
> Whatever action one performs—it is the dharmakāya.
> There is nothing that is not reality.[173]

And

These five [types of] beings are the five buddhas.
Just like a good dancer and painter,
likewise, the "great bliss" alone displays the multiple dances
of this *single* experience.[174]

Some might think that while it is correct to [speak about] the dharmakāya at the time of attaining buddhahood, it is not correct in
connection with sentient beings. It is not like this. Rather, as to the
essence of the naturally pure dharmakāya, there is not the slightest qualitative or quantitative difference among the three, that is
those who live in the prison of the six realms, those who abide
[on the bodhisattva levels starting] with the path [of seeing] until
the tenth [bodhisattva]level, and those who are on the level of a
buddha. As it is said in the *Sūtra [Requested by the Bodhisattva]
Dhāranīrājesvara*:

> As for the qualities of stainless buddhahood, by virtue of the
> very nature of their inseparability [from the mind], even with
> regard to ordinary beings who are completely obscured by
> their defilements, there is no difference between earlier and
> later. Thus, this ground [i.e. buddha nature] is inconceivable.
> So, [even] a sentient being who does not engage in the
> infinite wisdom of a tathāgata, in no way does [this sentient
> being] have the disposition of a [samsaric] sentient being.[175]

One might think: "If that is the case, all sentient beings would
become liberated [from cyclic existence] without any effort." But
this is also not correct. [This is already evident from the ways] it
was explained by the teachers of the precious Kagyü lineage who
taught by means of many analogies such as the sun [covered by]
clouds, silver [hidden] in ore, or a mustard seed in the ground.
Likewise, as it is said in a sūtra[176]:

> Butter, for example, is present in milk, permeating it,
> and in the same way buddha nature permeates all sentient
> beings.[177]

And in the [*Sūtra of*] *Candraprabha*: "All beings are pervaded by
sugatagarbha."[178]

And in the *Sūtra on Buddha Nature*:

> Like a buddha who is present [in a] withered lotus, honey [in
> the midst of] bees, grains [in] husks, gold in the midst of dirt,
> a precious image in earth, likewise is the sugata's element
> present in sentient beings who are obscured because of the
> stains of adventitious defilements.[179]

In the *Hevajra* it is also said:

> [Sentient beings are buddhas as such,][180]
> though they are covered by adventitious stains.
> Once these [defilements] are removed, they are buddhas.[181]

Accordingly, even though the element, the dharmakāya, pervades
sentient beings, they do not realize [their dharmakāya-mind], because it is covered by the obscuration of defilements. Thus, there
are three phases, this impure one [as mentioned right now], then,
the gradually slightly purer one, and [finally] a totally pure state.
Thus, the *Ultimate Continuum* states:

> According to the succession of impure,
> [partly] impure and [partly] pure, and perfectly pure,
> one speaks of a sentient being, of someone who abides
> on the path, and of a tathāgata.[182]

The *Sūtra of Śrīmāladevī* also explains this in detail. Having in mind
such explications, the noble teachers of the Kagyü lineage [first] in
India and [later also in] Tibet meticulously composed vajra-songs
and explanations on treatises in verses. So, neither did they teach
randomly according to their own assumptions nor [just] based on
their personal experience.

Also, in terms of reasoning, as it is taught in the *Sūtra on Buddha
Nature*:

> Since beginningless time, the [buddha-]element
> has been the basis for all phenomena.
> Because it exists [there are] all beings,
> and nirvāṇa is also attained."[183]

Thus, because the cause, [that is] emptiness, the dharmakāya, is present in all sentient beings—when this fruit has been actualized— the two kāyas[184] manifest as well. The fruit of awakening does not arise simply from ignorance [i.e. through ordinary concepts], just as a [white] conch cannot be transmuted from charcoal.

Therefore, by teaching "concepts are the dharmakāya", the previous authentic masters pinpointed the core. This actuality, that the essence [of mind] and concepts are not different—which is the profound point of the Secret Mantra, labelling [already] the cause [i.e. buddha nature] as the result [i.e. as dharmakāya]—is evident in the writings of the illustrious Khachö.[185]

> Those who harbor doubts regarding that which is
> trustworthy
> and whose eyes are blinded regarding the pure Dharma,
> even when they meet the Victor's teachings, [instead of
> being] mentally transformed,
> it is certain that they are carried away by the toxic water of
> their inner fixed ideas.
>
> In those who know the key instructions of the teachers'
> lineage
> and realize the intent of the teachings correctly,
> the water patterns of fixation[186] in their minds will be
> undone and
> it is certain that they will achieve experiences that are
> undeceiving.
>
> Instead of properly assessing with an unbiased mind,
> those damming up a muddy pond of crooked words do
> nothing but tire themselves.
> For the minds of noble ones, they are a shame.
> Those who are endowed with intelligence should regard
> [concept-dharmakāya]
> as a perfect and truthful teaching.

Here, in the great ocean of the Kagyüs' view,
[I am like a] frog aspiring to measure the dimension [of this ocean], which is not possible.
However, I who am a follower [of the Kagyüs] have just sprinkled a little of some water drops of this view.

I request forgiveness for any mistakes
caused by my lack of understanding.
May, through this virtue, all sentient beings realize the dharmakāya
and thus actualize the unsurpassable great awakening.

This "A Treasury of Immaculate Teachings. The Practice-Method of Concept-Dharmakāya", was written by [me,] Chökyi Dragpa Yeshe Pal Sangpo, the fourth holder of the Shamar crown upon the repeated request of a faithful Sakyapa in the region where previous masters have set their lotus feet known as the solitude of abundant happiness, the cave Zhedzong. It was written down by Mati Sāgara (Tib. Lodrö Gyamtso). May an abundance of virtue and happiness spread throughout space and time.

Part 4: The Sixty Verses on Mahāmudrā. Illuminating the Kagyüs' Intent, a Short Presentation of Mahāmudrā

By the Fourth Shamarpa, Chödrag Yeshe[187]

Homage to the noble masters, the spiritual teachers.

To that, where there is neither increasing nor diminishing,
which is the nature of all, saṃsāra and nirvāṇa,
the freedom from concepts, appearing as all things,
to Mahāmudrā I wholeheartedly prostrate.[188] [1]

[Masters] who have a view that is embedded in realization[189]—
[their] key instruction is the supreme light,
which illuminates the path for going toward
 unsurpassable attainment.
This is what shines in the Dagpo practice lineage. [2]

Nowadays there are but few who dedicate themselves to practicing,
and those who instruct [others] in tune with the mode of abiding
are very rare.

Thus, to match the meaning of the teachings to [one's] own thoughts, [everything]
is presumptuously analyzed down to the tiniest detail [causing]
many divisions. [3]

Those who take [the mind operating] with representations or without representations[190]
to be a real principle,
and thereby [attempt to] untie the reality of the middle [path],
do not understand the most unique Madhyamaka of Nonabiding [in the sense of] Unity.[191] [4]

Mahāmudrā, ornamented with the instructions of the spiritual teacher,
shows the key point of the last wheel [of Dharma][192]
of the perfection [vehicle] in accordance with the mantra [vehicle] [193]—
this is what the noble ones of this tradition teach.[194] [5]

Here, in order to clear away mistaken views,
to ascertain suchness and to
overcome doubts—in short it is in these three ways
that I wish to speak for the sensible ones. [6]

Some followers of emptiness proclaim, "Since there exists neither good nor bad, don't adopt and don't give up,"
thereby holding on to a distorted meaning of the view,
the cause for intolerable karmic ripening.[195] [7]

Also, those who say "Emptiness alone is the most unique among the paths
to defeat the hosts of defilements; thus, realizing it without relying on other methods gives rise to the dharmakāya,"
fall short of seeing the true mode of abiding as well.[196] [8]

[Others] proclaim "[We] don't maintain any standpoint, are free from [all] extremes."

With regard to the ineffable, such deceitful words [point to] a
path of delusion too.
It might also [just indicate] that they have no certainty in [their]
own view,
Through this, one is also not able to see the ultimate.[197] [9]

For some, similar to non-Buddhist propounders of [the principle
of] eternalism,
the aspect of the ultimate is permanent and enduring,
At the same time they proclaim that everything else is fictitious.
Confusing dualistic clinging as buddha nature[198] is but a source of
laughter.[199] [10]

Tediously, stringing together intellectual assumptions in one line,
they [try to]
determine the meaning of essencelessness, which is free from one
and many
and teach a lingering in the memory of the lack of reality.
This does not lead beyond a nonaffirming negation either.[200] [11]

"This nonaffirming negation is totally inappropriate"—
I do not raise such a categorical [objection],
yet [those who] wish to realize the actuality of this,
Mahāmudrā, an affirming negation,
should give up [the notion of it] being [a nonaffirming nega-
tion].[201] [12]

If even scholars, those inspired by deities, and siddhas
who say that they have realized the view of the true nature,
are completely fixated solely on biased perspectives
then there is no need to mention those who talk about ordinary
things. [13]

As for knowing the view of reality,
it is not by mere study of many scriptures,
it is not by meditating on instructions that are free from profound
key points,

it is also not by rational analysis and scrutiny, [14]

but by the unfolding of latent tendencies from previous lives
and by possessing an unwavering devotion to the spiritual friend
who
hails from the transmission line of realized spiritual teachers.
This way [you come] to realize the genuine view. [15]

With [the support] of a wise spiritual teacher, a fortunate student
should follow the Dharma and subsequently integrate it
because it is also not through faith alone that the instructions are
embraced.

Moreover, through meditation, the direct path[202] [16]
of experience and realization arises in the mind-stream.
Consequently, the gradual elements of the process of meditation
should be
given in concise instructions and then further elucidated to the
student,
so that a general idea is pointed out.
In that regard, there are the preliminaries, the actual [meditation
practice] and the subsequent [attainment].[203] [17]

In the first place, what is known as the causal condition[204] is explained:
Just as fruits [arise] without fault [from their respective] seeds,
so it is with wholesome and negative actions—this is to be contemplated carefully.
Thereafter, the remedies[205] should be applied extensively. [18]

To rely on a spiritual teacher who is endowed with knowing, car-
ing, and abilities
—[i.e. on a] spiritual friend who is himself endowed with realization,
gives the path [caringly] to others, and is able of bestowing blessing [on them]—
this is said to be the main condition. [19]

After having understood [the views of]
Non-Buddhists, the propounders of permanence or extinction[206],
as well as of those who speak of real minute particles and
of a [direct] contact between objects and consciousness,[207]
of the [propounders] of self-awareness and self-clarity,[208]
of real and false representations,[209] and in particular of the systems of the Madhyamaka [view] [20]
with representations and without representations,[210]
then, to ascertain a view surpassing these is the object condition.

When one is just floating in all kinds of concepts regarding [21]
what is to be meditated and the process of meditation, etc.,
there is no scope for stable meditative absorption.
Thus, to dispel expectations and fears is the immediate condition.

Having fully matured with these four [preliminary] conditions,
the steps leading to engagement in the actual [meditation prac-
tice] also need to be clarified: [22]

When there is total distraction due to attachment, there is excitement
and no entering into one-pointedness.
When drowsiness and the other weakness [of distraction][211]
have been relinquished, pliancy allows the experiences of joy,
clarity,
and nonconceptuality to unfold, and calm abiding arises. [23]

Then, someone who wishes for the realization of the connate[212]
[should understand that] all these phenomena [do not come
about from] other agents,
[but are] appearances from one's own mind, which is empty by
nature as well.
The meaning of this was also explained by master Nāgārjuna and
others [24]
who were aware of the true nature of Madhyamaka.

A spotted rope made up of many threads
will certainly give rise to fear in a person who mistakes it for a snake,
yet the snake is not established in this rope. [25]

The whirling firebrand appears like a wheel [of fire],
yet there is no wheel at the tip of the firebrand.
In just the same way, the very being of all of the illusory appearances of the manifold saṃsāra
is uncontrived, naturally abiding; this, primordially, [26]
is the nature of the luminosity of Mahāmudrā.

In particular, [as to] the very nature of the six complex [senses],[213]
—when the earlier has ceased and the later has not yet arisen—
this very moment is clear and nonconceptual [27]
and manifold relative appearances can equally arise.

Therefore, because these [manifestations and their emptiness] are
genuinely established as inseparable,
as a unity, as of one substance, of one essence,
as to the nature, there is absolutely no delusion. [28]

Therefore, the equal flavor of all phenomena is the primordial
nature
spontaneously present, not being just one [i.e. either manifesting
or empty].
This mode of abiding is one's own mind, primordial purity, the
dharmakāya,
unchanging in its continuity as cause, path, and result. [29]
This is buddha nature.

When one knows with certainty this equality [of manifestation
and emptiness]
free from refuting and establishing,
there is no chance anymore for the arising of even a hint of an
extreme view.
Thus, [the view of] the equal flavor of existence and peace
is the supreme of [all] views. [30]

Regarding delusion, when one does not understand one's own nature,
the wise explain—by means of the analogy of the clearing of contamination of water[214]—
the sustaining of an uncontrived natural awareness as meditation
to be practiced;
that is, to abide with whatever arises. [31]

Becoming familiar with this [in meditation] brings about the realization of self-aware wisdom.
"This self-awareness in regard to all phenomena, starting from
matter up to omniscience,
is just like the center of the sky, by nature pure, deep, clear, and
nondual"[32]
—this is what [I have] learned directly from the teachings of
Mañjuśrī.[215]

With your eyes closed, you do not see a vase,[216] likewise
mere nonthought[217] is not the [Buddha's] intent. [33]
[His intent] is the surmounting of clinging to the view that
knowing and objects of knowledge are separate.

This, the mind of awakening, [bodhicitta],
which is nondual as regards all sentient beings,
is not an object of thought and expression.
In the light of which—because there is nothing to analyze—
[this state of mind] is referred to as "mental nonengagement",[218] [34]
[as] explained by Maitrī and Sahajavajra.[219]

Having completed the supreme path [of meditation],
as for the steps of subsequent [attainment]:[220]
Fear of anything should be completely abandoned.
Thus, a lion-like conduct is to be practiced.[221] [35]

With the preliminary training of the yoga of powerfulness,
one connects to Mahāmudrā, the supreme powerfulness.[222]
By this, wisdom rapidly arises.
Some noble ones explain this to be the secret mantra path.[223] [36]

By cultivating meditation in this way, even a beginner
sees the all-ground directly by awareness, which is aware of itself
and, due to that, understands inferentially both the obscured and
the nonobscured.[224]

[Then,] at the time when defilements, coarse and subtle, [37]
are mingled indistinguishably with their antidotes,
the all-ground is truly seen [by direct yogic awareness].
This is called the attainment of the great path of seeing, the
awakened state,
thus explained by [Karmapa] Rangjung Dorje in his vajra verses.[225] [38]

It is said: "Even when there are doubts regarding the profound
teaching,
samsaric existence will be torn to shreds."[226]
Therefore, [I am] touching only briefly on [those points, which
are] grounds for uncertainty,
and elucidate them by means of straightforward speech. [39]

[Some] may [claim] that without relying on a karmamudrā,[227]
connate Mahāmudrā will not be realized.
Yet know that "the joy from sexual intercourse" is
what the unfortunate discuss, while the Buddha [40]
never taught that to be immutable joy.

[Also] master Indrabhūti[228] has clearly refuted this,[229]
and it is also explained in the commentary to the Kālacakra tantra.
Thus you [who propound this, merely] exhaust [yourself] with
the exertions of disputation. [41]

Some say that present-day Mahāmudrā[230]
and Heshang's claim are known to be similar in meaning.[231]
You friends, the claim of Heshang saying:
"Any kind of concept, good or bad, is to be blanked out"— [42]

[Do you really think] that present-day Mahāmudrā
is equivalent to that [in its views]?
Hey, did you give serious thought to the opponent's claim? [43]

If not conceptualizing anything were a blanking out—
in the *Madhyamaka Key Instructions*[232] by Atiśa and the songs
of Mahāsiddhas such as Saraha[233] [it is stated]:
"not conceptualizing anything, not grasping at anything,
all mindfulness and mental engagement is left behind"[234]— [44]
[so] how is it possible for you to repudiate these?

[Some] may [claim] that [the Mahāmudrā teaching]
"appearances are mind" is just a Mind-Only level[235] and that
this is not asserted from the Madhyamaka onwards.

Yet, are you proclaiming loudly that the king of tantras,[236]
the sūtras that teach the Madhyamaka,[237] [45]
and Nāgārjuna's teachings, such as the *Praise of the Vajra of
Mind*,[238]
teach the Mind-Only [view]?
What other scriptural authorities and arguments do [you] have? [46]

Some claim, "However good the [Mahāmudrā] meditation may be,
it remains nothing more than Madhyamaka meditation."[239]
[In this case], it is reasonable to ask yourself what you mean
when you say "Madhyamaka meditation": [47]

[As for its] two [ways, general Madhyamaka,] i.e.
emptiness analyzed through inferential reasoning,
and [the Mahāmudrā level of Madhyamaka,] i.e.
direct looking at natural luminosity:
[Only those who] by virtue of meditation make experiences,[240] see
[the latter] validly.

In particular, wise men with integrity also say that [48]
this Madhyamaka of Nonabiding [in the sense of] Unity,
which came down from the noble Saraha, father and sons,

and [was transmitted through] the glorious Dagpo Kagyü,
is superior to other Madhyamaka traditions as a method [49]

You too appear to respectfully endorse
the teachings of Maitrīpa and the tradition of Nāropa.
[So] also regarding the appropriateness or nonappropriateness
of the sequence of the four mudrās,[241]
it would be reasonable [for you first to] think clearly and then
speak.[242] [50]

"The [nontantric] Mahāmudrā meditation of the ignorant, it is
taught,
mostly becomes a cause of animal birth or leads to rebirth in the
formless realm,
or to falling into the śrāvakas' cessation."[243]

This pointless combination [51]
is not suitable for those of great learning:
This talk of a single cause that leads to the absorption of cessation,
which is difficult to practice even by the śrāvaka arhats,
to the four meditative concentrations,[244] and to rebirth in the animal [realm]: [52]

Not only does it contravene great scriptural traditions
and the noble ones' teachings, but it also merely debases one.
Although there are many sources of perplexities similar to this,
it is not possible to fool anyone in the ranks of the intelligent
ones. [53]

Yet, just like [in the story of] the rabbit and the splash,[245]
when an unfortunate person bereft of understanding has em-
barked on a deviant path,
if the compassion of the Victorious One cannot do anything,
then what [good] will my many words do? [54]

In the heart of noble ones there is no envy,
nor would they teach non-Dharma nor abandon the Dharma.
Yet, as far as the view and canonical treatises are concerned,
it does no harm to investigate these by means of logical reasoning. [55]

Thus, however much scholars may refute or affirm arguments,
it definitely does not change my respect [for them].
Those who [act otherwise], placing their trust on something else,
are ridiculous. [56]

Any view has to relate to the canonical treatises and reasoning,
because striving to put [the view] into practice [gives rise] to all qualities.
Thus, further and further development will be achieved.
This being the case, it [i.e. the view] should be embraced by
those who strive to follow the path. [57]

That which is the mudrā of unity,
engaging the whole of saṃsāra and nirvāṇa
as a dimension of a single nature,
is well described by the term Mahāmudrā. [58]

By the power of loving care, I have written this.
As for any errors in explaining the words and meanings,
no matter how small they might have been,
I request the mighty scholars and siddhas for forgiveness. [59]

By the good of this explanation, may those who uphold faith and
are thus followers of the Dharma
be entirely free from all disputation and make efforts to explore
the path.
May they internalize this correct view and
may all sentient beings attain the embodiment of wisdom. [60]

Having been urged for a long time by a spiritual friend who is endowed with much learning and dedicated to the profound teaching, [I,] the Buddhist monk Chökyi Dragpa Yeshe Pal Sangpo,[246] have composed these sixty verses. Śubhaṃ.

Part 5: The Point of Meditation, a Summary

By the Second Shamarpa, Khachö Wangpo[247]

With unwavering faith,
[I] always remember and pray [to you, my] master.[248]
[Your] compassionate blessing is unsurpassable
and [your] kindness is without equal. [1]

[After this prayer to his teacher, Shamar Khachö Wangpo now addresses his disciple:]
By virtue of pure karma and aspirations in previous [lives],
[you] achieved a flawless precious [human body with its] freedoms and endowments[249]
and met with supreme teachers endowed with a lineage of transmission.
My child, you have found which is hard to find.[250] [2]

[You] obtained the key instructions of the profound path,
developed certainty, and [your] wish to practice arose from within.
[Your] mind has by itself come to know its own nature.
My child, you have become the most fortunate. [3]

This life's appearances are just deceptions.
They appear to be so real but are unreliable.
Do not go along with delusory appearances,
My child, but firmly turn away from clinging. [4]

Practicing Dharma without reminding [oneself] that death can come at any time,
one [remains] a mere simulation of a Dharma practitioner.
Yet, a mere simulation will not bring about the Dharma's purpose.
My child, develop weariness and renounce [the samsaric world]. [5]

Sentient beings of the six realms, your [previous] fathers and mothers,
have been kind to you since beginningless time.
From your heart, generate [this] certainty again and again.
My child, practice the Mahāyāna mind training. [6]

If one's mind has not been purified from obscurations,
there is no chance for its qualities to arise.
The four powers [of purification]251 must be applied appropriately.
My child, understand this key point of the remedies. [7]

Without the auspicious accumulating of goodness,
no one can attain unsurpassable awakening.
To unify the two accumulations [of wisdom and merit],
my child, you should apply the maṇḍala as the path. [8]

Like mistaking a pile of stones for a human being,
one is deluded if one mistakes the pure as impure.
Comprehensively practicing the creation processes,
my child, ascertain the perfectly pure as pure. [9]

There is no buddha other than the teacher.
With a mind free from harboring doubts,
at all times, in all ways,
my child, get to the heart of your prayers. [10]

If one doesn't let go of distractive thoughts,
meditative absorption can hardly arise in one's mind.
The past, the future, and the present—
my child, give up all these agitating concepts. [11]

For a person [however] who is familiar with meditation,
distractive thoughts cause no harm [any longer].
If, [however] one [still] clings to obstacles as something concrete
that should be abandoned, one is mistaken.
My child, leave [concepts] self-liberate. [12]

The world of appearances, saṃsāra and nirvāṇa, are one's own
mind,
suchness, luminosity, free of limitations,
appearance and emptiness are inseparable, the primordial state.
My child, recognize this of your own accord, from within. [13]

First, undistracted mindfulness is essential.
With growing familiarity, mindfulness leads to a state of
non-[conceptual] mindfulness,[252]
—meaning beyond meditation, beyond distraction—
my child, meditate [in this way] like the flow of a river. [14]

As for your conduct, at all times
ensure that your behavior is consonant with the Dharma and is
free of negligence.
For pretensions to naturally dissipate,
my child, adorn [your] conduct with attention. [15]

The unity of appearance and emptiness is the meaning of the
ground.
Method and insight, the creation and perfection [processes], are
the meaning of the path.
Primordial spontaneous presence is the meaning of the fruition.
My child, these three meanings are inseparable. [16]

Being convinced that buddhahood is [one's own mind],
only by never being without this full dedication,
will one fully accomplish the dispelling of hindrances and the enhancement of [the practice].
My child, there is no doubt about this. [17]

Until one has familiarized oneself with meditation in formal sessions,
the key point is to bring the practice into flow.
Having familiarized oneself with meditation, day and night,
my child, sustain experiences and realization continuously. [18]

To achieve such certainty,
the key point is to practice on the spot.
If in your practice, stone cannot [crush] bone,[253]
my child, then [this] Dharma is [merely] superficial and [therefore] useless. [19]

Even if at present one seems to be a very good [practitioner],
upon encountering an adverse circumstance
one becomes an ordinary person with defilements ablaze like fire,
my child, rendering whatever you have practiced meaningless. [20]

When there is attachment toward those one is closely connected with,
and desire arises for wealth, enjoyment, and sense objects,
one is not a Dharma practitioner.
My child, eradicate desire and aversion. [21]

If you do not fool yourself,
others will not be able to fool you.
Do not lose control [of your life] to [other] people,[254]
my child, and guard all aspects[255] of your practice. [22]

The moment your mind-stream is merged with the Dharma,
no adverse condition will cause you distress.
Enemy and friend will be seen as essentially not different from
one another

My child, [at this point you] have set foot on the ultimate path. [23]

Although they are not endowed with the view of the true nature,
many are acclaimed as great meditators.
Yet, when a single difficult situation occurs,
my child, all of them will be unmasked. [24]

For this not to happen to you,
do whatever your teacher advises you.
Do not give in to [distracting] circumstances,
my child, and remain firm in your own way of being. [25]

The key instructions regarding dreaming, intermediate state,
transference,
luminosity, energy pathways, currents, and potencies
are methods for beholding the essence of the mind.
My child, they are to be practiced without attachment. [26]

In short, guru yoga and the key point,
which is looking at the very essence of one's mind,
are the quintessence of Candraprabhakumara's[256] intent.
My child, there is nothing superior to that. [27]

To accomplish the auspiciousness of all auspiciousness
and [to hoist] the victory banner of all victories,
this heartfelt gabble,
my child, was written by Khachö. [28]

May there be happiness!

Part 6: The Stages of a Meditation Practice of Unity

By the Second Shamarpa, Khachö Wangpo[257]

A condensed explanation of the stages of a meditation practice of unity. Homage to all the tathāgatas and their descendants.

To the question what "the practice of unity" and what "the stages of meditation" mean, [the answer is] as follows: "The practice of unity" is calm abiding that simultaneously is deep insight because [in this case these two] are connected with each other. "Stages of meditation" refers to the manner in which this is converted into the path.

At the onset one compassionately vows to liberate all sentient beings from cyclic existence, that is, [one generates] bodhicitta, taking no heed of one's own body and even one's own life. Having taken this vow, one should then engage with the six or ten perfections.[258] However, one should primarily abide in meditative absorption, the boundless types of which are summed up in just two [methods], as taught in the *Noble Unraveling the Intent* [*Sūtra*]:

> Therefore, one should understand that all of the teachings of the various types of meditative absorptions of śrāvakas,

bodhisattvas, and tathāgatas are summed up in calm abiding and deep insight.[259]

Moreover, regarding the great benefit [of these two aspects of meditation], the same [sūtra] states:

> Further, Maitreya, one should understand that the wholesome qualities of śrāvakas or bodhisattvas or tathāgatas, mundane happiness as well as all supramundane wellbeing are the outcome of calm abiding and deep insight.[260]

One's aspirations will not be fulfilled in the absence of [the required] causes, in the presence of the wrong causes or when the causes are not complete, just as [without] seeds seedlings [won't grow], [milk cannot be milked] from horns, and an echo [does not resound if not both a sound and a particular environment are present][261]. Instead, those who claim to be followers of the Buddha should assiduously apply these two meditative absorptions. As it is said in the *Noble Recitation of Dharma*:

> Whoever wishes to train according to my example
> should assert himself [or herself] in calm abiding and deep insight.[262]

Like someone who has reached the top of a high mountain [and thus has a panorama of everything], or like someone who lives in a home made from beryl [where everything is clear because it is transparent], when one abides therein [i.e. in calm abiding and deep insight], the ultimate nature of all phenomena will be realized. As it is said:

> Someone who has become familiar with deep insight
> and calm abiding will liberate himself [or herself]
> from the bondage of existential unease[263]
> and from the bondage of characteristics[264].[265]

With calm abiding alone, one will not accomplish one's purpose. As it is said in the *Noble King of Meditation* [*Sūtra*]:

> You may practice calm abiding, but by itself it will not surmount the notion of an identity. One will [after the

meditation again] be severely agitated by defilements, similar to the meditative absorption of Udraka.[266]

Deep insight without calm abiding will, by the same token, be unstable. As the *Great Parinirvāṇa Sūtra* states:

Śrāvakas do not see buddha nature[267] because their meditative absorption is very strong, but their insight is lesser. Bodhisattvas do behold it, yet it is unclear because their insight is very strong, and their meditative absorption is lesser. Tathāgatas behold it completely because they are equally endowed with calm abiding and deep insight.[268]

The prerequisites for [developing] calm abiding are initially elucidated by reference to six factors:[269]

[1] Staying in an environment that is conducive [to developing calm abiding] by virtue of [the following] five features:

(a) easy availability {of the necessities of life};

(b) a good place {without malicious people};

(c) a healthy place {where one does not get ill};

(d) good company {of ethical and like-minded people}; and

(e) a pleasant [environment]{in that it is always, day and night, quiet without people making meaningless noise}.

[2] Having few desires, {in that one does not crave for perfect and abundant pleasures}.

[3] Being content, {in that in regard to Dharma robes and the like one is satisfied with simple quality}.

[4] Completely avoiding excessive activity, {in that one does not engage in all kinds of pursuits such as buying, selling, and socializing}.

[5] Abiding by pure ethics, {in that one does not diverge from the fundamental precepts and, in case one does, one remedies the lapse immediately}.

[6] Completely renouncing concepts such as desire, {knowing that the many flaws that go along with them are the cause of severe defilements both in this and future lives}.

[Supported] by these [conditions, the mind] will become stable, just like a candle not exposed to wind. As the *Sūtra of Candraprabha* states:

> The power of calm abiding makes [the mind] unshakable.[270]

The prerequisites for deep insight are threefold:

[1] Relying on an authentic master who possesses the four qualities of learning, clarity of expression, compassion, and acceptance of setbacks. {In addition to these four, [the authentic master's] thoughts should have the strength of freedom from the three spheres,[271] as [being free from] these three sums up the prerequisite for deep insight.}

[2] Seeking much erudition {by discerning the meaning of the Buddha's teachings and by properly remembering what one has contemplated}, and

[3] correctly contemplating on the definitive meaning.

By means of these [factors the meditator] will accomplish his [or her] aspirations, as it is said in the *Jewel Heap* [*Sūtra*]:

> With insight one will attain perfect wisdom.[272]

Now, when practitioners engage in meditation, they should [find] congenial surroundings and [first generate] the intention to support all sentient beings such that they will attain [the state of] awakening. Then one should prostrate to the buddhas and their descendants of the ten directions by [touching the ground with] the five limbs.[273] In front of oneself, one places a representation [of the Buddha] such as a picture. It is also acceptable [to do] this otherwise, [for example, by visualizing the Buddha]. One [continues with] offerings and praises as much as possible, and the confession of negative deeds and so on.[274] Then, on a soft and comfortable seat, one takes either the full {or the half cross-legged} posture of the noble Vairocana; it is also acceptable to take any posture that is comfortable. The eyes should neither be wide open nor closed but look in the direction of the tip of the nose.[275] [The upper body] should be neither inclined forward nor inclined backward but be vertically aligned. Maintaining clear mindfulness [the meditator] sits and, first of all, practices calm abiding.

To the questions, "What is calm abiding? What is deep insight?" [the answer is] given in the *Noble Cloud of Jewels Sūtra*:

Calm abiding is one-pointedness. Deep insight is the discernment of reality.[276] Therefore, four foci are to be accomplished: [1] Calm abiding focuses on the illusory reflection of all phenomena without conceptual thoughts.[277] [2] Deep insight examines the suchness of all phenomena. By pursuing this, one will understand the ultimate nature [of all phenomena, i.e.] suchness, and [this understanding is] perfected. Accordingly, [as experienced through calm abiding] illusory reflections [are focused] nonconceptually and [as experienced through deep insight] illusory reflections [are initially focused] conceptually. [3] [Eventually,] the ultimate nature of all phenomena [is realized nonconceptually] until [4] the goal[278] [of awakening] is fully perfected.[279]

In [the context of this entire process of meditation], the practitioner [first] focuses the mind on the body of the Tathāgata, as it is described in the *King of Meditation* [*Sūtra*]:

The world's protector is most beautiful
with his physical appearance as radiant as gold.
The one who settles the mind on this focus,
that bodhisattva is known [as one] in equipoise.[280]

When [through this calm abiding meditation] the [visualized] body becomes clear [the practitioner] should [through the meditation of deep insight] investigate: where does this [mental image of the] tathāgata come from, where does it abide, and where does it go to? Such analysis leads to not-seeing [anything, because the tathāgata is inherently nonexistent]. One should meditate in the same way, analyzing all phenomena.[281]

[Generally] one should enquire: "is the mind well focused on its reference point, or is it drowsy or is it drawn to outer objects?"[282] In case of the second, [i.e. drowsiness], one should call to mind the perfectly joyful appearance of the Buddha, who is highly inspiring[283], or his twelve deeds [through which he benefits sentient beings], or the [topic of] dependent arising. If the last is the case [i.e. distraction], one should call to one's mind the characteristic that [things] are unreliable, in that everything conditioned is impermanent, [everything that is contaminated by clinging] involves suffering, etc.[284] At times when one is well focused, one should remain even-minded. In short, "the elephant of the samsaric mind should be tied with the rope of mindfulness and clear knowing to the treetrunk of focus."[285]

[As for deep insight:] Subsequently [i.e. grounded in calm abiding], the practitioner should explore reality, i.e. the emptiness of everything that is labelled either as a person or as phenomenon:

Where the person is concerned, [this] is not found apart from its psycho-physical constituents, elements, and sense fields,[286] and it is also not the very essence of the psycho-physical constituents, and so on. Therefore, what is referred to in the world as I and mine is nothing but a delusion. This is how one should investigate.

[Where phenomena are concerned:] any imputed outer and inner phenomenon is nothing but empty. In this context, the *Noble Descent into Laṅkā* [*Sūtra*], for example, also states that outer objects do not exist:

> There are no outer forms.
> It is one's own mind that appears as an outer
> [world].[287]

In this way, [it is taught] in different variations that everything that appears as object and subject is dream-like: [1] that objects [are by] nature consciousness, or [2] that the manifestation of an object occurs only in the mind because consciousness itself is the object, or [3] that in the absence of something beheld by the mind, there is also no consciousness, etc.

Thus, to help those who adhere to precisely this philosophical view, the statement [in the *Noble Descent into Laṅkā Sūtra*] formulated just above [i.e. "There are no outer forms. It is one's own mind that appears as an outer world"] and in the *Noble Sūtra on the Ten Levels*, "these three realms are mind only",[288] etc., were taught. However, [these teachings] are not to be taken as the ultimate meaning. To the question why, [the answer] is given in the [*Noble Descent into Laṅkā Sūtra*]:

> Once one has relied on [the notion of] Mind Only,
> external objects should not be imagined.
> Based on the apprehension of suchness,
> one should also pass beyond Mind Only.
>
> Having passed beyond Mind Only,
> one should go beyond, into a state that is without appearances.
> A practitioner who is established in a state without appearances
> sees the Mahāyāna.[289]

Therefore, everything, object and subject, are nothing but the very essence of dependent arising, magical illusions, and the like. This is how one should analyze. Accordingly and confirming all of this, the *Noble Cloud of Jewels* [*Sūtra*] teaches in detail:

> Those knowledgeable of the [handling of] errors should—in order to become free from all elaborations—apply the practice of unity in [their] meditation on emptiness.
> When they are meditating on emptiness extensively—fully exploring the various objects to which the mind is spreading out and the various objects with which the mind is enamored as well as their very essence—they will discern all of these [outer and inner phenomena] as empty. Examining the [perceiving] mind, this will [also] be realized as empty.
> Examining the mind that realizes—when this is also fully explored [as to its] very essence—it [too] will be identified as empty.
> Through such discernments, one engages in the practice of unity, which is devoid of [any clinging to] characteristics.[290]

For precisely this reason, the *Descent into Laṅkā* [*Sūtra*] also states:

> The arising of things is a conventional [perspective].
> Ultimately, they lack self-nature.[291]

The *Noble [Sūtra of] Detailed Playful Manifestations* also says:

> The descendant of the Śākyas [i.e. the Buddha],
> by seeing dependently arisen phenomena as being devoid of
> self-nature,
> became perfectly endowed with a mind that resembles
> space.
> When he saw the deceitful along with its hordes, there was
> no deceit anymore.[292]

The *Jewel Torch [Sūtra]* also states:

> That which has arisen out of conditions
> has not in fact arisen by its own nature.
> [But] the "body of reality",
> [this] is the body of the Victors.[293]

Master [Nāgārjuna] also says:

> That which is dependently arisen is not inherently arisen.
> That which is not inherently arisen is nonarisen.
> That which does not arise inherently
> How can this be called "arising"?[294]

It is therefore not plausible that ultimately there is an arising:
[1] from itself, [2] from other, [3] from both, or [4] without any
cause, for the [following] reasons:
[ad 1] Were there an [arising] from itself, [would the effect] exist
already [at the time of the cause] or not? In the former case, as it
existed already [it would not arise anymore, otherwise] it would
be an infinite. In the latter case, it would not happen that the
horns of a rabbit and so on do not arise.
[ad 2] [An arising from something other, necessitating that causes
and effects are of an entirely different nature, would mean that]
everything would arise from everything.
[ad 3] [An arising from both] would combine [the flaws of] both
[the above], and
[ad 4] [An arising of effects without any causes would imply that
things are] unconditioned, [which would mean that they would

either be there always or never because they would not depend on interacting causes and conditions].

As [arising] from other [and from itself] is not plausible, how should—as this is not plausible—the latter two [i.e. 3 and 4] be plausible?

Any linguistic designation in the three times is [therefore] a conventional imputation, nothing but an illusion. Ultimately, even buddhahood is without characteristics, not to mention everything else. [This is how] one should analyze. The [*Sūtras*] *on the Perfection of Wisdom* also states:

> Subhūti, even buddha[hood] is like an illusion, like a dream. Even nirvāṇa is like an illusion, {like a dream}. If there were something far superior to the phenomenon of nirvāṇa, this too would be like an illusion, like a dream.[295]

Thus, by perfectly knowing the ultimate, one [becomes] free from examining and analyzing. Being without verbalizing and whole[heartedly] and naturally engaged, without mental conditioning, one meditates very clearly on suchness and one should abide therein. When one does so, this continuity should be maintained without distraction. When one beholds a distraction, one should immediately pacify it. Clearing [the mind in case of] agitation etc. has [already] been described above.

One should not strive to augment or diminish one's [deep] insight and [calm] abiding but [simply] be aware. Otherwise, [one's mind] becomes flickering like a candle placed in a draft, or it becomes excessively relaxed like a person asleep.

Further, one should remedy the six types of weaknesses impeding meditative absorption by means of the eight mental factors which remove them:

[1] laziness should be counteracted by the four remedies of confidence, aspiration, effort, and pliancy;

[2] losing one's focus should be counteracted by the remedy of mindfulness;

[3] drowsiness and [4] agitation should be counteracted by the remedy of clear knowing; and

[5] lack of effort and [6] over-exertion should be counteracted by the two remedies of intention and equanimity.

From time to time, one should look at all the [things] in the world and consider them to be like an illusion, like a dream, like the reflection of the moon on water and like an optical illusion. The *Sūtra About Entering Non-Conceptuality* also states:

> [In meditation], the wisdom that transcends the world
> beholds all phenomena to be similar to the center of the sky.
> With subsequent attainment, they are beheld to be like an illusion,
> a mirage or the reflection of the moon on water.[296]

Seeing all sentient beings in this way as illusion-like, one generates great, limitless compassion.[297] Then, one takes a short rest, after which one should engage again in [meditative absorption] without appearances. As soon as one becomes physically or mentally weary, one should take a break [as described] above and then again engage as before [in meditative absorption].

Then, if one wishes, one rises from meditative absorption. Before one releases one's crossed leg posture, one should contemplate as follows: While ultimately all these phenomena are primordially unborn, by virtue of the gathering of manifold causes and conditions they manifest in all their diversity and appear to be convincingly real [as long as they are] not examined, just like the water of a mirage. Actually, they have no existence whatsoever. So why should one [cling to notions of] annihilism [or of permanence] and so on? In this regard, those who in their distorted perception lack the eye of insight and therefore strongly cling to [the notion of] self and other are wandering aimlessly [in saṃsāra]. It is utterly mistaken to turn one's back on them completely and, out of dislike, not fully engage in accumulations for their benefit, [considering them to be] hopeless cases.

One should rather be like a magician [who knows that everything is illusion-like]. Being skillful in accomplishing the vast accumulation [of the unity of wisdom and merit] without splitting them into two [discrete entities], one will quickly obtain the unsurpassable level [of awakening] and in samsaric existences, one will continually bring about benefit and happiness of all types. This is what we need to accomplish.

Regarding the question what "accumulation" in this context is about, the *Sūtra Revealing the Inconceivable Mystery of the Buddha* says:

> By virtue of the accumulation of wisdom,
> all defilements will be relinquished.
> By virtue of the accumulation of merit,
> all sentient beings will be healed.[298]

This is also explained in detail in the *Noble Sūtra About the Arising of Buddhas*

> The arising of tathāgatas is not due to one single cause. How so? Oh, bodhisattvas, tathāgatas have attained perfect accomplishment through ten myriads of immeasurable causes. What are these ten? Limitless merit and wisdom are the causes of acquiring an utterly unquenchable desire [to benefit others]....[299]

Having contemplated in this way, one should release one's crossed leg posture, prostrate to the buddhas and bodhisattvas of the ten directions, and make offerings and direct praises to them. Then one should engage in limitless aspirations.[300] At all times, without losing [the insight into] emptiness, which quintessentially is compassion, one should endeavor to fully engage in the accumulations such as giving.

Practitioners should at all times avoid consumption that is not in accord [with the teachings] such as fish, meat, alcohol etc. and practice meditative absorption in four or six sessions [each day]. They should live alone in a hermitage and [engage] in the practice of unity through just this practice.

This "Condensed Explanation of the Stages of a Meditation Practice of Unity" is a condensation of a work written by Ārya Vimalamitra and was summarized and composed by [me], a Buddhist monk who enjoys solitude. May there be goodness, may there be happiness.

Tibetan Texts

The Ornament of Gampopa's Intent.
Dispelling Doubts Regarding Concept-Dharmakāya

By the 14th Shamarpa, Mipham Chökyi Lodrö[301]

རྣམ་རྟོག་ཆོས་སྐུའི་དོགས་སེལ་སྒམ་པོའི་དགོངས་རྒྱན།།

Preface by Karmapa Thaye Dorje

བདུད་བཞི་མུན་པའི་དཔུང་རྣམས་གཏན་བཅོམ་ནས།།
ཇི་བཞིན་ལེགས་པར་གདམས་པའི་བདུད་རྩི་སྟེན།།
ཉེ་རིང་དབེན་པའི་ཐུབ་པའི་སྙེན་མོར་བྱེད།།
ཡེ་ཤེས་པད་མོ་འབྱེད་པར་འཚར་གྱུར་ཅིག།

འཇིག་རྟེན་གྱི་ཁམས་འདིར་སེམས་ཅན་སུ་འདུ་ཞིག་ཡིན་རུང་། མོ་མོའི་
བསོད་རྣམས་ཀྱི་བགོ་སྐལ་ལ་སྤྱོད་པ་དང་། རང་གི་བདེ་འབྲས་ལ་ལོངས་སུ

107

སྟོང་པའི་བསྐལ་བཟང་ཐོབ་པ་སོགས་བདེ་འབྲས་ཐམས་ཅད་ཀྱང་། དངོས་
བཀྱུད་ཅེ་རིགས་ནས་བདེ་བར་གཤེགས་པའི་བསྟན་པ་དང་སངས་རྒྱས་ཀྱི་
འཕྲིན་ལས་ཏེ་ད་ལ་རག་ལས་པ་དང་། དེ་དག་དང་འབྲེལ་བ་ཁོ་ན་ཡིན་པ་
ནི། ཅེ་སྐད་དུ། སྟོང་འཇུག་ལས།

ཇེ་ལྟར་མཚན་མོ་མུན་ནག་སྤྲིན་རུམ་ན།།
གློག་འགྱུ་སྐད་ཅིག་རབ་སྣང་སྟོན་པ་ལྟར།།
དེ་བཞིན་སངས་རྒྱས་མཐུ་ཡིས་བརྒྱ་ལམ་ན།།
འཇིག་རྟེན་བསོད་ནམས་བློ་གྲོས་ཐང་འགའ་འབྱུང་།།

ཞེས་གསུངས་པ་ལྟར་ཏེ། འཇིག་རྟེན་གྱི་ཁན་བདེ་ཐམས་ཅད་ནི་བདེ་བར་
གཤེགས་པའི་བསྟན་པ་དམ་པའི་ཚེས་ཀྱིས་དགེ་སྡིག་བླང་དོར་གྱི་ལམ་བསྟན་
པ་ལ་བློས་པ་ཁོ་ན་ཡིན་པ་དང་། རྩལ་ཏེ་སྟོན་པའི་ཐབས་ཀྱི་བློ་མོ་མཚོག་
ནི། དེའི་གསུང་རབ་བཀའ་དང་། དེའི་དགོངས་འབྲེལ་དུ་གཏོགས་པའི་
གཞུང་རྣམས་དང་། དེ་འབྲེལ་ཐུན་མོང་དང་ཐུན་མོང་མ་ཡིན་པའི་བསྟན་
བཅོས་རྣམས་ཡིན་ལ། དེ་ཡང་བཀའ་དང་བསྟན་བཅོས་ཀྱི་གཞུང་ལུགས་ཀྱི་
བྱ་བ་ཇེ་འདྲ་ཞིག་ཡིན་ཀྱང་། དེ་དག་ལ་ཐོས་བསམ་སྒོམ་སྒྲུབ་སོགས་ཚེས་
སྟོང་བཅུ་ཡི་སྒོ་ནས་འཇུག་པའི་འཇུག་གཞི་རྣམས་ཀྱི་གཙོ་བོ་ནི། གཙུག་ལག་
རག་པའི་ལམ་ནས་དྲངས་ཏེ་གཞུང་ལུགས་ཡིག་ཐོག་ཏུ་འཁོད་རིགས་རྣམས་
ཡིན་མོད། དེ་དག་དུས་རིང་ཞིག་ནས་རྣམས་ཆག་དུ་སོང་བས་ཡིད་ཐམ་
པའི་གནས་སུ་གྱུར། དེ་ལྟའང་སྙིགས་མ་ལྔ་བདོ་ཞིང་། རྒྱལ་བསྟན་ཕྱག་ཕྲ་
བའི་དུས་སྐབས་འདིར་ཡང་། ཕྱི་ཉི་ཤུ་ཀར་གཙུག་ལག་ལྷག་ཁང་ནས་དཔལ་རྒྱལ་
བ་ཀརྨ་པ་ཞུ་དམར་ནག་ཚེས་བཀྱུད་ཀྱི་པོད་ཕྲེང་ཞེས་ཆེན་གཙུག་ཀྱིས་ནང་
རིག་གི་གཞུང་ལུགས་དེ་དག་བདེ་བར་གཤེགས་པའི་བསྟན་པའི་གསོན་རྩ

ལ་སྐྱེན་པའི་རེ་འདུན་གྱིས་པར་དུ་བསྐྱེན་པ་དང་། འཕུལ་འཁོར་ལས་དཔར་
བའི་སྐྲོ་ནས་རིས་མེད་རྒྱ་ཆེ་སྐྱོབ་གཏེར་བ་རྣམས་ལ་ཆོས་སྐྱིན་འཛད་མེད་
ཉལ་འགྲོའི་རྒྱུན་བཞིན་སྐྱེལ་བའི་དགེ་བའི་ལས་བཟང་པོ་འདི་ལྷུ་བུ་ནི་ཤིན་
དུ་བསྔགས་པར་འོས་ཤིང་རྗེས་སུ་ཡི་རང་བའི་གནས་གྱུར་པ་དང་། གྲུབ་
འབྲས་རྟོགས་གྲུང་ལ་རིག་པའི་ལེགས་སྐྱོན་མཐུན་འགྱུར་བཅས།

གསུང་རབ་འོད་དཀར་ལྷ་ཡི་གཟིངས་རིང་ནས།།
འཆར་བའི་མོད་ལ་བློ་ལྡན་རྒྱ་ཡི་གཏེར།།
ཕྱོགས་བརྒྱར་སྐྱེལ་སྐྱེད་འདི་ཉིད་དཔར་བའི་དགོས།།
འཇིག་རྟེན་ཆོས་སྐྱོང་དགྱེས་པས་ཤིས་གྱུར་ཅིག།

ཅེས་པའི་སྐྱོན་ཚིག་འདི་ཡང་རྒྱལ་བ་ཀརྨ་པའི་མཚན་གྱི་ཕྲིན་ལྲབས་འཆང་བ་བཅུ་བདུན་
པ་མཐའ་ཡས་རྡོ་རྗེས་སངས་རྒྱས་ཀྱི་འདས་ལོ་༢༥༩༩ སྐྱེན་དྲུག་ཟླ་བའི་དཀར་
ཕྱོགས་ཟླ་བ་ཧྣ། ཕྱི་ལོ་༢༠༠༩ ཟླ་བ་ ༡༠ ཚེས་༣༢ ལ་བཟང་པོར་སྤེལ།།
ཕུབ་མཚུ་སགཏམ།།

Introduction by Prof. Sempa Dorje

སྤྱིར་སྐྱིད། ད་ལམ་རྒྱལ་བ་དོན་གྱི་བདག་པོ་ཀུན་གཟིགས་ཞུ་དམར་རིན་
པོ་ཆེས་ལྲགས་རྩོམ་གནང་བ་རྣམ་རྟོག་ཆོས་སྐྱེའི་དགོས་སེལ་སྐྲམ་པོ་པའི་
དགོངས་རྒྱན་ཞེས་བུ་བའི་བསྐྱེན་བཅོས་འདི་ནི་མཉམ་མེད་དྭགས་པོ་བཀའ་
བརྒྱད་ཀྱི་ཐུན་མིན་ལྲ་སྐྱོམ་སྐྱོད་པའི་གནད་གསང་སྐྱས་དོན་གྱི་རིམ་པ་རྣམས་
ཚིག་ཉུང་དུའི་དོན་ཆང་བར་སྐྱོན་པ་སོགས་ཁྱད་ཆོས་དུ་མ་དང་ལྡན་པ་
ཞིག་དུ་གྱུར་ཀྱང་། ཕྱིས་པ་རྣམས་ཀྱིས་མཁས་པའི་དགོངས་པ་རྟོགས་

109

དགའ་བར་བརྟེན་སྟོན་སྐྱིང་འཐུག་སྐྲོ་ཅུང་ཟད་འབྲི་བར་སྤྲོ་བ་ལ།   སྐུ་
བསྐྱར་ཀྱི་རྒྱལ་པོ་སློ་བྲག་མར་པ་ལོ་ཙོས་དགའ་བ་བརྒྱ་ཕྱག་ཏུ་མས་སྙེད་དོན་
མ་དོ་རྒྱུད་མཐའ་དག་གི་སྙིང་པོའི་དོན་ལ་མཚན་ཕྱག་རྒྱ་ཆེན་པོ་ཞེས་ཐྱབ་པ་
ཆེན་པོའི་དགོངས་པ་མཐར་ཕྱག་ཡིན་པར་གདེང་ཐོབ་ཅིང་རང་གིས་ཀྱང་
ཧྟོགས་པ་མངོན་དུ་གྱུར་པའི་ལམ་དེ་ཉིད་ཡིན་པ་ནི།   ཉིད་ཀྱི་བསྲུང་ལས།
ཐེག་པའི་མཐར་ཐུག་སྐྱིང་པོའི་དོན།།   མཐའ་བྲལ་ཡིད་ལ་མི་བྱེད་པ།།
ཆོས་ཕྱག་རྒྱ་ཆེ་ལ་དོ་སྤྱོད་ཀྱིས།།   ཞེས་པས་བསྟན།   དེ་ནས་ཟུང་
སྒྲུབ་བརྒྱུད་ཤིན་ཏུ་ཆེན་པོ་བརྒྱུད་ཀྱི་བྱེ་བྲག་ཕྱག་ཆེན་བརྒྱུད་པ་ཞེས་པའི་རིང་
ལུགས་དོ་མ་མེད་པ་འདི་ཉིད་གངས་ཅན་སའི་ཁྱོན་ཀུན་སུ་ཡོངས་སུ་གྲགས།
དེ་ནས་གྲུབ་མཐའ་དེ་ཉིད་ཀྱི་བཀྲུད་པ་ཟམ་མ་ཆད་ཅིང་མ་ངག་ནུམས་སུ་
བྱུང་བ་ལ་བརྟེན་པོད་དུ་ཐེག་ཆེན་འཕགས་པའམ་གྲུབ་ཐོབ་ཀྱི་ཚང་ཆེན་པོ་
བཙོལ།   ཁྱད་པར་དུ་མཉམ་མེད་དགས་པོ་རིན་པོ་ཆེས་ཕྱག་རྒྱ་ཆེན་པོའི་
བགའ་སྤྲལ་འདི་ཉིད་དབང་པོ་མཆོག་དམན་ཀུན་གྱིས་རང་འཆམས་ཀྱིས་
ཕྱིར་མི་བརློག་པའི་གནས་ཐོབ་ཐུབ་པའི་ཐབས་བླ་ན་མེད་པ་སེམས་དང་རྣམ་
ཧྟོག་ཆོས་སྐུ་གསུམ་གནད་གཅིག་ཏུ་སྐྱིལ་ཏེ་བསྟན་པར་མཛད་པས་རྗེ་ཉིད་ཀྱི་
སྤྱོབ་མ་སྐྲོམ་རྒྱུང་ཞིག་གིས་ཀྱང་མཁས་པ་ཆེན་པོའི་གོ་ས་རོས་པ་དུ་མ་བྱུང་
།   ཕྱིས་ལྟ་གྲུབ་འདི་ཉིད་ཀྱི་གནད་གསང་མ་ཞེས་པ་རྣམས་ཀྱིས་བླུན་སྤྱོམ་
སོ་ཕགས་སུ་བརྗོམ་སྟེ་འགགག་པ་དང་དོགས་གནས་ཅི་རིགས་པ་བྱུང་།   དེར
བརྟེན་དུས་དང་དུས་སུ་རང་གི་ལྟ་གྲུབ་ལ་དོགས་གཞི་ལང་ཚོ་དོགས་མེལ་
བྱ་རྒྱུ་ནི་བསྟན་པའི་བདག་པོ་རྣམས་ལ་བཀུར་བར་འོས་པའི་ཕྱག་ལས་ཡིན་
པར་སེམས།

དེས་ན་སྐྲབས་བབ་ཀྱི་དོགས་སེལ་བསྲུན་བཙོས་རིན་པོ་ཆེ་འདིའི་ཐོག་མར

སྒྲུབ་བསྒྲུབ་སྙིང་པའི་སོགས་སྦྱོག་གཅིག་གིས་སྟོན་པ་ཐུབ་པའི་དབང་པོ་ལ་
མཆོད་པར་བརྗོད་པ་བསྟན། དེ་རྗེས་ནུ་རོ་མེ་ཏེ་སོགས་སྦྱོག་གཅིག་གིས་
གདམ་ངག་བརྒྱུད་རིམ་སྙིར་བསྟན་ལ། སློས་སུ་ཚིགས་རྐང་ཐ་མས་རྩོམ་
པ་པོ་རང་ཉིད་དེ་ལུའི་གདམ་ངག་གི་སྐལ་བ་དང་ལྡན་པར་གྱུར་པ་བསྟན།
པའམ་དོན་གྱིས་བརྒྱུད་འཛིན་དུ་བཞུགས་པར་བསྟན། དེ་རྗེས་གང་དེའི་
སོགས་གཞུང་སྦྱོག་གཅིག་གིས་གཟུགས་རྒྱན་གྱི་ལམ་ནས་དངོས་དུ་བརྩམ་
པར་དམ་བཅའ་བ་བསྟན་ལ། ཤུགས་ལ་བསྟན་བཅོས་འདིའི་དགོས་
སོགས་ཚེས་བཞི་བསྟན་ཏོ།།

དེ་ནས་གཞུང་དོན་དངོས་སུ་འཆུག་པའི་ཐོག་མར་ཕྱོགས་སྟུའི་བཞེད་པ་བགོད་
དེ་དགག་བཞག་སྟོང་གསུམ་དོགས་སེལ་གྱི་རྒྱལ་རྣམས་ངེས་དོན་ཕྱུག་རྒྱ་
ཆེན་པོའི་ཐུན་མིན་གྱི་ཚེས་སྐད་དུ་རྣམ་ཧོག་ཚེས་སྐྱའི་ཐ་སྐྱད་རང་ལུགས་སུ་
འཁད་པ་ལ་ཚིག་དོན་གཉིས་ཀའི་ཆ་ལ་སྐྱོན་མེད་ཚུལ་ལུང་རིགས་གཉིས་གྱི་
སྒོ་ནས་རྒྱ་ཆེར་གཏན་ལ་ཕབ།

མཐར་ས་བོན་ཀུན་འཛིན་སོགས་གཞུང་སྦྱོག་གཉིས་ཀྱིས་བསྟན་བཅོས་ལུས་
ཡོངས་ཀྱི་བསྡུས་དོན་བསྟན་ཅིང་། རྩོམ་པ་པོ་ཉིད་ཀྱིས་སྐྱམ་པོ་པའི་ལུགས་
ཀྱི་ཕྱག་རྒྱ་ཆེན་པོའི་སྐྱབས་ཀུན་ཧོབ་དུ་རྣམ་ཧྲུན་ལུགས་ཀྱི་དབུ་མར་བཞེད་
པའི་སྲོ་མ་ཚིག་དུ་བསྟན། དེ་རྗེས་རྒྱལ་བས་ལུང་བསྟན་སོགས་ཚིགས་ཀང་
དང་པོ་གསུམ་གྱིས་སྐྲ་པོ་པའི་དགོངས་པའི་མཐིལ་འཁོར་འདས་ལམ་
གསུམ་གྱི་གནད་མ་ནོར་བར་བསྟན་ཏོ།། ཚིགས་ཀང་ཐ་མ་བཅུམས་
པའི་དགི་རྩ་བསྟན་འགྲོ་གཉིས་དོན་དུ་བསྔོ་བས་ལེགས་པར་རྒྱས་བཏབ་པའོ།།
མཛད་བྱུང་ཡང་ཡན་ལག་བཞི་ལྡན་གྱིས་སྲོ་ནས་ལེགས་པར་བསྟན་ཏེ་དོན་
ཡོངས་སུ་གྲུབ་པོ།།

ཞེས་པའི་སྟོན་སྐྱོང་འདི་བཞིན་ཕྱག་དཔེ་འདི་མཐའ་སྐྲབས་རྩོམ་པ་པོའི་བཞད་
སྒྲུབ་གཉིས་ཀའི་མཁས་རྒྱལ་ལ་ཡིན་མོས་ཤིང་དང་བ་སྐྱེས་ལ། བསྐུན་
བཅོས་འདི་ཉིད་རྒྱལ་བསྐུན་སྐྱེ་དང་ལྷག་པར་སྐྲབ་བཀུད་ཕུལ་འཛིན་པ་
རྣམས་ཕན་ཚེ་བར་སེམས། དེ་དང་ཆབས་ཅིག་ཕྱི༑ ༑ཁྱགར་དཔེ་སྐྲན་ཁང་
ནས་སྟོན་སྐྱོང་ཞིག་འབྲི་དགོས་པའི་བསྐུལ་མ་བྱུང་བར་བརྟེན་ཁྱུ་ཏུ་བ་སེམས་
རྡོར་པས་ཕྱི་ལོ་ ༢༠༡༡ སྐྲ་བ་ ༡༠ ཚེ་ ༥ ཉིན་ཀཱུ་པ་རྒྱལ་ཡོངས་ནང་པའི་
གཙུག་ལག་ཁང་གི་རང་ཁག་ཏུ་བྱིས་པ་ཕུལྦམ༎

རྣམ་རྟོག་ཚོས་སྒྱུའི་དོགས་སེལ་སྐྲམ་པོའི་དགོངས་རྒྱན་ཞེས་བྱ་བ༎

Text by the 14th Shamarpa, Mipham Chökyi Lodrö

ཕྱག་བསྐུལ་སྐྱེད་པའི་གཡང་ས་དོར་ནས་མི་གཞིག་ཐར་པའི་ལྭ་ལམ་
བརྟེས༎
ཞེ་མཐར་མནལ་བའི་མཚན་མོའི་གོས་སྒྲངས་ཡེ་ཤེས་དཀྱིལ་འཁོར་
ཀུན་ནས་གསལ༎
སྒོམ་པར་གཡེང་བའི་སྲིན་དུ་རྣམས་སངས་ཕན་བདེའི་འོད་ཟེར་འགོག་
མེད་འཕྲོ༎
མཐའ་ཀླས་འགྲོ་བའི་གཏན་སྐྱབས་ཁོན་ཕྱབ་དབང་ཉི་མ་གཙུག་གིས་
མཆོད༎

ན་རོ་མི་ཊིའི་གདམས་པ་མི་ཟད་མཛོད༎
འཛིན་ལ་དབང་ཐོབ་མར་པ་ལྷོ་བྲག་པའི༎
གཅེས་ནོར་མ་ལུས་འཕྲོག་མཁས་མི་ལ་རྗེའི༎
རྒྱལ་ཚབ་སྐྲམ་པོའི་འབངས་སུ་བདག་མཆེས་སོ༎

112

རྗེ་པོའི་ལེགས་པ་འདད་ཉོར་བུའི་ཕྲེང་།།
ཕྱོགས་ཀྱི་སྙོམ་པའི་བློན་པོའི་ཆེད།།
དབང་ཏྲགས་དུ་རྒྱུན་བསྒྱུར་བ་ལ།།
དྲངས་བས་བྱི་དོར་འདི་ན་སྤྲོ།།

དེ་ཡང་། ཆོས་ཀྱི་རྗེ་པོ་སྒམ་པོ་པའི་ཞལ་སྒྲོབ་བཀྲུད་པའི་ཞལ་རྒྱུན་དུ་རྣམ་
ཏོག་ཆོས་སྐུ་ཞེས་གྲགས་པ་ལ། ཀུན་མཁྱེན་འཇིགས་མེད་གླིང་པས་དོན་
གྱི་ཆ་ནས་མ་ནོར་ཡང་ཆིག་གི་ཆ་ནས་རྣམ་ཏོག་ཞེས་མ་དག་པའི་སེམས་
ཀྱི་མིང་ཡིན་པ་དང་། ཆོས་སྐུ་ནི་འཁྲུལ་པ་དང་བྲལ་བའི་མིང་ཡིན་པས་
དེ་གཉིས་གཅིག་ཏུ་སྦྱོར་ན་མཚོ་དཀར་ནག་གཉིས་གདོངས་བཞིབས་པ་ལྟར་
ཆིག་སྐྱོན་དུ་གསུང་། ཡང་བྱའུ་ཀན་ཆོས་ཀྱི་རྡོ་རྗེས་རྣམ་ཏོག་ཆོས་སྐུ་ཡིན་
ན་སངས་རྒྱས་ལས་ཀྱུན་ཏོགས་པ་མཐོབས་མི་འཐད་ཅེས་དོན་ཡང་ནོར་བར་
གསུང་པར་གྲགས། དེ་སར་པོད་དང་ཕྱི་རྒྱལ་བའི་བླ་མ་འགའ་ཞས་
ཀྱིས་ལོ་རྒྱས་འདི་དག་ལ་ཁུངས་སུ་བཙལ་ཏེ་བཀའ་བཀྲུད་པའི་ཕྱག་ཆེན་གྱི་
ཁྲིད་ལ་སྐྱོན་ཡོད་ཆུལ་སྐད་འཆལ་ཞིག་འགྲོ་བཞིན་འདུག་པས་ལུང་ཏོགས་
གི་བསྟན་པར་གནོད་པ་འགོག་ཅེད་དུ་དེ་ལྟའི་སྐྱོན་རྣམས་མེད་ཆུལ་གསལ་
བར་བསྟན་པ་ཞིག་འབྱི་རོགས་ཅེས་ཕོ་རར་སི་སྒྲུབ་དཔོན་བསྟན་འཛིན་དང་
བླ་མ་ཆོགས་གཉིས་རྣམ་གཉིས་ཀྱིས་རེ་བསྐུལ་གནན་བར་བརྟེན་ནས་འདིར་
རང་གིས་ཤེས་ཆོད་ཅུང་ཟད་ཅིག་འབྱི་བའི་སྤྱོབས་པ་བསྐྱེད་དོ།།

ཐོག་མར། སྒམ་པོ་པས་རྣམ་ཏོག་ཆོས་སྐུ་ཞེས་གསུང་པར་ཆིག་གི་ཆ་ནས་
སྐྱོན་མེད་ཆུལ་སྐྱིང་བ་ནི།

རྣམ་ཏོག་ཅེས་པའི་སྒྲ་དོན་ནི་མདོ་སྡུ་པ་ཡན་གྱི་ཆད་མའི་ལུགས་སུ་ཞེས་པས་
ཡུལ་འཛིན་པ་ལ་ཏོག་པ་དང་དེ་ཡང་བློ་དོར་ཕར་བའི་ཡུལ་གྱི་རྣམ་པ་དེ་འཛིན་

པ་ཡིན་པས་ན་རྣམ་པར་རྟོག་པ་ཞེས་དང་། བཟ་དག་སུམ་ཅུ་པ་ལས་རྣམ་
དབྱེ་གཉིས་པའི་བྱེ་བྲག་ཏུ་བྱུ་བའི་ཡུལ་དང་བྱེད་པ་པོ་གཉིས་ཐ་མི་དད་པ་ཞིག་
ལ། ལ་དོན་གྱི་ཕྱད་འཇུག་ཆལ་བསྟན་པ་ལ་གཞིར་བརྱུང་སྟེ་རྣམ་པར་རྟོག་པ་
ཅེས་པའི་བོད་ཀྱི་ཐ་སྐད་ཞིག་སྟོན་གྱི་མཁས་པས་མཛད་ལ། དེ་ཉིད་བསྒྱུས་
ཚིག་ཏུ་རྣམ་རྟོག་ཅེས་གྲགས་པ་ཡིན་འདུག

སྐྱམ་པོ་པས་རང་གི་སློབ་མ་རྣམས་ལ་ཁྲིད་བསྟན་སྐབས་རྣམ་རྟོག་ཅེས་པའི་
བོད་ཀྱི་ཐ་སྐྱད་དེ་རང་གསུང་སྟེ། དེ་ཉིད་གཅིག་ཏུ་མ་གྲུབ། དུ་མར་མ་
གྲུབ། གཉིས་ཀར་མ་གྲུབ། གཉིས་ཀ་མིན་པར་ཡང་མ་གྲུབ་ཅེས་
མཐར་བཞི་རིགས་པས་བཀག་ཕྱོགས་ནས་གནས་ལུགས་ཉིད་བསྟན་པའམ།
ཡང་ན།

རྣམ་རྟོག་ཐམས་ཅད་དུལ་སྐྱིགས་འདུ་བ་ཕྱིར་དོར་བུ་དང་དེ་དག་གི་གསེབ་
ནས་སེམས་ཀྱི་དོ་བོ་རྣམ་པར་དག་པ་ཞིག་འཚོལ་ཏེ་འཕྲ་དགོས་པ་ལྟ་བུ་མ་
ཡིན་པར། རྣམ་རྟོག་སྐྱད་ཅིག་མའི་དེ་ཀའི་དོ་བོར་མ་བཅོས་མ་སྐྱད་
དགག་སྒྲུབ་མེད་པར་ལྷ་བ་སོགས་རྣམ་རྟོག་ཉིད་ཀྱི་གནས་ལུགས་ཇེ་བཞིན་
པའི་དོ་ཐྱོག་ནས་དེ་དང་ཐ་མི་དད་པའི་སེམས་གནས་ལུགས་ཀུ་ས་ཡིའི་
འཛོག་སྐྱོམ་དུ་གྲགས་པའི་ཁྲིད་ཆུལ་གྱིས་དོ་སྟོང་མཛད་པ་ན། ཞལ་
སྐྱོབ་རྟེས་འཇུག་དང་བཅས་པས་དོན་ཇེ་བཞིན་དུ་རྟོགས་ན་ཅིག་སྐྱོན་མེད་པ་
ཡིན། གལ་ཏེ་ཐལ་ཆེ་བས་རྣམ་རྟོག་གང་ཤར་ཐམས་ཅད་ཆོས་སྐུ་
ཡིན་པས་ཐོས་བསམ་སྐོམ་གསུམ་ལ་བརྩོན་མི་དགོས་པར་གོ་ན་ཅིག་སྐྱོན་
དུ་ངེས་ཀྱང་དེ་ནི་མིན་པར་དགགས་པའི་ཞལ་སྐྱོབ་རྣམས་ཀྱི་གསུང་རབ་དང་
རྣམ་ཐར་ལས་གསལ། ཡང་དཔྱད་ཆུལ་གཞན་ཞིག་བྱེད་ན། མདོ་
རྒྱུད་ཐམས་ཅད་ནས་སྟོང་པ་ཉིད་དང་ཆོས་སྐུ་ཞེས་པ་གཉིས་དོན་གཅིག་ལ་

114

མིང་གི་རྣམ་གྲངས་ཐ་དད་པ་ཙམ་དུ་བསྟན་ཡོད། དེ་མིན་ན་མདོ་རྒྱུད་
ནས་གསུང་པའི་སྟོང་པ་ཉིད་དེ་ཁད་སྟོང་དང་། སྟོད་སྟོང་པ་ཟེར་བ་ལྟ་
བུའི་ལོས་འཛིན་གི་སྟོང་པར་གོ་བས་ཤིན་དུ་མི་འཐད། ཡུམ་ལས།
གཟུགས་སྟོང་པའི་སོགས་སྟོང་ཉིད་བཞི་སྟོར་གི་སྨྲོ་ནས་ཚོས་ཐམས་ཅད་སྟོང་
པ་ཉིད་དུ་གཏན་ལ་ཕབས་ནས།

དེ་ལྟ་བས་ན་གྲུང་ཆུབ་སེམས་དཔའ་རྣམས་ལ་ཐོབ་པ་མེད་པའི་
ཕྱིར། ཤེས་རབ་ཀྱི་ཕ་རོལ་དུ་ཕྱིན་པ་ལ་བརྟེན་ཅིང་གནས་ཏེ་
སེམས་ལ་སྒྲིབ་པ་མེད་པས་ཟག་པ་མེད་དེ་ཕྱིན་ཅི་ལོག་ལས་
ཤིན་དུ་འདས་ཏེ་མྱ་ངན་ལས་འདས་པ་མཐར་ཕྱིན་ཏོ།། དུས་
གསུམ་དུ་བཞུགས་པའི་སངས་རྒྱས་ཀུན་ཤེས་རབ་ཀྱི་ཕ་རོལ་
དུ་ཕྱིན་པ་འདི་ལ་བརྟེན་ནས་བླ་ན་མེད་པའི་བྱང་ཆུབ་དུ་མངོན་
པར་རྫོགས་པར་སངས་རྒྱས་སོ།།[302]

ཞེས་བསྟན་པས་ཏེ་ཆེ་བའི་སྟོང་ཉིད་ཀྱིས་[303] སངས་རྒྱས་མི་ནུས། འདི་
ཡི་དོན། ཏིང་ངེ་འཛིན་འཛིན་རྒྱལ་པོའི་མདོ་ལས།

རྣམ་ཤེས་རང་བཞིན་གཞན་ཡིན་ལ།།

སྟོང་ཉིད་གཞན་དུ་མ་གསུངས་སྟེ།།
གང་གིས་[304] རྣམ་ཤེས་རབ་ཤེས་པ།།

དེས་ནི་སྟོང་ཉིད་རབ་དུ་ཤེས།།
ཅེས་སོགས་ཕྱུང་ལྭ་སོ་སོར་སྣུར་སྟེ་གསུང་ངོ།། ཡུམ་གྱི་མདོ་ལས།

གཟུགས་སྟོང་པའི།།
སྟོང་པ་ཉིད་ནི་གཟུགས་སོ།།

115

གཟུགས་ལས་སྟོང་པ་ཉིད་གཞན་མ་ཡིན།།

སྟོང་པ་ཉིད་ལས་ཀྱང་གཟུགས་གཞན་མ་ཡིན་ནོ།།

ཞེས་སོགས་གསུངས་པ་ན་གཟུགས་དང་སྟོང་པ་གཉིས་མཚོ་གཉིས་གདོང་

བཞིབས་ལྡུ་བུའི་ཚིག་སྐྱོན་དུ་མི་འགྱུར་བ་ཇི་བཞིན། རྣམ་རྟོག་ཚོགས་སྐྱའོ།

ཚོགས་སྐྱ་ཉིད་ནི་རྣམ་རྟོག་གོ། རྣམ་རྟོག་ལས་ཚོགས་སྐྱ་གཞན་མ་ཡིན།

ཚོགས་སྐྱ་ལས་ཀྱང་རྣམ་རྟོག་གཞན་མ་ཡིན་ནོ།། ཞེས་བརྗོད་ནའང་ཚོག་

དོན་གཉིས་ཀ་སྐྱོན་དུ་མི་འགྱུར་བར་སེམས།།

སྐྱམ་པོ་པས།

མཚན་མར་སྨྲེས་པའི་རྣམ་རྟོག་འདི།།

ཚོས་སྐྱ་ཡིན་པར་ཚོར་གྱིས་བཟུང་།།

སྐྱེམ་པ་ཡིན་པ་ད་གཟོད་ཤེས།།

ཉམས་སུ་སྟོང་ན་སྐྱིང་པོ་མཐོང་།། ཞེས་གསུངས་པ་སྟེ།

དཔུ་མའི་རིགས་ལས་སྐྱ་བ་རྣམས་ལ། མཚན་མར་སྨྲེས་པའི་རྣམ་རྟོག་འདི།།

སྟོང་པ་ཡིན་པར་ཤེས་པར་གྱིས།། ཤེས་གསུང་ན་སྐྱན་དུ་འཇིབས་ངས་ལ།

རྣལ་འབྱོར་པ་རྣམས་ལ་ཚོས་སྐྱ་ཡིན་པར་ཚོར་གྱིས་བཟུང་སོགས་གསུངས་པ་

དེ་ཇེས་ཤེས་དང་སྟོང་ཐོག་ཏུ་འབྱུར་ཚེ་བ་ཚམ་ལས་འཆད་ཆུལ་དེ་གཉིས་ཀར་

ཚོག་དོན་གཉིས་ཀའི་སྐྱོན་མེད་པ་འདུ་མཉམ་དུ་སེམས།

དཔུ་མའི་རིགས་ལས་སྐྱུར་ན། རྣམ་རྟོག་ཚོས་ཅན། དོན་དམ་དུ་

ཚོས་སྐྱ་ཡིན་ཏེ། དེ་བོ་མཐའ་བཞི་དང་བྲལ་བའི་ཕྱིར། ཞེས་པས་རྣམ་

གྱངས་པའི་དོན་དམ་དང་། རྣམ་རྟོག་ཚོས་སྐྱ་ཡིན་ཏེ་མཐའ་བཞི་དང་

བྲལ་བའི་ཕྱིར་ཞེས་པས། རྣམ་གྱངས་མིན་པའི་དོན་དམ་བསྟན་ནུས་པར

སེམས་སོ། །

གཞི་རུ་སྣམ་པོ་པས་ཞལ་སྐྱོབ་རྣམས་ལ་རྣམ་རྟོག་གི་ངོ་བོ་དང་ཆོས་སྐུའི་གོ་དོན་ལེགས་པར་འགྱིལ་ཏེ་རྣམ་རྟོག་ཆོས་སྐུར་ངོ་སྤྲོད་ཐབ་ཅིང་རྒྱ་ཆེ་བ་མཛོད་ཡོད་པས་བསྒྱུས་དོན་གྱི་མིད་དུ་རྣམ་རྟོག་ཆོས་སྐུ་ཞེས་བཏགས་པ་ཡིན་པས་འདི་ནི་ཏིང་དོ་འཛིན་སྟོན་པའི་ཐ་སྣྱད་ཞིག་ཡིན།   གཞན་དུ་འཇིག་རྟེན་པའི་བབ་ཚལ་གྱི་གཏུམ་དཔེར་ན་ཕ་མས་བུ་ཕྱུག་ལ་རྣམ་རྟོག་ཚ་པོ་མ་བྱེད་ཅེས་སྐུ་བའི་ཚབ་ཐུའང་རྣམ་རྟོག་ཆོས་སྐུ་ཚ་པོ་མ་བྱེད་ཅེས་བཟོད་དགོས་པར་གསུང་པ་དེ་ག་ལ་ཡིན་ཏེ་མིན་ནོ། །

ད་ནི་རྣམ་རྟོག་ཆོས་སྐུ་ཞེས་གསུངས་པར་དོན་གྱི་ཆ་ནས་ཀྱང་སྐྱོན་མེད་པར་སྐྱིང་བ་ནི།   དཔགས་པོ་བཀའ་བརྒྱུད་ལུགས་ཀྱི་ཕྱག་ཆེན་སྤྲན་ཅིག་སྐྱེས་སྦྱོར་དུ་གྲགས་པའི་ཐབ་ཁྲིད་དུ་མ་ཞིག་ཡོད་པ་ལས།

རྗེ་སྐྱོམ་ཆུང་ཞབས་ཀྱིས།

        སེམས་ཉིད་ལྷན་ཅིག་སྐྱེས་པ་ཆོས་སྐུ་དངོས། །

        སྣང་བ་ལྷན་ཅིག་སྐྱེས་པ་ཆོས་སྐུའི་འོད། །

        རྣམ་རྟོག་ལྷན་ཅིག་སྐྱེས་པ་ཆོས་སྐུའི་རླབས། །

        དབྱེར་མེད་ལྷན་ཅིག་སྐྱེས་པ་ཆོས་སྐུའི་དོན། །

        ཅེས་གསུང་པ་དེའི་དོན།

མདོ་ཡི་དགོངས་དོན་བཞིན་འཆད་ན་སྒྱི་ལ་ཁྱབ་པས་འདི་ལྟར།   སྟོང་པ་ཞེས་པ་དང་ཆོས་སྐུ་ཞེས་པ་གཉིས་གཞི་ལམ་འབྲས་གསུམ་གྱི་རྣམ་བཞག་པོ་སོར་བཞད་པའི་སྐབས་ཀྱི་ཐ་སྙད་ཙམ་ལས་དོན་གཅིག་ཡིན་པ་གཞིར་བཞག་ནས།

སེམས་ཉིད་ལྷན་ཅིག་སྐྱེས་པ་ཆོས་སྐུ་དངོས།། ཞེས་པས། དངོས་བསྟན་དུ། སེམས་སྟོང་པའོ།། སྟོང་ཉིད་ནི་སེམས་སོ།། སེམས་ལས་སྟོང་པ་ཉིད་གཞན་མ་ཡིན། སྟོང་པ་ལས་ཀྱང་སེམས་གཞན་མ་ཡིན་ནོ།། ཅེས་དང་། ཕྱགས་བསྟན་དུ། མ་རྟོགས་ན་འཁོར་བའི་རྒྱུ་བ་སེམས་ཡིན་པར་བསྟན།

སྣང་བ་ལྷན་ཅིག་སྐྱེས་པ་ཆོས་སྐུའི་འོད།། ཅེས་པས། དངོས་བསྟན་དུ། སྣང་བ་སྟོང་པའོ།། སྟོང་པ་ཉིད་ནི་སྣང་བའོ།། སྣང་བ་ལས་སྟོང་པ་གཞན་མ་ཡིན།། སྟོང་པ་ལས་ཀྱང་སྣང་བ་གཞན་མ་ཡིན་ནོ།། ཅེས་དང་། ཕྱགས་བསྟན་དུ། མ་རྟོགས་ན་སེམས་ཉིད་ཡུལ་གཟུགས་སོགས་སུ་སྣང་བ་འོད་ཀྱི་དཔེ་ཡིས་བསྟན།

རྣམ་རྟོག་ལྷན་ཅིག་སྐྱེས་པ་ཆོས་སྐུའི་རླབས།། ཅེས་པས། དངོས་བསྟན་དུ། རྣམ་རྟོག་སྟོང་པའོ།། སྟོང་པ་ཉིད་ནི་རྣམ་རྟོག་གོ། །རྣམ་རྟོག་ལས་སྟོང་པ་ཉིད་གཞན་མ་ཡིན།། སྟོང་པ་ཉིད་ལས་ཀྱང་རྣམ་རྟོག་གཞན་མ་ཡིན་ནོ།། ཞེས་དང་། ཕྱགས་བསྟན་དུ། གཉིས་སུ་འཛིན་པའི་རྣམ་རྟོག་ཐམས་ཅད་སེམས་ཉིད་ཡུལ་དང་ཡུལ་ཅན་གྱི་རྣམ་པར་འཆར་བ་རླབས་ཀྱི་དཔེ་ཡིས་བསྟན།།

དབྱེར་མེད་ལྷན་ཅིག་སྐྱེས་པ་ཆོས་སྐུའི་དོན།། ཞེས་པས། དངོས་བསྟན་དུ། སེམས་དང་། སྣང་བ། རྣམ་རྟོག་གསུམ། རང་རང་གི་སྟོང་པ་ཉིད་དང་དོ་བོ་ལྷན་ཅིག་དབྱེར་མེད་དུ་སྐྱེ་བའི་ཕྱིར་ན། ཆོག་བཅད་དང་ཕོས་བདེན་གཉིས་དབྱེར་མེད། གཉིས་པས་སྣང་སྟོང་དབྱེར་མེད། གསུམ་པས་རིག་སྟོང་དབྱེར་མེད་ཀྱི་དོན་བསྟན་པ་དང་། ཕྱགས་བསྟན་དུ། དཔེར་ན་རྒྱ་དང་། རྒྱ་ནང་གི་གཟུགས་བརྙན། རྒྱ་ཡི་རླབས་གསུམ་ཀུན་རྫོབ་ཏུ་རྒྱ་ཡི་མཚན་ཉིད་གཅིག་པ་དང་། དོན་དམ་དུ་དེ་དག་གི་གནས་

ལུགས་སྟོང་པ་ཉིད་རྣམས་དོ་བོ་ཐ་མི་དད་པ་དབྱེར་མེད་ལྷན་སྐྱེས་ཡིན་པ་
ལྟར། སེམས་སྣང་ཏོག་གསུམ་ཡང་། གསུམ་ཞེས་དོ་བོ་ཐ་དད་དུ་མེད་
པ། མཐའ་བཞི་ལས་འདས་པའི་དབྱིངས་དང་དོ་བོ་དབྱེར་མེད་ལྷན་སྐྱེས་
སུ་ཡོད་པ་ནི་ཆོས་སྐུའི་དོན་ཡིན་ནོ་ཞེས་འབྲས་བུའི་ཆོས་སྐུའམ་དོ་བོ་ཉིད་ཀྱི་
སྐུ་བསྟན་པར་སེམས་སོ།།

དོན་འདི་དང་མཚུངས་པ་ན་རོ་པས་ཀྱང་གསུང་སྟེ།

སྣང་བ་རང་གྲོལ་ཆོས་ཀྱི་དབྱིངས།།
ཏོག་པ་རང་གྲོལ་ཨེ་ཤེས་ཆེ།།
གཉིས་མེད་མཉམ་པ་ཆོས་ཀྱི་སྐུ།། ཞེས་སོ།།

ཡང་། ཆོག་བཅད་དང་པོའི་ནང་། སེམས་ཉིད་ལྷན་ཅིག་སྐྱེས་པ་ཆོས་
སྐུ་དངོས་ཞེས་པས་གཞི་ཡི་ཆོས་སྐུ་བསྟན་ལ། དེའི་ལུགས་ལས། སྣང་
བ་དང་རྣམ་ཏོག་གཉིས་ཀ་སེམས་ལས་གུང་ན་མེད་པའི་ཆོས་སྐུའི་རང་
མདངས་ཡིན་པའི་གནད་སྟོན་པའི་སྐོ་ནས་དེ་ལ་ཇེ་བཞིན་མཉམ་པར་འཇོག་
ཆུལ་གྱིས་སྒོམ་པ་ལམ་གྱི་ཆོས་སྐུ་ཡིན་པར་བསྟན་ཏེ།

དང་པོ་སྣང་བ་ལ། གྲུབ་ཆེན་མི་ཏྲི་པས།

སྣང་བ་སྣ་ཚོགས་སེམས་ཀྱི་དོ་བོ་འདི།།
ཐུག་ཕྱད་ཙམ་གྱིས་མ་གྲུབ་ཕྱག་རྒྱ་ཆེ།། ཞེས་དང་།
ཇེ་མར་པས།

ཕྱི་སྣང་བ་སྣ་བའི་འཁྲུལ་འཁོར་འདི།།
སྐྱེ་མེད་ཕྱག་རྒྱ་ཆེན་པོར་ཏོགས།། ཞེས་དང་།

རྗེ་མི་ལས།

ཕྱི་སྣང་བ་རྗེ་བྱུར་སྣང་ལགས་ཀྱང་།།

མ་རྟོགས་དུས་ན་འཁོར་བ་སྟེ།།

ཕྱི་ཡུལ་གྱི་ཞེན་པས་འཆིང་བར་བྱེད།།

རྟོགས་པ་རྣམས་ལ་སྐྱ་མར་སྣང་།།

ཡུལ་སྣང་བ་སེམས་ཀྱི་གྲོགས་སུ་འགར།། ཞེས་དང་།

རྗེ་སྒྲམ་པོ་པས།

བཏགས་པའི་བག་ཆགས་སྣང་བྲགས་འདི།།

དོན་དམ་ཡིན་པར་ཙིར་གྱིས་བཟུང་།།

ཞེས་སོགས་ཀྱིས་སྣང་བ་ལས་ཀྱི་ཆོས་སྐུ་བསྟན་ཏོ།།

གཉིས་པ་རྣམ་རྟོག་ལའང་། མི་ཏྲི་པས།

མ་སྐྱེས་པ་ལས་རྟོག་པ་བློ་བུར་བ།།

རྟོག་པ་[305] དེ་ཉིད་དབྱིངས་ཀྱི་རོ་བོར་གནས།།

དེ་གཉིས་རོ་མཉམ་གྱུར་པ་ངས་བསྟན་ཏོ།། ཞེས་དང་།

རྗེ་མར་པས།

ཡིད་ཀྱི་གཡོ་བ་གཟུང་འཛིན་གཉིས།།

སྤྲོས་བྲལ་ཆོས་ཀྱི་སྐུ་རུ་ཐིམ།། ཞེས་དང་།

རྗེ་མི་ལས།

ནང་འགྱུ་བ་ཡིད་ཀྱི་རྣམ་རྟོག་འདི།།

120

མ་རྟོགས་.306 དུས་ན་མ་རིག་པ

ལས་རྟེན་མོངས་ཀུན་གྱི་གཞི་རུ་ཡིན།།

རྟོགས་ན་རང་རིག་ཡེ་ཤེས་ཏེ།།

དཀར་པོའི་ཡོན་ཏན་རྟོགས་པ་ལ་ལགས།། ཞེས་དང་།

རྗེ་སྒམ་པོ་པས།

མ་ཆོན་མར་སྨྲེས་པའི་རྣམ་རྟོག་འདི།།

ཆོས་སྐུ་ཡིན་པར་ཅིར་གྱིས་བཟུང་།།

སྒོམ་པ་ཡིན་པར་ད་གཟོད་ཤེས།།

ཉམས་སུ་མྱོང་ན་སྙིང་པོ་མཐོང་།།

ཅེས་སོགས་ཀྱིས་རྣམ་རྟོག་ལམ་གྱི་ཆོས་སྐུ་བསྟན་ཏོ།།

འབྲས་བུའི་ཆོས་སྐུ་ནི། དབྱེར་མེད་ལྷན་ཅིག་སྐྱེས་པ་ཆོས་སྐུའི་དོན།

ཞེས་གཞི་ལམ་འབྲས་གསུམ་དབྱེ་བ་མེད་པར་བསྟན་པ་དེའོ། ཡང་།

དཔལ་ཕྱོགས་ཀྱི་སྒྲུང་པོས།

རྣམ་པར་རྟོག་པ་མ་གཏོགས་པ།།

འཁོར་བ་ཞེས་བྱུ་ཙེ་.307 ཡང་མེད།།

རྣམ་རྟོག་དེ་དང་བྲལ་བས་ན།།

ཁྱོད་ནི་ཏྲ་ཏུ་སྨྲ་དྭ་འདའ།། ཅེས་གསུང་པས།

རྣམ་རྟོག་ཆོས་སྐུར་བཟྟོད་ན་སངས་རྒྱས་སྒྲིབ་ལམ་དུ་མི་འགྱུར་རམ། ཞེ

ན། དེའི་སྐྱོན་མེད་དེ། ཕུན་མོང་བའི་ཞི་ལྷག་ཟུང་སྒྲིལ་གྱི་ཏིང་ངེ་འཛིན་

གྱིས་རྣམ་རྟོག་སྟོང་བ་དང་། སྨྲོན་ལམ་དང་སྒྲུ་མ་ལྟ་བུའི་ཏིང་ངེ་འཛིན་

རྦུང་འབྱེལ་གྱིས་རྣམ་རྟོག་གྲོགས་སུ་བསླུར་བ་དང་། སླུན་ཚིག་སྐྱེས་སྦོར་གྱི་
ཏིང་ངེ་འཛིན་གྱིས་རྣམ་རྟོག་ཚོགས་སླར་འཚེར་བས་ན་ལམ་དུ་བྱེད་པ་སྟེ་རྣལ་
འབྱོར་གྱི་རིམ་པ་སོ་སོར་ཡོད་པ་དང་། སྤྱིར་འབྲས་བུ་ལམ་བྱེད་གྱི་སྐབས་
ཏོན་མོངས་པ་ཡེ་ཤེས་སུ་རྟོགས་དགོས་པ་ནི་རྒྱུད་ཐམས་ཅད་ལས་གསུང་
པ་དང་། གཞི་རྒྱུ་ཏོན་མོངས་པ་ནི་བྲི་བྲག་ཚམ་ལས་དོན་དུ་རྣམ་རྟོག་ཡིན་
པས་དེ་ཐམས་ཅད་ཀྱི་གནས་ལུགས་སྟོང་པ་ཉིད་ཡེ་ནས་ཡིན་བཞིན་པ་དེ་ཉིད་
མ་རྟོགས་པར་ཉན་རང་གིས་ཀྱང་སྟོང་བར་མི་ནུས་པ་ཡིན། མ་སྐྱེས་སྐྱེའི་
འགྱོད་པ་བསལ་བའི་མདོ་ལས་སྤྱིག་པ་འདག་པར་བྱེད་པའི་ཐབས་ནི་སྟྱིག་པ་
དམིགས་སུ་མེད་པའི་གནས་ལུགས་ལ་བལྟ་བ་ཉིད་ཡིན་པར་གསུངས་པའི་
ཕྱིར་རོ།།

དེ་མིན་པར་ཕྱོགས་ཀྱི་སྐྱང་པོས་སྐྱང་འདས་རྣམ་རྟོག་དང་བྲལ་བར་གསུང་
པ་དེ། སྟོང་ངའི་[308]ཕྱི་སྦྱོག་བཞིན་སངས་རྒྱས་ཀྱི་ཐུགས་རྒྱུད་ལས་བྲལ་བའི་
རྣམ་རྟོག་ཅེས་ནེ་ར་ཇ་ནའི་རྒྱུད་གི་དགོས་སུ་དོར་ཡོད་པར་གསུངས་པ་མ་
ཡིན་ནོ།།

དེའི་ཕྱིར་ན་འཕགས་པ་ཀླུ་སྒྲུབ་ཀྱི་དགོངས་པ་རྣམ་པར་ཕྱེ་བ་ལ་མཁས་པ་
ཀླུ་བ་གྲགས་པས་ཤེས་བྱའི་ཚེས་ཐམས་ཅད་ཀུན་རྟོབ་ཏུའང་ཚད་གྲུབ་ཏུ་མི་
བཞེད་པའི་གཏན་ཚིག་དུ་མ་ཞིག་བསྟན་པ་དང་། དཔལ་སྐྲ་པོ་པས་
ཀྱང་དགོངས་པ་དེ་དང་མཐུན་པར་སེམས་སྐྱང་རྟོག་གསུམ་ཀུན་རྟོབ་ཏུའང་
ཚད་གྲུབ་མིན་པར་སྟོན་པ་དང་ཆབས་ཅིག་བོད་ཀྱི་སྐྲོམ་སྨྲ་སོགས་ཕྱི་རབས་
རྣམས་ཀྱིས་སྟོང་ཉིད་གོལ་ཕོར་དུ་མི་འགྲོ་བའི་ཆེད་དུ་ཚེས་སྐུ་ཞིག་གསུངས་
པ་ནི་སྐྲད་དུ་བྱུང་བའི་ཐབས་ཡིན་པར་སེམས་སོ།།

དེ་བཞིན་སྐྲོམ་པའི་ཚེ་ནའང་ཀླུ་བ་དེ་དང་གཞི་མཐུན་སོ་སྣེའི་དོར་གྲགས་པའི

རྣམ་རྟོག་ཅེས་བརྗོད་པས་སྐྱུང་བུ་ངོ་སྤྲོད་པ་དང་། དེ་ཀུན་རྟོག་དང་དོན་དམ་
གཉིས་སུ་མི་བལྟ་བར་གནས་ལུགས་ཆོས་སྐུ་དེ་ཉིད་ལ་བལྟ་བའི་སྐྱོ་ནས་
གཅིག་སྤྱངས་སྟེ་གཅིག་ཤེས་ཤེས་པར་བྱེད་མི་དགོས་པར་གཅིག་ཤེས་ན་ཀུན་
ཤེས་པའི་གནད་ཀྱིས་ཉེན་པའི་མན་ངག་ཁྱད་པར་ཅན་ནི་སྤྱོང་བྱེད་འབྲས་བུ་
ལམ་བྱེད་དུ་བྲགས་པ་ཡིན།

དེའི་ཕྱིར་ན་རྗེ་མར་པས།

ཤེས་པ་གང་སྐྱེས་སྐྱེ་མེད་དུ་སྐྱོང་ཚ་ན་ཚོགས་དྲུག་ཡེ་ཤེས་སུ་
ཤར་བས་དབང་པོ་རང་ལོག་ཏུ་ཐིམ་ཞེས་གསུངས།

མདོ་སྡེ་རྒྱན་ལས་ཀྱང་།

བློ་དང་ལྡན་པས་མི་རྟོག་ཡེ་ཤེས་སྤྱོབས།།
ཐག་ཏུ་ཀུན་ནས་མཉམ་པར་བོང་བ་ཡིས།།
དེ་ལ་བརྟེན་ནས་ཉེས་པའི་ཚང་ཚིང་རྣམས།།
དུག་སྨན་ཆེན་པོས་དུག་བཞིན་འཇོམས་པར་བྱེད།།

ཅེས་གསུངས་པ་དང་།

ཀླུ་སྒྲུབ་ཀྱིས།

གཞན་ལས་ཤེས་མིན་ཞི་བ་དང་།། སྤྲོས་པ་རྣམས་ཀྱིས་མ་སྤྲོས་པ།།
རྣམ་རྟོག་མེད་དོན་ཐ་དད་མིན།། དེ་མིན་དེ་ཉིད་མཚན་ཉིད་དོ།། ཞེས་དང་།
རྒྱལ་བ་བྱམས་པས།

འདི་ལ་བསལ་བྱ་ཅི་ཡང་མེད།། བཞག་པར་བྱ་བ་ཅུང་ཟད་མེད།།
ཡང་དག་ཉིད་ལ་ཡང་དག་བལྟ།། ཡང་དག་མཐོང་ན་རྣམ་པར་

གྲོལ།། ཞེས་དང་།

མི་ཊི་པས།

ཏོན་མོངས་ཡེ་ཤེས་ཆེན་པོ་སྟེ།། དགས་ལ་མི་བཞིན་རྣལ་འབྱོར་གྲོགས།།

ཤེས་སོ་གས་རྡོ་རྗེའི་གསུང་ཤིན་ཏུ་མང་། དེ་ཡང་རིགས་པའི་དགག་ཕྲོགས་ནས་བསྐུན་པ་རྐྱང་པས་གྲོལ་བ་བདེ་བླག་ཏུ་མི་སྟེད་པ་དང་། མི་ཊི་པས།

བློ་མས་ངག་གིས་མ་རྐྱན་པའི།།

དབུ་མ་འང་འབྱེད་པོ་ཙམ་ཉིད་དོ།། ཞེས་སོ་གས་གསུངས་སོ།།

རྒྱལ་འདི་དག་དང་མཐུན་པར་རྗེ་བཙུན་རེ་མདའ་བ་ཆེན་པོས་འདི་སྐད་གསུངས་སྟེ།

གསལ་སྟོབ་བྱིང་རྣོད་སྤངས་པ་གདོད་མའི་དོན།།
བློམ་འདོད་བློ་ཡིས་མ་སྤྲད་རང་སར་བཞག
ལྷུག་པར་ཐོངས[309]ལ་དྲན་པའི་རྒྱུན་སོ་ཆུགས།།
རྒྱུ་མཚོའི་ཀློང་དུ་གཟིངས་ལས་འཕུར་བའི་བྱ།།
ཕྲོགས་རྣམས་སྐོར་ཞིང་དེ་རུ་འབབ་པ་ལྟར།།
ཅི་ཙམ་རྣམ་པར་རྟོག་པའི་ཚོགས་འཕྲོས་ཀྱང་།།
ཐ་མར་རང་གནས་ཆོས་ཀྱི་དབྱིངས་སུ་འབབ།།
དེ་ཕྱིར་རྣམ་རྟོག་ཆེད་དུ་དགག་མི་དགོས།།
ཕུལ་བར་ཐོངས་ལ་དྲན་པའི་བྱ་ར་གྱིས།
དུག་ལ་སྨུགས་ཀྱིས་བཏབ་པ་རྗེ་བཞིན་དུ།།

124

རྣམ་རྟོག་མ་རིག་ཡེ་ཤེས་ཆེན་པོར་འཆར།།

ཅེས་སོགས་གསུངས་སོ།།

མདོར་ན་ཕྱག་རྒྱ་ཆེན་པོ་སྒྲུན་ཅིག་སྐྱེས་སྦྱོར་གྱི་ཁྲིད་ཆུལ་འདི་ལ་ཙ་བ་རྩལ་འབྱོར་གྱི་རིམ་པ། ཙེ་གཅིག་སྟོས་བྲལ། རོ་གཅིག་སྒོམ་མེད་བཞི་དང་། དེ་རེ་རེ་ལ་ཡང་ཆུང་འབྲིང་ཆེ་གསུམ་གྱི་རིམ་པས་རྣལ་འབྱོར་གྱི་ཐེམ་སྐས་བཅུ་གཉིས་སུ་དབྱེ་བ་དང་། དེ་ཐམས་ཅད་ལ་ཐོག་མར་བཞག་ཐབས་དང་སྟོང་ཆུལ། གེགས་དང་གོལ་ཤོར་གྱི་ཕྱང་ལས་བཀྲལ་བའི་ཆུལ། བར་དུ་རྟོག་པ་ལམ་དུ་བྱེད་ཆུལ་གྱི་རིམ་པ་ནས་རྟེས་ཐོབ་སྒྱུ་མ་ལྟར་འཆར་བས་ཀུན་རྫོབ་ཏུ་ལས་འབྲས་ལ་རང་བྱུན་ཆུང་ཅིང་གཟུགས་སྐུའི་ས་བོན་ཐེབས་སམ་མི་ཐེབས་བཏག་པའི་ཆུལ་དང་། མཐར་མཉམ་རྗེས་འདྲེས་ཆུལ་ནས། རིམ་གྱིས། སྐྱེ་མེད་ཟང་ཐལ་དུ་ལ་བཟླ་བ། ཉིན་མཚན་འཁོར་ཡུག་ཏུ་བསྐྱེ་བ། ལམ་འབྲེས་ཀྱི་སྟོང་པས་ཉལ་སྟོང་བ་སོགས་མན་ངག་མཐའ་ཡས་པ་ལ་རྟེན་ནས་མཐར་ཕྱིན་སངས་རྒྱས་སྐུ་གསུམ་གྱི་གོ་འཕང་ཡོངས་སུ་རྟོགས་ཐུབ་པ་ཡིན་ནོ།།

ཡང་། གལ་ཏེ་བླ་མེད་རྟོགས་པ་ཆེན་པོའི་ལུགས་སུ་བྲིགས་ཆོད་ལོ་ནས་སངས་རྒྱས་མི་དགོས་པ་ཐོབ་བཀྲལ་དུ་འཇུག་དགོས་པར་བསྟན་པ་ལྟར། འདིར་ཡང་མཐར་ལམ་གཞན་ཞིག་ལ་འཇུག་དགོས་པ་མ་ཡིན་ནམ་སྙམས་ན། བྲིད་ཆུལ་འདི་ལ་གཞི་ལམ་འབྲས་གསུམ་ཆ་ཚང་བས་འདི་ཁོ་ནས་སངས་རྒྱས་ཐོབ་ནུས་པ་ཡིན་ཏེ། དེ་ཡང་།

གསང་བ་བསམ་གྱི་མི་ཁྱབ་པའི་རྒྱུད་ལས།

མེང་གི་རྣམ་པར་བསྒྱིངས་པའི་དིང་འཛིན་གྱིས།།

125

རྩེ་གཅིག་མི་གཡོ་དྭངས་པའི་ཞེས་པ་གསལ།།

རང་རིག་ཡེ་ཤེས་ཁོང་ནས་སད་པར་བྱེད།།

དོད་ཐོབ་ནས་ནི་སྐྱེ་ལ་དབང་བ་ཡིན།།

གཉིས་པ་སྐྱ་མ་ལྟ་བུའི་ཏིང་འཛིན་གྱིས།།

སྤྱོས་དང་སྤྱོལ་བའི་མཉམ་བཞག་ཆེན་པོ་ལས།།

བསམ་གྱིས་མི་ཁྱབ་ཏིང་འཛིན་རྩལ་དུ་འཆར།།

རྩེ་མོ་ཐོབ་ནས་འཕེལ་བ་རྒྱུན་མི་ཆད།།

གསུམ་པ་དཔའ་བར་འགྲོ་བའི་ཏིང་འཛིན་གྱིས།།

དུ་མ་རོ་གཅིག་ས་བཅུའི་རྟོགས་པ་འཁར།།

དུས་གསུམ་རྒྱལ་བའི་སྲས་པོས་གཞན་དོན་མཛད།།

བཟོད་པ་བརྟན་པས་དན་སོང་སྒྲུག་བསྒྲལ་སེལ།།

བཞི་པ་རྡོ་རྗེ་ལྟ་བུའི་ཏིང་འཛིན་གྱིས།།

སྒོམ་དུ་མེད་པའི་ཉམས་ལེན་བསྟོན་པ་ལས།།

རྣམ་མཁྱེན་སངས་རྒྱས་ཞིང་ཁམས་དཔག་མེད་ཐོག།

མ་བཙལ་ལྷུན་གྲུབ་ཆོས་མཆོག་ཆེན་པོ་ཡིན།།

ཞེས་གསུངས་པ་ལྟར་རོ།།

སྒྱུར་བུལ་ནི་གང་ཟག་སོ་སོའི་དབང་པོའི་ནུས་པར་རག་ལས་པ་ཡིན། དབང་
པོ་མཆོག་གི་མཆོག་གྱུར་ཊ་ན་མེད་པ་མཉམ་མེད་ཤྭགུའི་རྒྱལ་པོས་ཏིང་ངེ་
ཛིན་འདི་དག་ལ་བརྟེན་ནས་ལོ་དྲུག་གི་མཚམས་ན་སངས་རྒྱས་སྐུ་གསུམ་
གྱི་གོ་འཕང་བརྙེས་པ་ཡིན། འཛམ་མགོན་བློ་གྲོས་མཐའ་ཡས་ཀྱིས་ཕྱག
རྒྱ་ཆེན་པོ་ལྷན་ཅིག་སྐྱེས་སྦྱོར་གྱི་ཁྲིད་ཀ་འདི་ལ་སྐྱིང་པོའི་ཐེག་པ་ཞེས

བསྐྱངས་པའང་དོན་ནི་དང་འབྲེལ་བས་ཡིན་ནོ།།

རྟོགས་ཆེན་ཐོད་རྒྱལ་དུ་བསྟུན་པའི་ཐབས་ལམ་རྣམས་ནི་འཁད་ཚུལ་མི་འདྲ་
བ་ཚམ་ལས་གསང་སྔགས་རྒྱུད་སྡེ་རྣམས་ནས་བསྟུན་པའི་གཏུམ་མོ་སྐྲ་ལྭ་ལྱུས་
སྟེ་ལམ་འོན་གསལ་བར་དོ་འཕོ་བ་སྤོང་དུག་སོགས་རྟོགས་རིམ་མཚན་
བཅས་ཀྱི་ཐབས་ལམ་རྣམས་སུ་མ་འདུས་པ་མི་འདུག   བཀའ་བརྒྱུད་པའི་
ལུགས་སུ་རྟོགས་རིམ་མཚན་བཅས་ཀྱི་ཐབས་ལམ་བརྟེན་ན་དཔལ་ནུ་ལྱུ
དང༌། བི་ཀྲ་མ་ལ་ཤྲི་ལའི་པན་གྲུབ་རྣམས་ཀྱི་ཕྱག་རྒྱུན་ལྟར། ཧྲལ་ཚོན་
ནམ་བྲིས་པའི་དཀྱིལ་འཁོར་སོགས་ལ་བརྟེན་ཏེ་དབང་བཞི་རིམ་པར་ནོང་
པའམ། གལ་ཏེ་དབང་པོ་རབ་ཡིན་ན་རྡོ་རྗེ་ཨེ་ཤེས་ཀྱི་དབང་ནོད་དེ་རིགས་
ལྱའི་དམ་ཚིག་ནས་བཟུང་རུ་བ་དང་ཡན་ལག་གི་དམ་ཚིག་ཕུ་ཞིང་ཕུ་བ་དག་
སོག་དང་མིག་འབྱུས་བཞིན་དུ་བསྲུང་ནས་རྣམས་སུ་ལེན་དགོས་པ་ཡིན།

རྟོགས་ཆེན་ཐོད་རྒྱལ་ལའང་དེ་བཞིན་ཡིན་ཏེ་ཁྲིད་ཡེ་ཤེས་བླ་མ་ལས་སྤོ་
གསུམ་གྱི་གནད་སྤྱོན་པ་ནས་རང་སྲུང་ཨེ་ཤེས་ཀྱི་དཀྱིལ་འཁོར་ཆེན་པོར་
འཇུག་པའི་ཐབས་སུ་བླ་མ་ལ་གསོལ་བ་ལན་གསུམ་བཏབ། དེ་ནས་བླ་
མའི་ཕྱགས་ཀར་ཡེ་གེ་ཨ་མཐིང་ག་ཞིག་སྐོམ། བླ་མས་ཏ་ཏྲེ་སྐུ་དང་བཅས་
བྱིན་དབབ་པ་དང་ཕཏ་ཀྱི་སྐུ་དྲག་པོས་ཨེ་ཤེས་པ་དབབ་པ་སོགས་ནས་གཞིས་
ཐོག་ཏུ་རིག་པའི་རྩལ་དབང་བསྐུར་བ་བཅས་བསྟུན་ཏོ།།   དེའི་ཕྱིར་ན
རྟོགས་ཆེན་ཐོད་རྒྱལ་ནི་གསང་སྔགས་ཀྱི་ལམ་ཡིན་ནོ།།

འོ་ན་ལྷུན་ཅིག་སྐྱེས་སྦྱོར་གྱི་ཁྲིད་ཚུལ་འདི་ལ་ཕྱག་རྒྱ་ཆེན་པོའི་མིང་དུ་
བཏགས་པའི་དོན་ཅི་ཡིན་སྙམ་ན། སྤྱིར་བཏང་ལྟར་ན་ཕྱག་རྒྱ་ཆེན་པོའི་བླ་
པའད་དེ་རྒྱ་གར་ན་དབང་ལས་སྐྱེ་ཞིང་རིམ་གཞིས་ཀྱི་ཏིང་འཛིན་ལ་བརྟེན་
ནས་ཡོངས་སུ་རྟོགས་པའི་རང་བྱུང་གི་ཨེ་ཤེས་དེ་ལ་གདགས་པ་ཡིན་འདུག

127

སྐྱམ་པོ་པ་ལ་རྗེ་བོ་རྗེ་ཨ་ཏེ་ཤ་ནས་བརྒྱུད་པའི་བཀའ་གདམས་ལུགས་དང་
། མི་ཏྲི་པས་ཡིན་ལ་མི་བྱེད་པའི་གདམས་ངག་མ་ལུས་པ་ལྷོ་བྲག་མར་པར་
གནང་བ་གཉིས་ཀ་བཞུགས་ཞིང་གཉིས་ཀའི་རྒྱུན་གཅིག་ཏུ་སྦྱེལ་ཏེ་ཁོང་
གིས་ཁྲིད་སྟོན་པར་མཛད་པ་ན་སྤུགས་ནས་བསྟན་པའི་ཡེ་ཤེས་ཏེ་ཉིད་ལམ་
འདིས་བའི་བླག་ཏུ་ཐོབ་པར་བྱེད་པའི་རྒྱུ་མཚན་གྱིས་བསྟན་བཅོས་ཀྱི་མཚན་
དུ་དེ་ལྟར་བཏགས་པ་ཡིན་འདུག་པས་འབྲས་མིང་རྒྱུ་ལ་བཏགས་པ་ཡིན།
ཡང་། སྐྱབས་དེར་མི་རྣམས་གསང་སྔགས་ཀྱི་ཐ་སྙད་ཡོད་ན་བརྗེ་མཐོང་
ཆེ་བ་བྱེད་པས་གདུལ་བྱ་རིགས་མ་ངེས་པ་རྣམས་དག་ཚོས་ཟབ་མོ་འདི་ལ་
འཇུག་པར་སྒྲོ་བའི་ཆེད་དུའང་དེ་སྐད་བཏགས་པར་སེམས།

མདོ་སྔགས་ཐེག་པ་མཐོ་དམན་དེ་བསྐལ་བཟང་དང་སྐྱིགས་དུས་ཀྱི་སྐབས་སོ་
སོར་འཚམས་པའི་ཚོས་ལ་དགོས་དབང་གིས་ཆེ་བ་རྗེ་ལྟར་བརྗོད་རུང་དོན་དུ་
མཐོ་དམན་ཞིག་སངས་མ་རྒྱས་པའི་གང་ཟག་སུས་ཀྱང་མཐོང་བ་དང་རྟོགས་
པ་མི་ནུས་པར་སེམས་སོ།།

ས་བོན་ཀུན་འཛིན་ཀུན་གཞིའི་རྣམ་ཤེས་ལས།།
ཡིན་པའི་རྣམ་ཤེས་གྲངས་མེད་སྐུ་མར་ལྱངས།།
གང་ཚེ་གཅིག་སྐྱིན་དེ་ཚེ་ཁམས་ལུས་སོ་གས།།
སྣང་ཡུལ་འཇིག་རྟེན་གཟུགས་བརྙན་མཆེད་ཅིང་གྲུབ།།

སྐྱར་ཡང་ཡུལ་གྱི་རྣམ་ལྱན་ཤེས་པ་གང་།།
གསལ་ཞིང་རིག་པ་ཉིད་ལ་རྣམ་རྟོག་སྟེ།།
གདོད་ནས་མ་སྐྱེས་རང་སྟོང་ཚོས་སྐྱུའི་གནད།།
གཅིག་ཤེས་ཀུན་གྲོལ་ནུས་པའི་གསོང་ལམ་བསྒྲགས།།

རྒྱལ་བའི་ལུང་བསྟན་མ་ཉམ་མེད་སྐྱམ་པོ་པས།།

ཐ་མལ་ཤེས་པ་རང་འཚོ་མ་ཉིན་ཉིན།།

འཁོར་འདས་རྒྱུ་རུ་བསྟན་པའི་ཐབ་ལམ་ཀུན།།

འགྲོ་བ་དགྲོལ་ཕྱིར་ནམ་ཡང་མི་ནུབ་ཤོག

ཅེས་ཞུ་དམར་ཁྲི་འཛིན་པ་མི་ཕམ་ཚེས་ཀྱི་བློ་གྲོས་སུ་འབོད་པས། དལ་མ་སྒྲི་ལོ 2001 ཟླ་བ 7 ཚེས 14 ནས 24 བར་ཞག་བཅུའི་རིང་ཡུ་རོབ་རྒྱལ་ཁབ་ཀྱི་ཕྱི་བག་ཡི་རན་སི་ནང་ཀཱུ་བགཱད་བརྒྱུད་ཀྱི་སྒྲུབ་སྡེ་ཀུན་གྲོལ་གླིང་དུ་སྒྲུབ་ཐེངས་གསར་ཞུགས་དགེ་འདུན་ཞལ་གྲངས་བརྒྱ་ཐམ་པ་ལ་དབང་ལུང་འཆད་སྤྱངས་བར་གསེང་རྣམས་སུ་བྱིས་ཏེ 2001-7-24 ཧོར་ཟླ་༦ ཚེས་༤ རྒྱལ་བའི་ཚེས་འཁོར་བསྐོར་བའི་དུས་ཚེན་ཉིན་ཧྲོགས་པར་བྱས་སོ།། ||

129

A Treasury of Immaculate Teachings.
The Practice-Method of Concept-Dharmakāya,

By the Fourth Shamarpa, Chödrag Yeshe[310]

རྣམ་པར་རྟོག་པ་ཆོས་སྐྱུའི་སྒྲུབ་ཐབས་དྲི་མེད་གསུང་རབ་གཏེར་
མཛོད་ཅེས་བྱ་བ་བཞུགས་སོ།། ༎

ན་མོ་མཉྫུ་ཤྲཱི་ཡེ།

དཔལ་ལྡན་གདོད་ནས་རྣམ་དག་རིན་ཆེན་བཞིན།།
ཆོན་མོངས་དྲི་མས་སྒྲིབས་པར་གྱུར་ན་ཡང་།།
འགྱུར་མེད་དེ་བོ་ཆོས་སྐུའི་རོལ་པ་ཅན།།
གང་དེར་མི་འཕྲོགས་དང་པས་ཕྱག་འཚལ་ལོ།།
ཀུན་མཁྱེན་བླ་མེད་སྟོན་པའི་གསུང་རབ་གངས་ཀྱི་རིར།།

131

ཨོན་ཏན་དུ་མས་ལེགས་གཏམས་བློ་ཡི་ཉིན་བྱེད་ཀྱི།།

ཤེས་རབ་ཐིགས་མེད་འོད་ཟེར་རྟེན་པའི་མཐུས་བསྐུལ་ཏེ།།

དམ་ཆོས་བདུད་རྩིའི་རྒྱ་རྒྱུན་མངོན་འབེབས་བཀའ་བརྐྱུང་རྒྱལ།།

བདག་བློའི་ཐེ་ཚོམ་དུ་བ་རབ་གཙོད་ཅིང་།།

ལུང་རིགས་ངང་ལྷུན་ཆོར་བུའི་ཡུ་བ་ཅན།།

མ་རིག་བདུད་ཀྱི་གཡུལ་ངོར་འདེབས་མཁས་པའི།།

འདྲེན་པའི་བླ་མ་རྣམས་ལ་གུས་བཏུད་དེ།།

གང་འདིར་དད་ལྷུན་བརྒྱུད་པའི་གསུང་རབ་ལ།།

རྗེ་གཅིག་མོས་པས་ཆོས་སྐུའི་འདོད་ལུགས་དག

ཇི་ལྟ་བུ་ཞེས་བསྐུལ་དོན་འབྲས་སྟེར་ཕྱིར།།

མོད་ཙམ་གསལ་བ་ཉིད་དུ་འདིར་བྱིའོ།།

དེ་ལ་འདིར་རྣམ་པར་རྟོག་པ་ཆོས་ཀྱི་སྐུ་ཞེས་སྟོན་ཀྱི་བཀའ[311]བརྒྱུད་བླ་མ་ དག་གིས་གསུངས་ཏེ། འདི་ལ་ཁ་ན་མ་ཐོ་བའི་ཉེས་པ་མེད་ཅིང་རྒྱལ་བའི་ བཀའ་ཚད་མས་གསལ་བའི་ཕྱིར། མང་དུ་སྨོས་པ་ལ་དགོས་པ་མེད་མོད། ཞོན་ཀྱང་བློ་མིག་ལྡོངས་པ་ཁ་ཅིག་ཅི་སྨྲ་གཏོལ་མེད་པར་མི་རིགས་པའི་ཞེས་ སྨྲ་བ་ནི་བདེན་ཏེ། གསུང་རབ་མ་མཐོང་བར་ཟད་པའི་ཕྱིར་རོ།། འདི་ ལ་ཆོས་ཀྱི་རྒྱལ་པོ་དགའ[312]པོ་ལྟ་རྗེས་ཆོས་སྐུ་སྟོང་ཉིད་ཀྱིས་སེམས་ཅན་ ཐམས་ཅད་ལ་ཁྱབ་པའི་ཕྱིར་ཞེས་དང་། མ་ཚན་མ་སྣེས་པའི་རྣམ་རྟོག་ འདི།། ཆོས་སྐུ་ཡིན་པར་ཚེར་གྱིས་རྱུང་།། ཉམས་སུ་སྟོང་ན་སྙེང་པོ་ མཐོང་།། ཞེས་གསུངས་པའི་དོན་འདི་ལ་གྲུབ་མཐའ་འདི་སྐུ་བར་འདོད་པ་ ཁ་ཅིག་རྣམ་པར་རྟོག་པ་གང་སྐྱེས་ཆད་ཆོས་ཀྱི་སྐུ་ཡིན་དེ། སེམས་ཅན་ དང་སངས་རྒྱས་གཉིས་བཟང་ངན་མེད་དོ་ཅེས་ཟེར་བ་དག་ཀྱང་ཆོས་རྒྱལ་

ཀྱུང་བའི་རྟགས་ཁོ་ནར་བས་སོ། །དེ་ལྟར་མ་ཡིན་ཏེ། རྣམ་རྟོག་གི་
དོ་བོ་ཆོས་ཀྱི་སྐུ་ཉིད་ཡིན་ལ། རྣམ་རྟོག་གང་སྐྱེས་ནི་མ་ཡིན་ནོ། །ཧེ་
 རུ་ཀ་ལས། བླ་མོ་དཔལ་ཕྱིང་གིས་ཞུས་པའི་མདོ་ལས།

ཕུ་རིའི་བུ་སེམས་ཅན་གྱི་ཁམས་ཞེས་བྱ་བ་ནི། དེ་བཞིན་
གཤེགས་པའི་ཚིག་བླ་དགས་སོ། །ཕུ་རིའི་བུ་དེ་བཞིན་
གཤེགས་པའི་སྙིང་པོ་ཞེས་བྱ་བ་ནི། ཆོས་ཀྱི་སྐུའི་
ཚིག་བླ་དགས་སོ། །ཕུ་རིའི་བུ་དེའི་ཕྱིར་སེམས་ཅན་གྱི་
ཁམས་ཀྱང་གཞན་ལ། ཆོས་ཀྱི་སྐུ་ཡང་གཞན་མ་ཡིན་ཏེ།
སེམས་ཅན་གྱི་ཁམས་ཉིད་ཆོས་ཀྱི་སྐུ་ལ། ཆོས་ཀྱི་སྐུ་ཉིད་
སེམས་ཅན་གྱི་ཁམས་ཏེ། འདི་ནི་དོན་གྱིས313 གཉིས་སུ
མེད་དེ། ཡི་གི་ཚིག་ཏུ་ཐ་དད་པ་ཡིན་ནོ། །
ཞེས་དང་།

གསང་བ་བསམ་གྱི་མི་ཁྱབ་པའི་མདོར།

ཞི་བའི་བློ་གྲོས་འདི་ལྟ་སྟེ། དཔེར་ན། རྣམ་མཁའ་ནི་
གཟུགས་སུ་སྣང་བ་ཐམས་ཅད་དུ་ལྗགས་པའོ། །ཞི་བའི་བློ་
གྲོས་དེ་བཞིན་དུ། དེ་བཞིན་གཤེགས་པའི་སྐུ་ཡང་སེམས་
ཅན་དུ་སྣང་བ་ཐམས་ཅད་དུ་ལྗགས་པའོ། །ཞི་བའི་བློ་གྲོས་
འདི་ལྟ་སྟེ། དཔེར་ན་རྣམ་མཁའི་རང་དུ་གཟུགས་སུ་སྣང་བ་
ཐམས་ཅད་དུ་འདུས་སོ། །ཞི་བའི་བློ་གྲོས་དེ་བཞིན་དུ་དེ་
བཞིན་གཤེགས་པའི་སྐུའི་རང་དུང་། སེམས་ཅན་དུ་སྣང་
བ་ཐམས་ཅད་དུ་འདུས་སོ། །

ཞེས་གསུང་པས་སེམས་ཉིད་གདོད་མ་ནས་སྟོང་པ་འདི་ཉིད་ཆོས་སྐུ་ཡིན་པར

གྲུབ་སྟེ། མིང་གི་རྣམ་གྲངས་ཙམ་དུ་བདེ་གཤེགས་སྙིང་པོ་ཁམས་ཤེས་
བྱ་བ་ལ་སོགས་པ་གསུངས་ཏེ། དེ་ལྟར་ཡང་པ་རཱི་ཨ་བྷ་ལཱ་ཀ་རས་སྒྲུབ་
དགོངས་རྒྱན་དུ།

གནས་དང་ས་བོན་དང་། ཁམས་དང་། རང་བཞིན་ཞེས་
པ་རྣམ་གྲངས་རྣམས་ཀྱིས་བརྗོད་དོ།།

ཅེས་རྒྱས་པར་གསུངས་སོ།།

རྒྱུད་ལས་ཀྱང་།

ཀུན་ལ་ཁྱབ་པའི་ཆོས་ཀྱི་སྐུ།། ཞེས་དང་།

ཉི་བཟྡུ་ལས།

སེམས་ཅན་རྣམས་ནི་སངས་རྒྱས་ཉིད།། ཅེས་དང་།

འཁོར་ལོ་སྡོམ་པར།

གང་དུ་ཕྱིན་ཀྱང་གཞལ་ཡས་ཁང་།།
སུ་དང་འགྲོགས་ཀྱང་ཧེ་རུ་ཀ།
ཅི་ལྟར་བྱས་ཀྱང་ཆོས་ཀྱི་སྐུ།།
དོན་དུ་མ་གྱུར་གང་ཡང་མེད།། ཅེས་དང་།

འགྲོ་ལྷ་འདི་དག་སངས་རྒྱས་ལྷ་ཡིན་ཏེ།།
གར་མཁན་བཟང་དང་རི་མོ་མཁན་ལྷ་བུ།།
དེ་བཞིན་བདེ་ཆེན་ཞེས་བྱ་གཅིག་པུས་ནི།།
གཅིག་པུའི་ཉམས་ནི་དུ་མའི་གར་མཛད་དོ།།

ཅེས་གསུངས་པ་ཡིན་ནོ།

ཁ་ཅིག་སངས་རྒྱས་ཐོབ་པའི་དུས་ཚོས་སྐྱར་འབད་ཀྱང་། སེམས་ཅན་
ལ་མི་འཐད་དོ།། ཅེས་བསམ་ན། དེ་ལྟར་མ་ཡིན་ཏེ། འགྲོ་དྲུག་
བཙོན་རར་གནས་པ་དང་། ལས་ལ་གནས་པ་ནས་ས་བཅུ་པའི་བར་དང་
། སངས་རྒྱས་ཀྱིས་གསུམ་པོ་ལ་རང་བཞིན་གྱིས་དག་པའི་ཆོས་སྐུའི་ངོ་
བོ་ལ་བཟང་ངན་ཆེ་ཆུང་གང་ཡང་མེད་དོ།།

དེ་སྐད་དུ་གཟུངས་ཀྱི་དབང་ཕྱུག་རྒྱལ་པོས་ཞུས་པའི་མདོ་ལས།

དེ་ལ་དེ་མ་མེད་པའི་སངས་རྒྱས་ཀྱི་ཡོན་ཏན་ནི། གཅིག་
དུ་ཀུན་ནས་ཉོན་མོངས་པའི་སོ་སོ་སྐྱེ་བོ་ལ་ཡང་རྣམ་དབྱེར་
མེད་པའི་ཆོས་ཉིད། སྤྱི་ཕྱི་ཁྱད་མེད་པར་ཡོད་པའི་ཕྱིར།
གནས་འདི་བསམ་གྱིས་མི་ཁྱབ་སྟེ། གང་གི་ཕྱིར་གང་ལ་དེ་
བཞིན་གཤེགས་པའི་ཡེ་ཤེས་མཐའ་དག་རྟེས་སུ་མ་ཞུགས་པའི་
སེམས་ཅན་ནི། སེམས་ཅན་གྱི་རིགས་གང་ཡང་མེད་དོ།།
ཅེས་གསུངས་སོ།།

དེ་ལྟར་ན་སེམས་ཅན་ཐམས་ཅད་འབད་པ་མེད་པར་གྲོལ་བར་འགྱུར་རོ།
ཞེས་སེམས་པར་བྱེད་ན། དེ་ཡང་ཆ་མ་ཡིན་ཏེ། བཀའ་རྒྱུད་རིན་པོ་
ཆེའི་བླ་མ་དག་གིས། དྲི་སྟིན་མ་དངུལ་རོམ། ཡུང་གཞི་མ་ཞེས་
སོགས་དཔེ་མང་པོས་བསྟན་ཏེ་དེ་བཞིན་དུ། མདོ་ལས་ཀྱང་།

དཔེར་ན་འོ་མ་ལ་མར་གྱིས་ཁྱབ་པར་གནས་སོ།
།དེ་བཞིན་དུ་སངས་རྒྱས་ཀྱི་སྙིང་པོས་སེམས་ཅན་ཐམས་ཅད་ལ་
ཁྱབ་པོ ། ཞེས་གསུངས་ཤིང་།

བླ་བ་སྟོན་མར་བདེ་གཤེགས་སྙིང་པོས་འགྲོ་ཀུན་ཡོངས་ལ་ཁྱབ། །ཅེས་དང་།

དེ་བཞིན་གཤེགས་པའི་སྙིང་པོ་བསྟན་པའི་མདོ་ལས། སངས་
རྒྱས་པ་ཅན་འན་སྣང་སྟེ་སྣང་མ་ལ། །སྐྱུར་མ་སྙིང་པོ་མི་གཙང་ནང་ནས་
གསེར། །

།ས་ནང་རིན་ཆེན་གཟུགས་ཡོད་དེ་ལྟ་བར།

།བློ་བུར་ཉོན་མོངས་དྲི་མས་བསྒྲིབས་པ་ཡི།
།སེམས་ཅན་རྣམས་ལ་བདེ་གཤེགས་ཁམས་འདི་གནས། །ཞེས་དང་།

ཉེ་བརྫོ་ལས་ཀྱང་།

ཚོན་ཀྱང་བློ་བུར་དྲི་མས་བསྒྲིབས།།
དེ་ཉིད་བསལ་ནས་སངས་རྒྱས་སོ།།

ཞེས་གསུངས་པ་བཞིན་དུ་སེམས་ཅན་རྣམས་ལ་ཁམས་ཆོས་སྐུས་ཁྱབ་པར་
གནས་ཏེ། ཚོན་ཀྱང་ཉོན་མོངས་པའི་སྙིབ་པས་གཡོགས་ནས་སེམས་ཅན་
རྣམས་ཀྱིས་མི་རྟོགས[314]དེ། དེ་ཉིད་མ་དག་པ་དང་། རིམ་གྱིས་སྦྱང་
བད་དག་པ་དང་། མ་ལུས་པ་དག་པའི་གོ་རིམ་གསུམ་དུ་འགྱུར་ཏེ།
རྒྱུད་བླ་མར།

མ་དག་མ་དག་དག་པ་དང་།།
ཤིན་དུ་རྣམ་དག་གོ་རིམ་བཞིན།།
སེམས་ཅན་ལམ་ལ་གནས་པ་དང་།།
དེ་བཞིན་གཤེགས་རྣམས་རིམ་པ་བཞིན།། ཞེས་གསུངས་ཤིང་།

དཔལ་ཕྱེང་གིས་ཞུས་པའི་མདོ་ལས་ཀྱང་རྒྱུ་ཆེར་གསུངས་ཏེ། ཚོན་
འདི་ལྟ་བུའི་ཚུལ་ལ་དགོངས་ནས་བཀའ་རྒྱུད་བླ་མ་དག་མ་པ་རྒྱ་བོད་དུ་
རིམ་གྱིས་བྱོན་པ་དག་གིས། རྡོ་རྗེའི་མགུར་དང་། ཚོགས་སུ

བཅད་པ་བསྐུན་བཙོས་ཀྱི་རྣམ་བཤད་ཞིབ་ཏུ་མཛད་པ་ཡིན་གྱི། རང་
ཁ་ཆོད་བཟེ་དང་རང་གིས་ཉམས་སུ་མྱོང་བ་ལ་བརྟེན་ནས་ཀྱང་
གསུངས་པ་མ་ཡིན་ནོ།།

འདི་ཉིད་རིགས་པའི་རྩལ་ཡང་། དེ་བཞིན་གཤེགས་པའི་སྙིང་པོ་བསྟུན་
པའི་མདོ་ལས།

ཐིག་མ་མེད་དུས་ཅན་གྱིས་ཁམས།།
ཆོས་རྣམས་ཀུན་གྱི་གནས་ཡིན་ཏེ།།
དེ་ཡོད་པས་ན་འགྲོ་ཀུན་དང་།།
མྱ་ངན་འདས་པ་ཐོབ་པ་ཡིན།

ཞེས་གསུངས་པ་ཡིན་པས། རྒྱུ་སྟོང་ཉིད་ཆོས་ཀྱི་སྐུ། སེམས་ཅན་
ཐམས་ཅད་ལ་གནས་པའི་ཕྱིར་ན། འབྲས་བུ་དེ་མཛིན་དུ་གྱུར་ནས་སྐུ་
གཉིས་ཀྱང་འབྱུང་བ་ཡིན་ཏེ། རྒྱུ་རིག་པ་ཁོ་ན་ལས་འབྲས་བུ་སངས་
རྒྱས་མི་འབྱུང་སྟེ། སོལ་བ་ལས་དུང་བཞིན། དེ་ལྟ་བས་ན་རྣམ་པར་
རྟོག་པ་ཆོས་ཀྱི་སྐུ་ཡིན་ནོ་ཞེས་གོང་མ་ཆོད་མར་གྱུར་པ་དག་གིས་དགོངས་པ་
གནད་དུ་ཕོག་པ་ཡིན་ནོ།། གསང་སྔགས་ཀྱི་ཐབ་གནད་རྒྱ་ལ་འབྲས་བུར་
བཏག་པ་ངོ་བོ་དང་རྣམ་རྟོག་ཐ་དད་མེད་པའི་དོན་ནི། དཔལ་མ་ཁའ་སྙིང་
པས་མཛད་པ་ལས་གསལ་བར་ཡོད་དོ།།

ཡིད་ཆེས་གནས་ལ་ཐེ་ཚོམ་ཟ་བ་དང་།།
དག་པ་ཆོས་ལ་བློ་མིག་ལྡོངས་པ་དག
རྒྱལ་བའི་གསུང་རབ་མཐོང་ཡང་ཡིན་མི་འགྱུར།།
ནང་གི་ཞིན་ཏོག་དུག་རྒྱས་བརྒྱགས་པར་རེས།།
བླ་མ་བརྐུད་པའི་མན་ངག་ཤེས་པ་དང་།།
གསུང་རབ་དགོངས་པ་ཇེ་བཞིན་ཏོགས་པ་དག

137

རང་བློ་ཞེན་པ་རྒྱུ་ཡི་པ་ཏུ་བཞིག །
ཡང་དག་དྲང་པོའི་སྲུང་བ་འཐོབ་པར་རིས།།
གཟུར་གནས་བློ་ཡིས་ལེགས་པར་མི་གཞལ་བར།།
ཀྱིག་འཕན་འདྲམ་སྐྱིལ་རང་ཉིད་ངལ་བར་བས།།
དེ་དག་དམ་པའི་ཕྱོགས་ཀྱིས་ཁྲིལ་བའི་གནས།།
བློ་གྲོས་ལྡན་དག་ལེགས་གསུང་ཚད་མར་བྱུ།།
འདིར་ནི་བཀའ་རྒྱུད་བཞེད་དོན་རྒྱ་མཚོ་ཆེར།།
སྦྱལ་བས་མཐའ་བཟུང་སེམས་པ་ག་ལ་ཞིག །
འོན་ཀྱང་རྗེས་འཇུག་བདག་གིས་ཅུང་ཟད་ཙམ།།
བཞེད་དོན་རྒྱ་ཐིགས་གཏོར་བར་གྱུར་པ་ཡང་།།
མི་ཤེས་ནོངས་པ་གང་མཆིས་བཟོད་པར་གསོལ།།
དགེ་བས་འགྲོ་ཀུན་ཚོས་ཀྱི་སྐུ༹[315] རྟོགས་ནས།།
བླ་མེད་བྱང་རྒྱུབ་ཆེན་པོ་མངོན་གྱུར་ཅིག

ཅེས་རྣམ་པར་རྟོག་པ་ཚོས་སྨྲའི་སྐྱབ་ཚུལ་དུ་མེད་གསུང་རབ་ཀྱི་གཏིར་མཛོག་འདི་ནི་
དད་པ་དང་ལྡན་པ་ས་སྐྱ་པས་ཡང་ཡང་གསོལ་བ་བཏབ་པའི་ངོར།། ཞུ་དམར་ཚོད་
པན་འཛིན་པ་བཞི་པ་ཚོས་ཀྱི་གྲགས་པ་ཡེ་ཤེས་དཔལ་བཟང་པོས། གོང་མ་དག་གི་
ཞབས་ཀྱི་པད་མོ་མཛོན་པར་གཀོད་པའི་དོགས་བདེ་དགུའི་དབེན་ནས་ཞེས་འཛོང་ཕྱག
པར་སྒྱུར་བའི་ཡི་གེ་པ་ནི་མ་ཏི་སྭ་ག་རས་བགྲིས་པའོ།། དགེ་ལེགས་རྒྱ་ཆེན་པོ་
ཕྱོགས་དུས་ཀུན་ཏུ་འཕེལ་བར་གྱུར་ཅིག །།

The Sixty Verses on Mahāmudrā.
Illuminating the Kagyüs' Intent,
a Short Presentation of Mahāmudrā

By the Fourth Shamarpa, Chödrag Yeshe[316]

ཕྱག་རྒྱ་ཆེན་པོ་དྲུག་ཅུ་[317]པ་བཞུགས་སོ།   །

ཕྱག་རྒྱ་ཆེན་པོ་མཚོན་པར་བྱེད་པའི་གཏམ་མདོར་བསྡུས་པ་བཀའ་བརྒྱུད་ཀྱི་
དགོངས་པ་གསལ་བ་ཞེས་བྱ་བ།   རྗེ་བཙུན་བླ་མ་དམ་པ་རྣམས་ཀྱི་ཞབས་
ལ་ཕྱག་འཚལ་ལོ།།

གང་ལ་སྨིན་དང་འགྲི་མེད་པར།།
འཁོར་དང་མྱང་འདས་ཀུན་རང་བཞིན།།
ཐོག་བྲལ་དངོས་པོ་མ་ལུས་འཆར།།
ཕྱག་རྒྱ་ཆེ་ལ་རབ་ཏུ་འདུད།།   [1]
གང་ཞིག་རྟོགས་པ་དང་འབྲེལ་ལྟ་བ་ཡོད།།

139

མན་ངག་དེ་ནི་སློན་མེ་མཚོག་ཡིན་ཏེ།།

བླ་མེད་ཐེག་སྤྱད་ཆས་པའི་ལམ་སྣང་བྱེད།།

དེ་ནི་དགས་[318] པོའི་སྐྱབ་བརྒྱད་འདི་ལ་སྣང་   [2]

དེང་ཚེ་སྐྱབ་ལ་གཞོལ་བའང་བསྒྲུབས་གྱུར་ཅིང་།།

གནས་ལུགས་རྗེ་བཞིན་འདོམས་པ་རབ་ཏུ་དགོན།།

དེས་ན་རང་བློ་འཚོམ་པར་གསུང་རབ་དོན།།

ཞིབ་མོར་དཔྱད་རྟོག་རྣམ་དབྱེ་དུ་མར་གྱུར།།   [3]

རྣམ་བཅས་རྣམ་མེད་ཉིད་དུ་ཡོངས་གཟུང་ནས།།

དབུ་མའི་དེ་ཉིད་དགྱོལ་བར་བྱེད་པ་དག

རབ་ཏུ་མི་གནས་ཟུང་དུ་འཇུག་པ་ཡི།།

དབུ་མ་མཚོག་ནི་ཤེས་པར་མ་གྱུར་ཏོ།།   [4]

བླ་མའི་མན་ངག་གིས་བརྒྱུན་ཕྱུག་རྒྱུ་ཆེ།།

སྤྱགས་དང་རྗེས་འབྲེལ་ཕ་རོལ་ཕྱིན་པ་ཡི།།

འཁོར་ལོ་ཕྱི་མའི་གནད་རྣམས་སྟོན་པ་ནི།།

བརྒྱུད་པ་འདི་ཡི་དགས་པ་རྣམས་བཞེད་དོ།།   [5]

འདིར་ནི་ལྷ་བ་སྐྱོན་ལྡན་སེལ་བ་དང་།།

དེ་ཁོ་ན་ཉིད་གཏན་ལ་འབེབས་པ་ལ།།

དགོས་པ་སྐྱོང་བར་བྱེད་པའི་ཚུལ་གསུམ་དུ།།

བསྡུས་ཏེ་བློ་ལྡན་དག་ལ་སྐྱ་བར་འདོད།།   [6]

ལ་ལས་སྐྱོང་པ་ཉིད་པས་དགེ་དང་སྡིག

གང་ཡང་ཡོད་པ་མིན་ཕྱིར་བླང་དོར་དུ།།

མི་བུ་ཞེས་རབ་སྟོག་པས་ལྷ་བའི་དོན།།

ལོག་པར་གཟུང་གྱུར་རྣམ་སྨྲིན་མི་བཟད་སྐྱུ།། [7]

ཉོན་མོངས་ཚོགས་འཇོམས་ལམ་གྱི་མཆོག་གྱུར་པ།།

སྟོང་ཉིད་ཁོ་ནར་གསུངས་པས་ཐབས་གཞན་ལ།།

ལྦོས་མིན་དེ་རྟོགས་ཚོ་སྨྲ་འབྱུང་དོ་ཞེས།།

ཟེར་བ་དག་ཀྱང་གནས་ལུགས་མཐོང་ལས་ཉམས།། [8]

གང་དུའང་ཁས་ལེན་མེད་པ་མཐའ་བྲལ་ཞེས།།

གཡོ་ཚིག་ལྷུར་སྟོག་འདི་ཡང་བརྗོད་བྲལ་ལ།།

འཁྲུལ་ལམ་ཡང་ན་རང་ལྷ་ངེས་མེད་པས།།

འདིས་ཀྱང་དོན་དམ་མཐོང་བར་མི་ནུས་སོ།། [9]

ཕྱི་རོལ་རྟག་པར་སྨྲ་བ་ལ་ལ་ལྟར།།

དོན་དམ་ཆ་གང་རྟག་དང་བརྟན་པ་སྟེ།།

ཅིག་ཤོས་བརྟན་པར་སྨྲ་བའི་གཉིས་འཛིན་དུ།།

བདེ་གཤེགས་སྙིང་པོར་འཁྲུལ་པ་བཞད་གད་གནས།། [10]

ཡིད་དཔྱོད་ཕྱིན་བར་སྙིལ་བའི་ངལ་བ་ཡིས།།

གཅིག་དང་དུ་མ་བྲལ་བའི་བདག་མེད་དོན།།

གཏན་ལ་ཕབ་ནས་བདེན་མེད་དུན་རྒྱུན་བསྒྲུ།།

འདི་ཡང་མེད་དགག་ཉིད་ལས་མ་འདས་སོ།། [11]

མེད་དགག་འདི་ནི་ཀུན་དུ་མི་རུང་ཞེས།།

གཅིག་ཏུ་བདག་ནི་སྟོང་པར་མི་བྱེད་ཀྱང་།།

ཕྱག་རྒྱ་ཆེན་པོ་མ་ཡིན་དགག་འདིའི་དོན།།

རྟོགས་པར་འདོད་པས་སྒྲུང་བར་བྱ་བ་ཉིད།། [12]

དེ་ལྟར་མཁས་དང་ལྟ་ཡིས་བྱིན་རླབས་དང་།།

གྲུབ་ཐོབ་གནས་ལུགས་ལྟ་བ་རྟོགས་སྒྲུ་རྣམས།།

ཕྱོགས་རེ་ཚམ་ལ་རབ་ཏུ་འཆེལ་གྱུར་ན།།

གྲི་ནར་སྒྲུ་བ་རྣམས་ཀྱིས་སློས་ཅི་དགོས།། [13]

དེ་ཁོ་ན་ཉིད་ལྟ་བ་ཞེས་པ་ནི།།

གཞུང་ལུགས་མང་དུ་ཐོས་པ་ཙམ་གྱིས་མིན།།

ཟབ་གནད་བྲལ་བའི་མན་ངག་སློམ་པས་མིན།།

རིགས་པས་དཔྱད་དང་བཙལ་བ་ཡིས་ཀྱང་མིན།། [14]

སྐྱེ་བ[319.]སྔོན་ནས་བག་ཆགས་བཏུས་པ་དང་།།

རྟོགས་ལྡན་བླ་མ་བརྒྱུད་པ་ལས་འོངས་པའི།།

དགེ་བའི་བཤེས་ལ་མོས་གུས་འགྱུར་མེད་ལྡན།།

དེ་འདྲ་དེས་ནི་ཡང་དག་ལྟ་བ་རྟོགས།། [15]

མཁས་པའི་བླ་མས་སྐལ་ལྡན་སློབ་མ་ནི།།

ཆོས་ཀྱི་རྗེས་སུ་འབྲང་སྐྱད་སྒྱུར་བྱ་སྟེ།།

དད་པ་ཁོ་ནས་གདམས་པ་བརྗུང་མི་བྱ།།

དེ་ཡང་སློམ་པས་རྣམས་དང་རྟོགས་པ་ཡི།། [16]

མཚན་སུམ་ལམ་ནི་རྒྱུད་ལ་སྐྱེ་འགྱུར་བས།།

སློམ་རིམ་ཚོགས་རིམ་ཚོགས་བཞད་མདོར་བྱས་བསྟད་བྱ་ཞིང་།།

སློབ་མ་ལ་བཞད་ཕྱོགས་ཙམ་མཚོན་པར་བཞད།།

དེ་ལའང་སློན་དུ་འགྲོ་བ་དངོས་དང་རྗེས།། [17]

ཐོག་མར་རྒྱུ་ཡི་ཀྱེན་ཞེས་གང་གསུངས་པ།།

ས་བོན་དག་ལས་མ་འཚོལ་འབྲས་བུ་ལྟར།།

དགེ་སྦྱིག་ལས་ནི་ཞིབ་མོར་བསམ་བྱས་ནས།།

གཉེན་པོ་དག་ནི་ཀུན་ནས་རྒྱས་པར་བགྱི།། [18]

དགེ་བའི་བཤེས་གཉེན་རང་ཉིད་ཏྟོགས་པ་ [320] ལྟར།།

གཞན་ལ་ལམ་སྟྱིན་བྱིན་གྱིས་ཏྟོབ་པར་ནུས།།

མཁྱེན་དང་བརྩེ་དང་ནུས་པ་ [321] ལྟན་པ་ཡི།།

བླ་མ་བསྟེན་པ་བདག་པོའི་ཀྱེན་དུ་འདོད།། [19]

ཕྱི་རོལ་རྟག་དང་ཆད་པར་སྨྲ་རྣམས་དང་།།

རྟལ་ཕྱན་ཉིད་དང་ཡུལ་ཞེས་ཐུག་ཕྱད་སྨྲ།།

རང་རིག་རང་གསལ་བདེན་དང་རྣམ་པ་བརྟེན།།

ཁྱུད [322] པར་དབུ་མ་རྣམ་བཅས་རྣམ་མེད་ལུགས།། [20]

དེ་དག་ཞེས་ནས་དེ་ལས་ཕྱལ་བྱུང་བའི།།

ལྟ་བ་གཏན་ལ་འབེབས་གང་དགོགས་པའི་ཀྱེན།།

བསྒོམ་པར་བྱ་དང་སྒོམ་བྱེད་ལ་སོགས་ཀྱི།།

རྣམ་ཏྟོག་དུ་མས་ཀུན་ནས་གཟིངས་གྱུར་པ།། [21]

དེ་ཡིས་ཏྱིང་འཛིན་བཏུན་པར་མི་ནུས་པས།།

རེ་དོགས་བསལ་བ་དེ་མ་ཐག་ཀྱེན་ནོ།།

དེ་ལྟར་ཀྱེན་བཞིས་ཡོངས་སུ་སྟྱིན་གྱུར་པས།།

དངོས་གཞི་ལ་འཇུག་རིམ་པ་གསལ་བ་ཡང་།། [22]

ཆགས་པས་རབ་གཡེངས་ཏྟོད་པར་གྱུར་པ་དང་།།

ཙེ་གཅིག་མི་འཁྲུག་ཏྲྀང་བ་ཉིད་དང་གཞན།།

སློན་རྣམས་སློང་ལས་བདེ་གསལ་མི་རྟོག་ཉམས།།

ཕེན་སྤྱངས་ཀྱིས་བསྐྱེན་ཞི་གནས་སྐྱེ་བར་འགྱུར།། [23]

དེ་ནས་ལྷན་ཅིག་སྐྱེས་གང་རྟོགས་འདོད་པས།།

ཚོས་འདི་ཐམས་ཅད་བྱེད་པོ་གཞན་མེད་དེ།།

རང་གི་སེམས་སྐྱང་དེ་ཡང་རང་བཞིན་སྟོང་།།

ཞེས་བྱའི་དོན་འདི་སྒྲུབ་དཔོན་སྐུ་སྒྲུབ་སོགས།། [24]

དཔའ་མའི་དེ་ཉིད་རིག་པ་དག་ཀྱང་བཞིན།།

གང་དག་སུ་[323] རྣམས་ཚོགས་པའི་ཐག་ཁྲ་ལ།།

སྒྱུལ་དུ་འཁྲུལ་བའི་སྐྱེ་བོ་སྐྲག་འགྱུར་མོད།།

ཐག་པ་དེ་ལ་སྒྱུལ་དུ་གྲུབ་པ་མེད།། [25]

མགལ་མེ་སྐོར་བས་འཁོར་ལོ་ལྟར་སྣང་ཡང་།།

མགལ་དུམ་རྩེ་ལ་འཁོར་ལོ་ཡོད་མིན་ལྟར།།

སྣ་ཚོགས་འཁོར་བའི་འཁྲུལ་སྣང་ཀུན་གྱི་གཞིས།།

མ་བཙས་རང་བབས་གནས་འདི་ཐག་མ་ནས།། [26]

འོད་གསལ་ཕྱག་[324] རྒྱ་ཆེན་པོའི་རང་བཞིན་ནོ།།

བྱེ་བྲག་ཚོགས་དྲུག་འདི་དག་ངོ་བོ་ཡང་།།

སྤྲ་མ་འགགས་ཤིང་ཕྱི་མ་མ་སྐྱེས་ལ།།

སྐད་ཅིག་མ་འདི་གསལ་ལ་རྟོག་མེད་ཅིང་།། [27]

ཀུན་རྟོབ་སྣང་བ་དུ་མ་འང་འཆར་རུང་བ།།

དེ་སྐྱེད་ཟུང་འཇུག་ཆོས་གཅིག་ངོ་བོ་གཅིག།།

དབྱེར་མེད་ཉིད་དུ་ཚད་མས་གྲུབ་པའི་ཕྱིར།།

རང་བཞིན་ལ་ནི་འཁྲུལ་པ་གཏན་མེད་དོ།། [28]

དེས་ན་ཚོས་ཀུན་རོ་མཉམ་གཏོང་མའི་བབས།།

སྤྲུན་གྲུབ་ཕྱོགས་སུ་མ་ལྷུང་གནས་ལུགས་འདིས།།

རང་སེམས་ཡེ་ནས་རྣམ་དག་ཚོས་ཀྱི་སྐུ།།

རྒྱ་ལམ་འབྲས་བུར་རྒྱུན་ཆགས་འགྱུར་བ་མེད།། [29]

འདི་ནི་བདེ་བར་གཤེགས་པའི་སྙིང་པོ་སྟེ།།

དགག་སྒྲུབ་དང་བྲལ་མཉམ་ཉིད་འདི་ངེས་ན།།

མཐར་ལྟ་ཆ་ཚམ་སྐྱེ་བའི་སྐབས་མེད་པས།།

སྤྱད་ཞི་རོ་མཉམ་ལྷ་བའི་མཆོག་ཡིན་ནོ།། [30]

རང་ཉིད་རང་གིས་མ་རྟོགས་འཁྲུལ་གྱུར་པ།།

དེ་ལ་རྒྱུ་ཡི་རྟོག་པ་སེལ་བའི་དཔེས།།

མ་བཅོས་ཐ་མལ་ཤེས་པ་སྐྱོང་བ་ནི།།

གང་ཕྱར་འཛིན་སྐོམ་བྱ་བར་མཁས་རྣམས་གསུང་།། [31]

དེ་གོམས་རང་རིག་ཡེ་ཤེས་རྟོགས་པར་འགྱུར།།

རང་རིག་དེ་ཡང་གཟུགས་སོགས་ཚོས་རྣམས་ནས།།

ཐམས་ཅད་མ་བྲིན་པའི་བར་གྱི་ཚོས་ཀུན་ལ།།

རྣམ་མཁའི་དཀྱིལ་ལྟར་རྣམ་དག་རང་བཞིན་ནི།། [32]

ཟབ་གསལ་གཉིས་མེད་ཡིན་ཞེས་འཇམ་དཔལ་གྱི།།

ཞལ་གྱི་ལུང་ལས་རབ་ཏུ་གསུངས་པའང་ཐོས།།

མིག་བཙུམས་པ་ན་བྲམ་པ་མི་མཐོང་ལྟར།།

བསམ་མེད་ལྷོན་དགོངས་པ་མ་ཡིན་ཏེ།། [33]

ཞེས་དང་ཤེས་བུ་པོ་སོར་འཛིན་པ་སྤོང་།།

འགྲོ་ཀུན་གཉིས་སུ་མེད་པའི་བྱང་ཆུབ་སེམས།།

དེ་ནི་བསམ་དང་བརྗོད་པའི་ཡུལ་མིན་པས།།

དཔྱད་དུ་མེད་ཕྱིར་ཡིད་ལ་མི་བྱེད་ཅེས།། [34]

མི་ཏི་པ་དང་སྒྲུན་སྙེས་རྗེ་རྗེས་བཤད།།

ལམ་མཆོག་མཆར་འབྱིན་རྗེས་ཀྱི་རིམ་པ་ནི།།

གང་ལའང་འཇིགས་པ་རྣམ་པར་སྤངས་ནས་ནི།།

སེང་གེའི་ཆལ་གྱི་སྤྱོད་པ་བྱ་བ་དང་།། [35]

གཏུམ་མོའི་རྣལ་འབྱོར་བསྒོམ་པ་སྟོན་འགྲོ་བས།།

མཆོག་གི་གཏུམ་མོ་ཕྱག་རྒྱ་ཆེ་ལ་སྟོར།།

དེ་ཡིས་ཡེ་ཤེས་སྐྱུར་དུ་སྐྱེ་འགྱུར་ཞེས།།

གསང་སྔགས་ལམ་ནི་དམ་པ་ལ་ལས་བཞིད།། [36]

དེ་ལྟར་བསྒོམས་པས་དང་པོའི་ལས་ཅན་ཡང་།།

ཀུན་གཞི་རང་.325 རིག་མཛོན་སུམ་གྱིས་མཐོང་ཞིང་།།

དེ་ལས་སྒྲིབ་བཅས་སྒྲིབ་པ་མེད་པ་ཡང་།།

རྗེས་དཔག་ཆུལ་རྟོགས་ཉོན་མོངས་རགས་དང་ཕྲ།། [37]

གཉིན་པོ་ཐ་དད་མེད་པར་འཇེས་པར་འགྱུར།།

དེ་ཚེ་ཀུན་གཞི་མཛོན་དུ་མཐོང་བ་སྟེ།།

མཐོང་ལམ་ཆེན་པོ་ཐོབ་ལ་སངས་རྒྱས་ཞེས།།

རང་བྱུང་རྡོར་རྗེས་རྗེ་རྗེའི་ཆོག་ཏུ་གསུངས།། [38]

146

ཟབ་མོའི་ཆོས་ལ་ཐེ་ཚོམ་སྐྱེས་པས་ཀྱང་།།

སྲིད་པ་རྒྱལ་པོར་བྱེད་ཅེས་གསུངས་པས་ན།།

དོགས་པ་སྐྱེ་བར་རིགས་རྣམས་མངོན་ཚམ་ཞིག

བགོད་ནས་གཟུ་བོའི་ངག་གིས་བསལ་བར་བྱ།། [39]

ལས་ཀྱི་ཕྱག་རྒྱ་དག་ལ་མ་བརྟེན་པར།།

ལྷན་སྐྱེས་ཕྱག་རྒྱ་ཆེན་པོ་མི་རྟོགས་ལོ།།

དབང་པོ་གཉིས་སྦྱོར་བདེ་བ་དེ་ཉིད་ཅེས།།

སྐལ་ངན་སྨྲ་མོ་དེ་ནི་སངས་རྒྱས་ཀྱིས།། [40]

ནམ་དུའང་འགྱུར་མེད་བདེ་བར་མ་གསུངས་ཤེས།།

སྒྱིབ་དཔོན་ཡེ་ནད་བྲུ་ཏིས་གསལ་བར་བཀའ

དུས་ཀྱི་འཁོར་ལོའི་རྒྱུད་འགྱེལ་ལས་ཀྱང་གསུངས།།

དེས་ན་བྱེད་ཅག་ཀོལ་བ་ངལ་བར་ཟད།། [41]

ཁ་ཅིག་ད་ལྟའི་ཕྱག་རྒྱ་ཆེན་པོ་དང་།།

དྲུ་ཕྱང་འདོད་པ་དོན་ལ་མཚུངས་ཤེས་ཟེར།།

བྱོགས་དང་ཁྱོད་ནི་དྲུ་ཕྱང་འདོད་པ་གང་།།

དགེ་སྦྱིག་གང་དུའང་བསམ་པ་འགོག་པ་འདི།། [42]

ཡིན་ཟེས་སྨྲ་མོད་ད་ལྟའི་ཕྱག་ཆེན་པས།།

དེ་དང་མཚུངས་པའི་ཁས་བླངས་གང་ཡིན་པའི།།

ཕྱོགས་སྟེའི་འདོད་པ་ཕྱགས་ལ་བྱོན་ནམ་ཀུའི།།

གལ་ཏེ་ཅེར་ཡང་མི་རྟོག་པ་འགོག་ན།། [43]

ཅེར་ཡང་མི་རྟོག་ཅེར་ཡང་མི་འཛིན་པར།།

དྲན་དང་ཡིད་བྱེད་ཐབས་ཅད་སྤྱོང་དོ་ཞེས།།

ཨ་ཏི་ཤ་ཡི་དབུ་མའི་མན་ངག་དང་།།

ས་ར་ཧ་སོགས་གྲུབ་ཆེན་རྣམས་ཀྱི་སྐུ།།   [44]

བྱེད་ཚག་རྣམས་ཀྱིས་དགག་པར་གལ་ནུས།།

སྣང་བ་སེམས་ཤེས་སྨྲ་བ་སེམས་ཚམ་སྟེ།།

དེ་སྐྱེད་དབུ་མ་ཡན་ཆད་མི་འདོད་ལོ།།

རྒྱུད་རྒྱལ་དབུ་མ་སྟོན་པའི་མདོ་སྡེ་དང་།།   [45]

སེམས་ཀྱི་རྡོ་རྗེའི་བསྟོད་པ་ལ་སོགས་པར།།

གྲུ་སྒྲུབ་ཀྱིས་བཤད་སེམས་ཙམ་སྨྲས་སོ་ཞེས།།

བྱེད་ཚག་སྐད་གསང་མཐོན་པོས་སྒྲོགས་བྱེད་དག།

གཞན་དུ་ལྱུང་དང་རིགས་པ་ཅི་ཞིག་ཡོད།།   [46]

ལ་ལས་འདི་ནི་རྗེ་སྒྲུ་སྒོམ་ལེགས་ཀྱང་།།

དབུ་མའི་སྒོམས་ལས་ལྷག་པ་མེད་ཅེས་སྒྲོག

བྱེད་ཀྱིས་དབུ་མའི་སྒོམ་ཞེས་གསུངས་པ་ཡི།།

དགོངས་དོན་དེ་ནི་གང་ཡིན་དཔྱད་པར་རིགས།།   [47]

རྗེས་དཔག་རིགས་པས་དཔྱད་པའི་སྟོང་ཉིད་དང་།།

རང་བཞིན་འོད་གསལ་མངོན་སུམ་ལྷ་བ་གཉིས།།

བསྒོམས་པས་རྣམས་སུ་སྐྱོང་རྣམས་ཆད་མས་མཐོང་།།

བྱེད་པར་གཟུ་བོའི་མཁས་པ་དག་ཀྱང་གསུང་།།   [48]

ཟུང་འཇུག་རབ་ཏུ་མི་གནས་དབུ་མ་ནི།།

རྗེ་བཙུན་ས་ར་ཏ་པ་ཡབ་སྲས་ནས།།

དཔལ་ལྡན་དྭགས་³²⁶ པོའི་བཀའ་བརྒྱུད་འདི་དག་བཞིན།།

དེ་ནི་དབུ་མ་གཞན་ལས་ལྷག་པའི་ཚུལ།།   [49]

མི་ཏྲི་པས་བཤད་དེ་དང་དུ་རོ་པའི།།

གཞུང་འདི་ཁྱེད་ཀྱང་གུས་པས་ལེན་པར་སྤྱད།།

ཕྱག་རྒྱ་བཞི་པོའི་གོ་རིམས་མ་ཐུན་མི་མཐུན།།

དེ་ཡང་རྣལ་དུ་མཛོད་ལ་བཞད་པར་རིགས།།   [50]

བླུན་པོའི་ཕྱག་རྒྱ་ཆེ་བསྒོམ་ཕལ་ཆེར་ནི།།

དུད་འགྲོའི་རྒྱར་གསུངས་ཡང་ན་གཟུགས་མེད་སྐྱེ།།

ཡང་ན་ཉན་ཐོས་འགོག་པར་ལྡང་ཞེས་པའི།།

གྲི་ན་འདི་ལྟར་རབ་ཏུ་བཀོད་པ་ནི།།   [51]

མཁས་པ་ཆེན་པོ་དག་ལ་མི་ཉེས་སོ།།

ཉན་ཐོས་དགྲ་བཅོམ་པས་ཀྱང་སྐྱབ་དཀའ་བའི།།

འགོག་པའི་སྙོམ་འཇུག་བསམ་གཏན་བཞི་པོ་དག།།

དུད་འགྲོར་སྐྱེ་དང་རྒྱ་གཅིག་གཏམ་འདི་ནི།།   [52]

གཞུང་ལུགས་ཆེ་དང་འཁགས་པ་དག་གི་གསུང་།།

དེ་དག་རྣམས་ལ་རྙོལ་བར་མ་ཟད་ཀྱི།།

རང་ཉིད་ལ་ཡང་ཚ་འདི་བྱེད་པར་ཟད།།

དེ་བས་འདི་མཆོངས་དོགས་གནས་མང་མོད་ཀྱང་།།   [53]

བློ་ལྡན་ཚོགས་ནི་སུས་ཀྱང་བསྐུ་མི་ནུས།།

རི་བོང་ཅལ་ལྤར་ཏོགས་³²⁷དང་བྲལ་བ་ཡི།།

སྐྱེ་བོ་སྐྲལ་ངན་ལམ་གོལ་ཞུགས་གྱུར་ན།།

149

རྒྱལ་བའི་ཕྱག་རྒྱས་རྗེས་དེ་ལ་བགྱུར་མེད་ན།། [54]

བདག་གི་སྨྲ་བ་མང་པོས་ཅི་བྱུར་ཡོད།།

དམ་པ་དག་གི་ཕྱག་ལ་ཕྱག་དོག་མེད།།

ཚོས་མིན་སྟོན་དང་ཚོས་སྟོང་ག་ལ་ཞིག

དེ་ལྟ་ན་ཡང་ལྟ་བ་ལུང་དང་ནི།། [55]

རིགས་པས་གཏན་ལ་འབེབས་ལ་ཉེན་མེད་མཆི།།

དེ་སྐྱེད་བདག་ནི་མཁས་པའི་དགག་སྒྲུབ་དང་།།

ཇི་ལྟར་མཛད་ཀྱང་གུས་པ་མི་ལྡོག་མོད།།

གཞན་དུ་དོན་པ་ལྟུན་རྣམས་བཞད་གད་འགྱུར།། [56]

ལྟ་བ་གང་ཞིག་ལུང་དང་རིགས་པར་འབྲེལ།།

ཉམས་སུ་བླང་སྐྱེད་འབད་པས་ཡོན་ཏན་ཀུན།།

ཁྱད་པར་ལས་ཀྱང་ཁྱད་པར་ཐོབ་³²⁸ འགྱུར་པ།།

དེ་འདུ་གང་ཡིན་ལམ་འདོད་དག་གིས་གཟུང་།། [57]

བྱུང་དུ་འཛུག་པའི་ཕྱག་རྒྱ་གང་ཡིན་འདི།།

འཁོར་དང་མྱུ་འན་འདས་པ་ཇེ་སྟེད་པ།།

རང་བཞིན་གཅིག་པའི་དང་དུ་སྟོར་བྱེད་པས།།

ཕྱག་རྒྱ་ཆེན་པོ་ཞེས་ནི་རབ་ཏུ་བཏོད་³²⁹ [58]

བསྟེ་བའི་དབང་གིས་བདག་གིས་འདི་བྱས་ཏེ།།

ཚིག་དོན་རྣམས་ལ་ལོག་པར་བཤད་པའི་སྐྱོན།།

ཤུང་ཟད་ཙམ་ཞིག་ཆགས་པར་གྱུར་ན་ཡང་།།

མཁས་དང་གྲུབ་པའི་དབང་པོ་དག་བཟོད་མཛོད།། [59]

150

འདི་བཞད་དགེ་བས་དད་དང་ཚོས་ཀྱི་རྗེས་འབྲང་བ།།

དེ་དག་ཀུན་ཏུ་ཙོད་པ་མེད་ཅིང་ལམ་ཚོལ་བརྩོན།།

ཨང་དག་ལྟ་བ་འདི་ནི་ཁོང་དུ་ཆུད་གྱུར་ཏེ།།

ཡེ་ཤེས་སྐུ་ནི་འགྲོ་བ་ཀུན་གྱིས་ཐོབ་གྱུར་ཅིག [60]

ཅེས་པ་འདི་ནི་མང་དུ་ཐོས་པ་དང་ལྡན་ཞིང་ཚོས་ཟབ་མོ་ལ་མོས་པའི་བཤེས་གཉེན་གྱིས་

ཡུན་རིང་པོ་ནས་བསྐུལ་བ་ལས།   ཤྲཱཀུའི་དགེ་སྦྱོང་ཚོས་ཀྱི་གྲགས་པ་ཡེ་ཤེས་དཔལ་

བཟང་པོས་སྦྱར་བ་སློ་ཀ་དྲུག་ཅུ་པའོ།། །།ༀ་སྭ་མ།།

The Point of Meditation, a Summary

By the Second Shamarpa, Khachö Wangpo[330]

སྐོམ་དོན་མདོར་བསྡུས་པ་བཞུགས་སོ།།   །།

ཐུགས་རྗེས་གྱུར་བསྐྱབས་བླ་མེད་པ།།
བཀའ་དྲིན་མཚུངས་པ་མེད་པའི་རྗེ།།
ལྷིམ་ཀྱུང་མེད་པའི་དད་པ་ཡིས།།
དུན་པ་བརྗེད་མེད་གསོལ་བ་འདེབས།།   [1]

སྟོན་གྱི་ལས་སྟོན་རབ་དགར་བས།།
སྟོན་མེད་དལ་འབྱོར་རིན་ཆེན་ཐོབ།།
བརྒྱུད་.331 ན་བླ་མ་མཆོག་དང་མཉལ།།
རྙེད་པར་དགའ་བ་སྐྱེད་དོ་བུ།།   [2]

153

ཟབ་ལམ་གནད་ཀྱི་གདམས་པ་ཐོབ།།

ངེས་ཤེས་སྐྱབ་བློ་ནང་ནས་སྐྱེས།།

རང་སེམས་རང་ངོ་རང་གིས་ཤེས།།

སྐལ་པ་རབ་ཏུ་གྱུར་རོ་བུ།། [3]

ཚེ་འདིའི་སྣང་བ་སྒྱུ་མ་ཚམ།།

བདེན་བདེན་འཛིན་ཡོང་བློ་གཏད་མེད།།

འཁྲུལ་སྣང་རྗེས་སུ་མ་འབྲང་བར།།

ཞེན་པ་གཏིང་ནས་བསྐྱོག་ཅིག་བུ།། [4]

ནམ་འཆི་ཆ་མེད་མ་དྲན་པའི།།

ཆོས་བྱེད་ཆོས་པའི་གཟུགས་བརྙན་ཚམ།།

གཟུགས་བརྙན་ཆོས་ཀྱིས་དོན་མི་འགྲུབ།།

བློ་ཤས་ཡིད་འབྱུང་བསྐྱེད་ཅིག་བུ།། [5]

འགྲོ་དྲུག་སེམས་ཅན་ཕ་དང་མ།།

ཐོགས་མེད་དུས་ཀྱི་རིན་ཆན་དུ།།

སྐྱིང་ནས་ཡང་ཡང་ངེས་ཤེས་བསྐྱེད།།

ཐེག་ཆེན་བློ་སྦྱོང་བསྒོམ་332 ཤིག་བུ།། [6]

རང་རྒྱུད་སྐྱོབ་པ་མ་དགག་ན།།

ཡོན་ཏན་འབྱུང་བའི་གོ་སྐབས་མེད།།

སྤོབས་བཞི་ཆོད་དུ་སྐྱོལ་བ་ཡི།།

གཉེན་པོ་333 གནད་དུ་ཐོ   ག་བུ། [7]

ལེགས་ཚོགས་རྟེན་འབྲེལ་མ་འགྲིག་པའི།།

བླ་མེད་བྱུང་རྒྱབ་ག་ལ་འང་མེད།།
ཚོགས་གཉིས་བྱང་དུ་འཇུག་པའི་དོན།།
དཀྱིལ་འཁོར་ལམ་དུ་བྱའོ་བུ།། [8]

ཐོ་མེར་འཁྱལ་པ་ཅི་ལྟ་བར།།
དག་ལ་མ་དག་འཛིན་པ་འཁྱལ།།
རྣམ་དག་དག་པ་ཉིད་ངེས་པའི།།
བསྐྱེད་རིམ་རྒྱུ་འབྲུམས་བསྒོམ་མོ་བུ།། [9]

བླ་མ་ལས་གཞན་སངས་རྒྱས་མེད།།
ཐེ་ཚོམ་སོམ་ཉི་མེད་པའི་བློས།།
དུས་དང་རྣམ་པ་ཐམས་ཅད་དུ།།
གསོལ་འདེབས་གནད་དུ་བཏང་ངོ་བུ།། [10]

རྣམ་རྟོག་གཡེང་བ་མ་དོར་ན།།
སེམས་ལ་ཏིང་འཛིན་སྐྱེ་བར་བཀའ།།
འདས་དང་མ་འོངས་དུ་ལྟར་གྱི།།
རྟོག་པའི་ཞིང་ལོང་སྟོང་ངོ་བུ།། [11]

གོམས་པར་གྱུར་པའི་གང་ཟག་ལ།།
རྣམ་རྟོག་གཡེང་བས་གནོད་པ་མེད།།
སྟོང་འགྱོགས་མཆན་མར་འཛིན་ན་འཁྱལ།།
རང་གྲོལ་དང་དུ་ཞོག་ཅིག་བུ།། [12]

སྣང་སྲིད་འཁོར་འདས་རང་གི་སེམས།།
མཐའ་བྲལ་འོད་གསལ་དེ་བཞིན་ཉིད།།

སྣང་སྟོང་དབྱེར་མེད་གཏོད་མའི་གཤིས།།

རང་ངོས་རང་གིས་ཤེས་བྱ་བུ།། [13]

དང་པོར་མ་གཡེངས་དྲན་པ་གཅེས།།

གོམས་ནས་དྲན་པས་དྲན་མེད་དང་།།

བསྒོམ་མེད་གཡེང་བ་མེད་པའི་དོན།།

ཆུ་བོའི་རྒྱུན་བཞིན་སྐྱོམས་ ³³⁵ ཤིག་བུ།། [14]

སྐྱོད་ལམ་རྣམ་པ་ཐམས་ཅད་དུ།།

ཚོས་དང་མཐུན་ཞིང་ཐོ་ཚོ་མེད།།

རྩུལ་ཚོས་དང་གིས་གྲོལ་བའི་དོན།།

བག་ཡོད་མཇེས་པར་སྐྱོད་ཅིག་བུ།། [15]

སྣང་སྟོང་ཟུང་འཇུག་གཉིས་ཡི་དོན།།

ཐབས་ཤེས་བསྐྱེད་རྫོགས་ལམ་གྱི་དོན།།

གཏོད་ནས་ལྷུན་གྲུབ་འབྲས་བུའི་དོན།།

དོན་གསུམ་དབྱེར་མེད་ཉིད་དོ་བུ།། [16]

སངས་རྒྱས་ཉིད་དུ་ཐག་ཆོད་པའི།།

མོས་གུས་འབྲལ་མེད་ཁོ་ན་ཡིས།།

གེགས་སེལ་བོགས་འདོན་མ་ལུས་པ།།

འགྲུབ་ལ་ཐེ་ཚོམ་མེད་དོ་བུ།། [17]

མ་གོམས་བར་དུ་ཕྱུན་ངེས་པས།།

རྣམས་ལེན་བསྱངས་ ³³⁶ སུ་གཞུག་པ་གནད།།

གོམས་ནས་ཉིན་མཚན་ཁོར་ཡུག་དུ།།

ཉམས་རྟོགས་རྒྱུ་འབྱམས་བསྐྱང་རོ་བུ།། [18]

དེ་ལྟའི་ངེས་པ་ཐོབ་པ་ལ།།

འཕྱལ་འཕྱལ་སྐྱབ་པ་གནད་དུ་ཆེ།།

ཉམས་ལེན་རོ་རུས་མ་ཐུབ་ན།།

བྱས་ཡོའི་ཚོས་ལ་དགོས་མེད་བུ།། [19]

ད་ལྟ་བཟང་བཟང་ལྟར་སྣང་ཡང་།།

ཀྱེན་ངན་ཞིག་དང་ཕྲད་པའི་ཚེ།།

ཊོ་བཟངས་ནོན་མོངས་མི་ལྟར་འབར།།

བསྐྱབས་ཚད་དོན་མེད་འགྱུར་རོ་བུ།། [20]

ཉེ་དུ་གཉེན་འབྲེལ་ཞེན་པ་དང་།།

ནོར་རྫས་ལོངས་སྤྱོད་འདོད་ཡོན་གྱི།།

ཞེན་འཁྲིས་བྱུང་ན་ཚོས་པ་མིན།།

ཆགས་སྤྱང་རུད་ནས་ཕྱུངས་ཞིག་བུ།། [21]

རང་མགོ་རང་གིས་མ་བསྐོར་ན།།

གཞན་གྱིས་བསྐོར་བར་མི་ནུས་ཀྱི།།

སྣ་ཐག་མི་ལ་མ་འོར་བར།།

སྐྱབ་པའི་སོ་འཕྱང་སྲུངས་ཞིག་བུ།། [22]

རང་རྒྱུད་ཚོས་དང་འདྲེས་ཚམ་ན།།

ཀྱེན་ངན་གང་གིས་རྟེ་བ་མེད།།

དགྲ་གཉེན་དབྱེར་མེད་རོ་བོ་མཐོང་།།

དོན་དམ་ལམ་སྣ་ཟིན་རོ་བུ།། [23]

གནས་ལུགས་དགོངས་དང་མི་ལྡན་པའི།།
མིང་བཏགས་སྒོམ་ཆེན་གྲངས་མང་ཡང་།།
ཀྲེན་ངན་རེ་རེ་རྗུང་རྗུང་གིས།།
ཐམས་ཅད་ཚམ་ལ་ཐབ་པོ་བུ།། [24]

ཁྱོད་ནི་ནེ་ལྷར་མི་འགྱུར་བར།།
བླ་མས་337 ཅེ་གསུང་བསྐུལ་པ་དང་།།
ཡུལ་ཀྲེན་དབང་དུ་མི་གཏོང་ཞིང་།།
རང་ས་བརྟན་པར་རྗུང་ཅིག་བུ།། [25]

རྟེ་ལམ་བར་འཕོ་འོད་གསལ་དང་།།
ཅུ་རྐྱང་ཐིག་ལེའི་མན་ངག་རྣམས།།
སེམས་ཀྱི་དོ་བོ་མཐོང་ཐབས་ཏེ།།
མ་ཞིན་ཉམས་ལེན་བྱའོ་བུ།། [26]

མདོར་ན་བླ་མའི་རྣལ་འབྱོར་དང་།།
རང་སེམས་རང་དོ་ལྟ་བའི་གནད།།
བླ་འོད་གཞེན་ཉུའི་ཕྱགས་ཀྱི་བཅུད།།
འདི་བས་ལྷག་པ་མེད་དོ་བུ།། [27]

བཀྲ་ཤིས་ཀུན་གྱི་བཀྲ་ཤིས་པ།།
རྣམ་པར་རྒྱལ་བའི་རྒྱལ་མཚན་དུ།།
འགྱུབ་ཕྱིར་སྙིང་གཏམ་བབ་ཚལ་དུ།།
མཁན་སྦྱོང་པ་ཡིས་བྲིས་སོ་བུ།། [28]
མངྒ་ལོ།།

The Stages of a Meditation Practice of Unity

By the Second Shamarpa, Khachö Wangpo[338]

རྣལ་འབྱོར་སྒོམ་པའི་རིམ་པ་བཤུགས་སོ།། ༎

རྣལ་འབྱོར་སྒོམ་པའི་རིམ་པ་མདོར་བསྡུས་ཏེ་བསྟན་པ། སུས་དང་བཅས་
པའི་དེ་བཞིན་གཤེགས་པ་ཐམས་ཅད་ལ་ཕྱག་འཚལ་ལོ།།

དེ་ལ་རྣལ་འབྱོར་ནི་གང་དེ་སྒོམ་པའི་རིམ་པ་ནི་གང་ཞེ་ན།། བཤད་པ།
ཞི་གནས་དང་ལྷན་ཅིག་པའི་ལྷག་མཐོང་ནི་རྣལ་འབྱོར་ཏེ་བྱུང་དུ་འབྱེལ་བའི་
ཕྱིར་རོ།། དེ་རྗེ་ལྟར་ལམ་དུ་བྱ་བའི་ཚུལ་ལ་སྒོམ་པའི་རིམ་པ་ཞེས་མིང་
གིས་བཏགས་སོ།།

དེ་ལ་དང་པོར་སེམས་ཅན་ཐམས་ཅད་སྙིང་རྗེས་འཁོར་བ་ནས་གདོན་བར་དམ་
བཅས་ཏེ་རང་གི་ལུས་དང་སྐྱོག་ལ་ཡང་མི་ལྟ་བའི་བྱང་ཆུབ་ཀྱི་སེམས།

དེའི་སྒོམ་པ་དང་ལྔན་པ་དང་པོར་མཚོས་ནས་དྲུག་གམ་བཅུའི་ཕ་རོལ་ཏུ་ཕྱིན་
པ་ལ་འཇུག་པར་བྱའོ།། གཙོ་ཆེར་ཏིང་ངེ་འཛིན་འབའ་ཞིག་ལ་གནས་པར་
བྱ་སྟེ། དེའི་ཚོགས་མཐའ་དག་ཀུན་གཞིའི་ཁོ་ནས་བསྒྲུས་པར་འཕགས་པ་
དགོངས་པ་ཇེས་པར་འགྲེལ་བར་བཀའ་སྩལ་.339 བ

དེས་ནན་ཐོས་རྣམས་དང་བྱང་ཆུབ་སེམས་དཔའ་རྣམས་དང་དེ་
བཞིན་གཤེགས་པ་རྣམས་ཀྱི་ཏིང་ངེ་འཛིན་རྣམ་པ་དུ་མ་བསྟུན་པ་
གང་དག་ཡིན་པ་དེ་དག་ཐམས་ཅད་ཞི་གནས་དང་ལྷག་མཐོང་
གིས་བསྡུས་པར་རིག་པར་བྱའོ།། ཞེས་དང་།

ཕན་ཡོན་ཆེན་པོ་ཡང་དེ་ཉིད་ལས། ཇེ་སྐད་དུ།

བྱམས་པ་ཡང་ནན་ཐོས་ཀྱི་.340 འམ་བྱང་ཆུབ་སེམས་དཔའ་
རྣམས་ཀྱི་འམ་དེ་བཞིན་གཤེགས་པ་རྣམས་ཀྱི་དགེ་བའི་ཚོས་
དང་འཇིག་རྟེན་པའི་བདེ་བ་དང་། འཇིག་རྟེན་ལས་འདས་པ་
ཐམས་ཅད་ཀུན་ཞི་གནས་དང་ལྷག་མཐོང་གི་འབྲས་བུ་ཡིན་པར་
རིག་པར་བྱའོ།། ཞེས་གསུངས་སོ།།

དེ་ལ་མེད་པ་པ་དང་སོར་བ་དང་མ་ཆང་བའི་རྒྱས་འདོད་པ་མཚོན་དུ་མི་བྱེད་དེ།
ས་བོན་དང་མྱུ་གུ་དང་རྩ་དང་ལོ་མ་དང་སྨྱུ་བརྐྱེན་བཞིན། དེ་ལས་བརྫོག་པ་
ཏིང་དེ་འཛིན་གཤེས་པོ་འདི་ལ་ནི་སྒོན་པའི་རྟེས་.341 སུ་ཞུགས་པར་ཁས་ཆེ་
བ་དག་ནན་ཏན་དུ་བྱས་ཏེ་འཐགས་པ་ཚོས་ཡང་དག་པར་སྒྲུང་.343 པ་ལས

གང་དག་ང་ཡི་རྟེས་སུ་སློབ་འདོད་དེས།།
ཞི་གནས་ལྷག་མཐོང་དག་ལ་འབད་པར་བྱ།། ཞེས་སོ།།

གང་དག་རེ་ཆེན་པོའི་སྟེར་ཕྱིན་པ་དང་བེདུ་བུའི་ཁང་པ་ན་འདུག་པ་ལྟར།
འདི་ལ་གནས་ན་ཚོས་ཐམས་ཅད་ཀྱི་མཆན་རྟོགས་པར་འགྱུར་རོ།། བཀའ

སྤུལ་པ།

སྐྱེ་བ་པོ་ཡིས་ལྔག་མཐོང་དང་།།
ཞི་གནས་གོམས་པར་བྱུན་ནི།།
གནས་དང་ལེན་གྱི་འཆིང་བ་དང་།།
མཚན་མའི་འཆིང་བ་ལས་འགྲོལ་³⁴⁴འགྱུར།།   ཞེའོ།

ཞི་གནས་འབབ་ཞིག་གིས་དོན་མངོན་དུ་མི་བྱེད་དེ་འཕགས་པ་ཏིང་ངེ་འཛིན་
རྒྱལ་པོ་ལས།

ཏིང་ངེ་འཛིན་དེ་སྒོམས་པར་བྱེད་མོད་ཀྱི།།
དེ་ནི་བདག་ཏུ་འདུ་ཤེས་འཇིག་³⁴⁵ མི་བྱེད།།
དེ་ནི་ཉོན་མོངས་ཕྱིར་ཞིང་རབ་འཁྲུགས་ཏེ།།
ལྔག་སྐྱོད་འདི་ན་ཏིང་འཛིན་སྒོམ་པ་བཞིན།།   ཞེས་སོ།།

ཞི་གནས་དང་བྲལ་བའི་ལྔག་མཐོང་ཡང་བཏན་པར་མི་འགྱུར་ཏེ་ཡོངས་སུ་མྱ་
ངན་ལས་འདས་པ་ཆེན་པོའི་མདོ་ལས།

ཉན་ཐོས་རྣམས་ཀྱིས་ནི་དེ་བཞིན་གཤེགས་པའི་རིགས་ལ་མཐོང་
སྟེ་ཏིང་ངེ་འཛིན་ཤས་ཆེ་བའི་ཕྱིར་དང་ཤེས་རབ་ཆུང་བའི་ཕྱིར་
རོ།།   བྱང་ཆུབ་སེམས་དཔའ་རྣམས་ཀྱིས་ནི་མཐོང་མོད་
ཀྱི་མ་གསལ་ཏེ་ཤེས་རབ་ཤས་ཆེ་བའི་ཕྱིར་དང་ཏིང་ངེ་འཛིན་
ཆུང་བའི་ཕྱིར་རོ།།   དེ་བཞིན་གཤེགས་པ་རྣམས་ཀྱིས་ནི་
ཐམས་ཅད་གཟིགས་ཏེ་ཞི་ལྔག་མཉམ་པར་སྦྱོར་པར་ལྡན་པའི་ཕྱིར་རོ།།
ཞེས་སོ།།

དེ་ལ་རེ་ཞིག་རྣམ་པ་དྲུག་གིས་ཞི་གནས་ཀྱི་ཚོགས་བསྒྲུན་ཏེ། ⌠ ཡོ་བྱད་སླབ་
པ་ཚོགས་མེད་པས་   ⌡³⁴⁶ སྙེད་སླ་བ་དང་། གནས་ ⌠ མི་སྡུན་

པའི་སྐྱེ་བོ་མེད་པས་ ༑བཟང་བ་དང་། ༑རྟད་མེད་པས་ ༑ས་བཟང་
བ་དང་། ༑ཚུལ་ཁྲིམས་དང་ལྡ་བ་མཐུན་པས་ ༑གྲོགས་བཟང་བ་དང་།
༑རྟེན་མཚན་ཐབས་ཅད་དུ་སྐྱེ་བོའི་སྐྱ་ཅ་ཚོ་མེད་པས་ ༑ལེགས་པར་
ལྡན་པ་སྟེ། ཡོན་ཏན་ལྔས་ ༑དང་ལྡན་པ་ ༑མཐུན་པའི་ ཡུལ་
༑དེ་དེ་ ༑བསྟེན་པ་དང་། འདོད་པ་ ༑བཟང་ཞིང་མང་པོའི་ལོངས་
སྤྱོད་ལ་སྒྲེད་པ་མེད་པས་ ༑རྒྱུ་བ་དང་། ༑ཚོས་གོས་སོགས་འདན་དོན་
གྱིས་ ༑ཚོག་ཤེས་པ་དང་། ༑ཏེ་ཚོང་སྐྱོས་འདི་རིགས་དུ་མ་འམ་ ༑བྲ་བ་
མང་པོ་ཡོངས་སུ་སྤུངས་པ་དང་། ༑སྒྲུབ་པའི་གཞི་མི་འཕྲལ་ཞིང་རང་
ན་མོད་ལ་གསོ་བས་ ༑ཚུལ་ཁྲིམས་རྣམ་པར་དག་པ་དང་། ༑ཉེས་པ་དུ་
མས་འདི་དང་ཕྱི་མར་ཞེན་ཏུ་གདུང་བར་རིག་ནས་ ༑འདོད་པ་ལ་སོགས་པའི་
ཏོག་པ་ཡོངས་སུ་སྤུངས་པའོ།། འདིས་རྐྱང་མེད་པའི་མར་མེ་བཞིན་བཏན་
པར་འགྱུར་ཏེ་རླ་བ་སྐྲོན་པའི་མརོ་ལས།།

            ཞི་གནས་སྤོབས་ཀྱིས་གཡོ་བ་མེད་པར་བྱེད།། ཅེས་སོ།།

ལྷག་མཐོང་གི་ཚོགས་ནི་རྣམ་གསུམ་སྟེ། མང་དུ་ཐོས་པ། ཚོག་
གསལ་བ། སྒྲིང་རྗེ་དང་ལྡན་པ། སྒྲོ་བ་བཟོད་པ་བཞི་ལྷུན་གྱི་སྒྲིས་བུ་
དམ་པ་བསྟེན་པ་ ༑དེ་བཞི། ད་དུང་བསམ་པས་འཁོར་གསུམ་མི་དམིགས་
པའི་སྤོབས་པར་འགྱུར་བར་འདི་གསུམ་གྱིས་ལྷག་མཐོང་གི་ཚོགས་བསྒྲུས་
༑ དང་། ༑བདེ་བར་གཞིགས་པའི་གསུང་རབ་ཀྱི་དོན་ལ་སོས་པས་
བསམས་པའི་དོན་ཏེས་པ་སྲེད་ལེགས་པར་འཛིན་པས་ ༑མང་དུ་ཐོས་པ་
ཡོངས་སུ་བཙལ་བ་དང་ཏེས་པའི་དོན་ལ་ཚུལ་བཞིན་སེམས་པའོ།། འདིས་
ནི་འདོད་པ་མཐོན་དུ་བྱེད་དེ་འཕགས་པ་དགོན་མཚོག་བརྟེགས་པ་ལས།།

            ཤེས་རབ་ཀྱིས་ནི་ཡེ་ཤེས་རྣམ་པར་དག་པ་ཐོབ།། ཅེས་སོ།།

དེ་ལ་རྣལ་འབྱོར་པས་སྒོམ་པའི་ཚོ་ཡིད་དུ་འོང་པའི་ཕྱོགས་སུ་སེམས་ཅན

ཐམས་ཅད་གྱུར་རྒྱབ་ལ་ཡོངས་སུ་འགྱོད་པའི་བསམ་པས་ཕྱོགས་བཅུའི་

སངས་རྒྱས་སྲས་དང་བཅས་པ་ལ་ཡན་ལག་བདུན་ཕྱག་བྱུག་ནས་རེ་མོ་ལ་

སོགས་པའི་སྐུ་གཟུགས་མདུན་དུ་གཞག་པའམ། གཞན་དུ་རུང་སྟེ།

མཆོད་པ་དང་བསྟོད་ཏེ་ཉེ་ནས་པ་བྱས་ལ་སྨྱིག་པ་བཞགས་པ་ལ་སོགས་པ་

བྱས་ནས་སྨྱན་འཇམ་ཞིང་བདེ་བ་ལ། རྗེ་བཙུན་རྣམ་པར་སྣང་མཛད་ཀྱི་

སྐྱིལ་མོ་དྐྱུང་ ༼འམ་སྐྱིལ་མོ་དྐྱུང་ ༽ ཕྱེད་དམ་ཡང་ན་ཅི་བདེ་བར་གནས་

གྱང་རྔུང་། མིག་ད་ཅང་ཕྱེ་བཙུམས[347] མ་ཡིན་པ་སྣའི་རྩེར་གཏད་

ཏུ་ཅང་སྐྱི་སྨྲ་མ་ཡིན་པ་ལུས་དང་པོར་བསྲངས་ལ་དྲན་པ་མཛོན་དུ་བཞག་སྟེ་

འདུག་ནས། ཐོག་མར་ཞི་གནས་བསྐྱབ་པར་བྱའོ།།

དེ་ལ་ཞི་གནས་ནི་གང་ལྡག་མཐོང་ན་གང་ཞེ་ན། འཕགས་པ་དགོན་

མཆོག་སྤྲིན་མཛོར་

ཞི་གནས་ནི་རྩེ་གཅིག་པ་ཉིད་དོ།། ལྡག་མཐོང་ནི་ཡང་དག་པར་

སོ་སོར་རྟོག[348]པའོ།། དེ་བས་ན་དམྱིགས་པ་རྣམས་བཞི་བསྒྲུབ་

པར་བྱ་སྟེ་དེ་ལ་ཞི་གནས་ཀྱིས་ཚོས་ཐམས་ཅད་ཀྱི་གཟུགས་བརྐན་ལོ་

དམྱིགས་ཏེ་རྣམ་པར་མི་རྟོག་པར་བྱས་པ་དང་། ལྡག་མཐོང་གིས་

ཚོས་ཐམས་ཅད་ཀྱི་དེ་ཁོ་ན་ལ་རྟོག་པ་དང་། དེ་གོམས་པས་དེ་ཉིད་ཀྱི་

མཐའ་རྟོགས་པ་དང་མཐར་སོན་པས་རྣམ་པར་མི་རྟོག་པའི་གཟུགས་

བསྐྱེན། རྣམ་པར་རྟོག་པའི་གཟུགས་བསྐྱེན། དངོས་པོའི་

མཐའ། དགོས་པ་ཡོངས་སུ་སྨྲུབ་པ།། ཞེས་བྱའོ།།

དེ་ལ་རྣལ་འབྱོར་པས་དེ་བཞིན་བཤེགས་པའི་སྐུ་ལ་སེམས་གཏད་པར་བྱ་སྟེ་

འཕགས་པ་ཏིང་ངེ་འཛིན་གྱི་རྒྱལ་པོ་ལས།

གསེར་གྱི་ཁ་དོག་ལྟ་བུ་སྐུ་ལུས་ཀྱིས།།

འཇིག་རྟེན་མགོན་པོ་ཀུན་དུ་མཛེས་པ་སྟེ།།

དམིགས་པ་དེ་ལ་གང་གིས་སེམས་འཛིག་པ།།

བྱང་ཆུབ་སེམས་དཔའ་དེ་མཚམ་གཞག་ཅེས་བྱ།།

ཞེས་སོ།།

སྐུ་གསལ་བར་གྱུར་བའི་ཚེ་འདི་ལྟར་ཏེ་བཞིན་གཤེགས་པ་གང་ལས་གང་དུ་
གང་གི་ཚེ་གཤེགས་བཞུགས་བཞུད་ཅེས་བརྟགས་པས་མ་མཐོང་བ་ལྟར་ཚེས་
ཐམས་ཅད་ཀྱང་དཔྱད་དེ་བསྒོམ་པར་བྱའོ།།

ཅི་དམིགས་ལ་ལེགས་པར་འཛིན་ཏམ། འོན་ཏེ་བྱིང་ངམ། འོན་ཏེ་ཕྱིའི་
ཡུལ་ལ་སེམས་གཡེངས་ཞེས་བརྟག་པར་བྱའོ།། གཉིས་ལྟར་ན་མཆོག་ཏུ་
དགའ་བར་མཛད་པས་ཀུན་ཏུ་རོལ་པའི་སངས་རྒྱས་ཀྱི་སྐུ་འམ། མཛད་
པ་བཅུ་གཉིས་སམ། རྟེན་ཅིང་འབྲེལ་པར་འབྱུང་བ་ཡིད་ལ་བྱའོ།། ཐ་མ་
ལྟར་ན་འདུ་བྱེད་ཐམས་ཅད་མི་རྟག་པ་དང་སྡུག་བསྔལ་བ་སོགས་ཡིད་བཏུན་
ཏུ་མི་རུང་བའི་མཚན་ཉིད་ཡིད་ལ་བྱའོ།། གང་ལེགས་པར་འཛིན་པའི་
ཚེ་བཏང་སྙོམས་སུ་བྱའོ།། མདོར་ན་དྲན་པ་དང་ཤེས་བཞིན་གྱི་ཐག་པས་
ཡིད་ཀྱི་གླང་པོ་དམིགས་པའི་སྟོང་པོ་ལ་གདགས་སོ།།

དེའི་རྗེས་སུ་རྩལ་འབྱོར་པས་དེ་ཁོ་ན་བཅལ་བར་བྱ་སྟེ་གང་ཟག་དང་ཆོས་སུ་
བཏགས་པ་ཐམས་ཅད་སྟོང་པ་སྟེ། དེ་ལ་གང་ཟག་ནི་ཕུང་པོ་ཁམས་སྐྱེ་
མཆེད་ལས་གུད་ན་མི་དམིགས་ཕུང་སོགས་ཀྱི་ངོ་བོ་[ཉིད་]ཀྱང་མ་ཡིན་
དེ་བས་ན་འཛིག་རྟེན་གྱི་ང་དང་ང་ཡི་ཞེས་བྱ་བ་ནི་འཁྲུལ་པ་ཁོ་ནའི་ཞེས་དཔྱད་
པར་བྱའོ།།

གང་ཕྱི་དང་། ནང་གི་ཆོས་བཏགས་པ་རྣམས་ཀྱང་སྟོང་པ་ཁོ་ན་
སྟེ། དེ་ལ་རེ་ཞིག་ཕྱི་རོལ་གྱི་དོན་མེད་པ་ཉིད་དུ་འཐགས་པ་ལང་ཀར་[349]
གཤེགས་པ་ལས་ཀྱང་གསུངས་ཏེ།

ཕྱི་རོལ་གཟུགས་ནི་ཡོད་མ་ཡིན།།

རང་གི་སེམས་ནི་ཕྱི་རོལ་སྣང་།།   ཞེས་སོ།།

དེ་ལྟར་ན་ཡུལ་རྣམ་པར་ཤེས་པའི་རང་བཞིན་རྣམ་རྣམ་པར་ཤེས་པ་ཙྟེད་ཡུལ་
གྱི་ཕྱིར་ཡུལ་སྣང་ཤེས་པ་ཙན་རྣམ་སེམས་པ་མེད་ཀྱང་ཤེས་པ་མེད་པ་སོགས་
དུ་མ་ཉིད་ཀྱི་ཕྱིར་ཡུལ་ཡུལ་ཙན་དུ་སྣང་བ་ཐམས་ཙད་རྨི་ལམ་བཞིན་ནོ།།

དེ་བས་ན་བརྗོད་མ་ཐག་པའི་ལུང་དང་འཐགས་པ་ས་བཅུ་པ་ལས་གང་འབད་
པ་ཁམས་གསུམ་པ་འདི་དག་སེམས་ཙམ་མོ །།   ཞེས་སོགས་ཁོ་ནའི་
གྲུབ་པའི་མཐའན་གདོན་པར་སོས་པ་རྣམས་ལ་ཕན་གདགས་པའི་ཕྱིར་ཏེ།
ཡང་དག་པའི་དོན་དུ་མི་གཟུང་ངོ།།   དེ་ཅིས་ཤེས་ཞེ་ན།

སེམས་ཙམ་ལ་ནི་བརྟེན་ནས་སུ།།

ཕྱི་རོལ་དོན་ལ་མི་བརྟག་གོ།

དེ་བཞིན་ཉིད་ལ་གནས་ནས་སུ།།

སེམས་ཙམ་ལས་ཀྱང་བརྒལ་བར་བྱ།།

སེམས་ཙམ་ལས་ནི་བརྒལ་ནས་སུ།།

སྣང་བ་མེད་ལ་བརྒལ་བར་བྱ།།

སྣང་མེད་གནས་པའི་རྣལ་འབྱོར་པ།།

དེ་ཡིས་ཐེག་པ་ཆེན་པོ་མཐོང་།།

ཞེས་བཤད་པས་སོ།།

དེའི་ཕྱིར་ཡུལ་ཡུལ་ཙན་ཐམས་ཙད་ཏེན་ཅིང་འབྲེལ་པར་འབྱུང་བ་དང་སྒྱུ་མ་
ལ་སོགས་པའི་ཏོ་བོ་ཉིད་ཁོ་ནའི་ཞེས་དཔྱད་པར་བྱའོ།།

དེ་ལྟར་འདི་དག་གི་ཏེས་པ་འཐགས་པ་དགོན་མཆོག་སྦྱིན་ལས་ཀྱང་བཀའ་

སྐུལ་ཏེ་དེ་ལྟར།

སྤྱོན་ལ་མ་ཁབས་པ་དེས་ ³⁵⁰ སྤྱོས་པ་ཐམས་ཅད་དང་བྲལ་བར་བྱ་
བའི་ཕྱིར་སྤྱོང་པ་ཉིད་སྤྱོམ་པ་ལ་རྣལ་འབྱོར་དུ་བྱེད་དོ།། དེས་
སྤྱོང་པ་ཉིད་སྤྱོམ་པ་མང་བས་གནས་གང་དང་གང་དག་ཏུ་
སེམས་འཕྲོ་ཞིང་སེམས་མཚན་པར་དགའ་བའི་གནས་དེ་དང་
དེ་དག་གི་ངོ་བོ་ཉིད་ཡོངས་སུ་བཅལ་ན་སྤྱོང་པར་རྟོགས་སོ།།
སེམས་གང་ཡིན་པ་དེ་ཡང་བརྟགས་ན་སྤྱོང་པར་རྟོགས་སོ།།
སེམས་གང་གིས་རྟོགས་པ་བརྟགས་ན་ ³⁵¹ དེ་ཡང་ངོ་བོ་ཉིད་
ཀྱིས་བཅལ་ན་སྤྱོང་པར་རྟོགས་སོ་ ³⁵²།། དེ་དེ་ལྟར་རྟོགས་པས
མཚན་མ་མེད་པའི་རྣལ་འབྱོར་ལ་འཇུག་གོ ཞེས་རྒྱ
ཆེར་འབྱུང་ངོ།།

དེ་ཉིད་ཀྱི་ཕྱིར་འཕགས་པ་ལང་ཀར་གཤེགས་པ་ལས་ཀྱང་།

དངོས་རྣམས་སྐྱེ་བ་ཀུན་རྟོབ་ཏུ།།
དམ་པའི་དོན་དུ་རང་བཞིན་མེད།། ཅེས་དང་།།

འཕགས་པ་རྒྱ་ཆེར་རོལ་པ་ལས་ཀྱང་།

ཤཱཀྱའི་སྲས་པོས་རྟེན་ཅིང་འབྱུང་བའི་ཆོས།།
རང་གི་ངོ་བོ་མེད་པར་མཐོང་ནས་ནི།།
རྣམ་མཁའ་ལྟ་བུའི་སེམས་དང་རབ་ལྡན་པ།།
གཡོ་ཅན་དཔུང་བཅས་མཐོང་བས་གཡོ་བ་མེད།། ཅེས་སོ།།

དཀོན་མཆོག་ཏ་ལ་ལར་ཡང་།

རྒྱུན་ལས་སྐྱེས་པ་རང་གི་དངོས་མ་སྐྱེ།།

ཚོས་ཀྱི་ལུས་ནི་རྒྱལ་བ་རྣམས་ཀྱི་སྐུ།། ཞེས་སོ།།

སློབ་དཔོན་གྲུས་ཀྱང་།

ཏེན་ཅིང་འབྲེལ་པར་གང་འབྱུང་བ།།

རང་བཞིན་གྱིས་ནི་དེ་མ་བསྐྱེད།།

རང་བཞིན་གྱིས་ནི་གང་མ་སྐྱེ།།

དེ་ལ་སྐྱེས་ཞེས་ཅི་སྐད་བྱ།། ཞེས་འབྱུང་ངོ།།

དེ་བས་ན་གང་དོན་དམ་པར་བདག་དང་གཞན་དང་གཉིས་ཀ་དང་རྒྱུ་མེད་པ་ལས་སྐྱེ་བར་མི་རུང་སྟེ།

ཅི་བདག་ལས་ན་ཇེན་པའི་མ་ཇེན་པ། སྐྱ་མ་ལྟར་ན་གྲུབ་པ་དང་ཕུག་པ་མེད་དོ།། ཕྱི་མ་ལྟར་ན་རེ་བོང་ད་སོགས་རྣམས་ཀྱང་མི་སྐྱེ་བར་མི་འགྱུར་རོ།། ཐམས་ཅད་ལས་ཐམས་ཅད་ཀྱི་ཕྱིར་དང་གཉིས་ཀ་འདུ་བའི་ཕྱིར་དང་། འདུ་བྱས་མེད་པའི་ཕྱིར། གཞན་སོགས་ལས་མི་རུང་དོ་དེ་མི་རུང་བས་ཕྱི་མ་དག་ཇེ་ལྟར་རུང་།

གནས་སྐབས་གསུམ་རྣམ་པར་བརྟོད་པ་ཐ་སྙད་བཏགས་པ། སྐྱ་མ་ཚམ་ཁོ་ན་སྟེ་དོན་དམ་པར་སངས་རྒྱས་ཉིད་ཀྱང་མཚན་མར་མེད་ན་གཞན་ལྷ་སློས་ཀྱང་ཅི་དགོས་སྐྱ་མ་དུ་དཔྱད་པར་བྱའོ།།

དེ་སྐད་དུ་ཡང་རྒྱལ་བའི་ཡུམ་ལས།

རབ་འབྱོར་སངས་རྒྱས་ཀྱང་སྐྱུ་མ་ལྟུ་བུ་སྟེ་ལམ་ལྟུ་བུ། སྨུ་
ངན་ལས་འདས་པ་ཡང་སྐྱུ་མ་ལྟུ་བུ། སྟེ་ལམ་ལྟུ་བུ།།
སྐྱུ་ངན་ལས་འདས་པའི་ཚོས་ལས་ཆེས་ལྷག་པ་ཞིག་ཡོད་ན་དེ་
ཡང་སྐྱུ་མ་ལྟུ་བུ་སྟེ་ལམ་ལྟུ་བུའོ།། ཞེས་གསུངས་སོ།།

དེ་ལྟ་བས་ན། དོན་ཡོངས་སུ་ཤེས་པས་རྟོག་པ་དང་དཔྱོད་པ་དང་བྲལ་བ་
བརྗོད་པ་མེད་པ་དང་གཅིག་ཏུ་པ་རང་གི་ངང་གིས་འཇུག་པ་མཚོན་པར་འདུ་
བྱེད་པ་མེད་པས་དེ་ཁོ་ན་ཉིད་ཤིན་ཏུ་གསལ་བ་བསྒོམ་ཞིང་། འདུག་
པར་བྱའོ།། དེ་ལྟར་གྱུར་ན་དེའི་རྒྱུན་མི་གཡེང་བར་བྱའོ།། གཡེང་བར་
མཐོང་ན་མོད་ལ་ཞི་བར་བྱའོ།། ཤོད་པ་ལ་སོགས་པ་གསལ་བ་ནི་
སྱར་བརྗོད་པ་ཉིད་དོ།། གང་ཤེས་རབ་དང་གནས་པ་ཆེ་བ་དང་རྒུང་བ་མི་
འབད་པ་དང་ནན་ཏན་དུ་བྱའོ་གཞན་དུ་རྩུང་ལ་གཞག་པའི་མར་མེ་དང་གཏིང་
གྱིས་ལོག་པའི་མི་བཞིན་མི་གནས་པ་དང་དུ་ཅང་གནས་པར་འགྱུར་རོ།།

སྱར་ཡང་ཏིང་ངེ་འཛིན་གྱི་ཉེས་པ་རྣམ་པ་དྲུག་སྤོང་བའི་འདུ་བྱེད་བརྒྱད་ཀྱིས་
གསལ་བར་བྱ་སྟེ། ལེ་ལོའི་གཉེན་པོར་དད་པ་འདུན་པ་རྩོལ་བ་ཤིན་ཏུ་
སྱངས་བ་བཞི་དང་དྲན་པས་དམིགས་པ་བརྗེད་པ་དང་བྱིང་བ་དང་རྒོད་པ་
ཤེས་བཞིན་གྱིས་དང་མི་རྩོལ་བ་དང་། རྩོལ་བར་སེམས་པ་དང་བཏང་
སྙོམས་སྙོམ་མོ།།

སྐབས་སྐབས་སུ་འཛིགས་ཏེན་མཐའ་དག་ལ་བལྟས་ལ་སྒྱུ་མ་དང་སྨི་ལམ་
དང་རྒྱུ་ལྔ་དང་མིག་ཡོར་ལྟ་བུར་བལྟའོ།། དེ་སྐད་དུ་ཡོང་རྣམ་པར་མི་རྟོག་
པར་འཇུག་པའི་མདོ་ལས་

འཛིག་རྟེན་ལས་འདས་པའི་ཡེ་ཤེས་ཀྱིས་ཆོས་ཐམས་ཅད་ནམ་
མཁའི་དཀྱིལ་འདྲ་བར་མཉམ་པར་མཐོང་ངོ།། དེའི་རྗེས་
ལ་ཐོབ་པས་ནི་སྒྱུ་མ་དང་སྨིག་རྒྱུ་དང་རྒྱ་ལྔ་ལྟར་མཐོང་ངོ་ཞེས་
འབྱུང་ངོ།།

དེ་ལྟར་འགྲོ་བ་སྒྱུ་མ་ལྟར་བྱར་མཐོང་ནས་ཆད་མེད་པའི་སྙིང་རྗེ་ཆེན་པོ་བསྐྱེད་
དེ་ཅུང་ཟད་ངལ་གསོས་ནས་སྱར་ལ་སྱང་བ་མེད་པ་ལ་འཇུག་པར་བྱའོ།།
ཇི་སྲིད་ལུས་དང་སེམས་ངལ་བས་སྒོ་བར་གྱུར་ན་སྱར་བཞིན་སྐབས་ཕྱེ་སྟེ་སྱར་

168

ཡང་དེ་བཞིན་དུ་འཇུག་གོ

དེ་ནས་འདོད་ན་ཏིང་ངེ་འཛིན་དེ་ལས་ལངས་ཏེ་སྒྱེལ་མོ་དགྱུང་མ་བཞིག་པར་ འདི་སྐྲ་དུ་ཚོས་འདི་དག་ཐམས་ཅད་དོན་དམ་པར་གཏོད་མ་ནས་མ་སྐྱེས་ བཞིན་དུ་སྒྱིག་རྒྱུའི་རྒྱ་སྤྱར་རྒྱུ་དང་ཀྱེ་སྐུ་ཚོགས་པ་འདུས་པའི་དབང་གིས་ མ་བརྟགས་ན་ཉམས་དགའ་བ་དུ་མ་དགའ་སྟུང་སྟེ་དོན་དུ་ན་འདི་ལ་ཅུང་ཟད་ ཚམ་མ་དམིགས་པས་ཅིའི་ཕྱིར་ཆད་པ་ལ་སོགས་པར་འགྱུར།

དེ་ལ་གང་དག་ཕྱིན་ཅི་ལོག་གི་བློ་ཅན་ཞེས་རབ་ཀྱི་མིག་དང་བྲལ་བས་བདག་ དང་གཞན་དུ་མངོན་པར་ཞེན་པས་ལོག་པར་འཁོར་བ་དེ་ལ་གཅིག་ཏུ་མི་ ཕྱོགས་ཞིང་མི་དགའ་བས་དེའི་དོན་དུ་ཚོགས་ཡོངས་སུ་སྒྲུབ་པར་མི་བྱེད་པ་ དེ་དག་ནི་ཐབས་མེད་པས་ཡོངས་སུ་གོལ་ལོ།།

གང་དག་སྒྱུ་མ་མཁན་བཞིན་དུ་གཉིས་སུ་མ་ཆད་པའི་ཚོགས་རྒྱ་ཆེན་པོ་སྒྲུབ་ པར་མཁས་པ་དེ་དག་ཡུན་སྲུང་དུས་བླ་ན་མེད་པའི་གོ་འཕང་བརྙེས་ནས་སྒྲིན་ པ་ན་ཐབ་པ་དང་བདེ་བའི་རྣམ་པ་ཐམས་ཅད་སྒྲུབ་ཅིང་བཞུགས་པ་དེ་ཁོ་བོ་ ཅག་རྣམས ⌠ ཀྱིས ⌡ བསྒྲུབ་པར་བྱ་དགོས་སོ།།

དེ་ལ་ཚོགས་གང་ཞེ་ན་དེ་བཞིན་གཤེགས་པ་གསང་བའི་མདོ་ལས།

ཨེ་ཞེས་ཀྱི་ཚོགས་ཀྱིས་ཏོན་མོང་ས་པ་མཐའ་དག་སྤྱོང་བར་འགྱུར་བ་ལགས་ སོ།།

བསོད་ནམས་ཀྱི་ཚོགས་ཀྱིས་ནི་སེམས་ཅན་ཐམས་ཅད་ནི་བར་འཚོ་བར་འགྱུར་ བ་ལགས་སོ།།   ཞེས་དང་།

འཕགས་པ་དེ་བཞིན་གཤེགས་པ་སྐྱེ་བ་འབྱུང་བའི་མདོར་ཡང་བཀའ་སྩལ་པ།

གང་དེ་བཞིན་གཤེགས་པ་རྣམས་འབྱུང་བ་དེ་ནི་རྒྱ་གཅིག་བུ་མ་
ཡིན་ནོ་དེ་ཅིའི་ཕྱིར་ཞེ་ན།   ཀྱི་རྒྱལ་བའི་སྲས་དག་དེ་བཞིན

> གཤེགས་པ་རྣམས་ནི་ཡང་དག་པར་འགྲུབ་པའི་རྒྱུ་ཚད་མེད་པ་འབུམ་ཕྲག་བཅུས་ཡང་དག་པར་འགྲུབ་སྟེ་བཅུ་གང་ཞེ་ན་འདི་ལྟ་སྟེ། བསོད་ནམས་དང་ཡེ་ཤེས་ཚད་མེད་པས་མི་ངོམས་པ་ཡང་དག་པར་འགྲུབ་པའི་རྒྱུ་དང་ཞེས་བྱ་བ་ལ་སོགས་པ་རྒྱ་ཆེར་གསུངས་སོ།།

དེ་ལྟར་བསམ་ནས་རང་གིས་སྐྱིལ་མོ་དཀྲུང་བཤེག་སྟེ་ཕྱོགས་བཅུའི་སངས་རྒྱས་སྲས་དང་བཅས་པ་ལ་ཕྱག་བྱས་ཏེ་མཆོད་ཅིང་བསྟོད་པ་ནས་ཚད་མེད་པའི་སྨོན་ལམ་ཡང་གདབ་བོ།། དེ་ནས་ཐམས་ཅད་དུ་སྙིང་རྗེའི་སྙིང་པོ་ཅན་གྱི་སྟོང་པ་ཉིད་དང་མི་འབྲལ་བས་སྦྱིན་པ་ལ་སོགས་པའི་ཚོགས་ཡོངས་སུ་སྒྲུབ་པ་ལ་བརྩོན་པར་བྱའོ།། རྣལ་འབྱོར་པས་ནི་དུས་ཐམས་ཅད་དུ་ཉ་དང་ཤ་དང་ཆང་ལ་སོགས་པ་མི་མཐུན་པའི་བཟའ་བ་རྣམས་སྤྱངས་ལ་ཐུན་བཞིའམ་དྲུག་ཏུ་སམྤུཊི་བྱའོ།། གཅིག་ཏུ་དགོན་པ་ལ་གནས་ཏེ་རྣལ་འབྱོར་འདི་ཁོ་ནས་རྣལ་འབྱོར་དུ་བྱའོ།།

རྣལ་འབྱོར་སྒོམ་པའི་རིམ་པ་མདོར་བསྡུས་ཏེ་སྨད་པ། ཨཙརྻ་བི་མ་ལ་མི་ཏྲས་མཛད་པ་ལས་ཤཱཀྱའི་དགེ་སློང་དབེན་པ་ལ་དགའ་བས་བསྡུས་ཏེ་སྦྱར་བ་སྭ་སྟི།། མངྒ་ལཾ་བྷཝནྟུ།།

Bibliography

Abbreviations of Kangyur and Tengyur editions

D   Derge edition of Kangyur and Tengyur. *The Tibetan Tripiṭaka*, Taipei
         Edition. Taipei, Taiwan: SMC Publishing, 1991.

H   Lhasa edition of the Kangyur and Tengyur. Lhasa: Zhol par khang,
         1934.

Q   Peking edition of Kangyur and Tengyur. *The Tibetan Tripiṭaka*, Peking
         Edition. Tokyo/Kyoto: Tibetan Tripiṭaka Research Institute, 1957.

Sūtras and Indian śāstras:

Abhisamayālaṃkāra. Maitreya/Asaṅga. Tibetan translation: *Mngon par rtogs pa'i
         rgyan*, Tengyur D 3786 (*shes phyin, ka*) 1b1–13a7.

Ajātaśatrukaukṛtyavinodanānāmamahāyānasūtra. Tibetan translation: *Ma skyes
         dgra'i 'gyod pa bsal ba zhes bya ba theg pa chen po'i mdo*, Kangyur D 216,
         vol. 62, (*mdo sde, tsha*) 211b2–268b7.

Avataṃsakasūtra. Tibetan translation: *Phal po che zhes bya ba shin tu rgyas pa
         chen po'i mdo*, Kangyur D 44, vol. 35–38, (*ka, kha, ga, a*).

Avikalpapraveśadhāraṇī. Tibetan translation: *Rnam par mi rtog par 'jug pa zhes bya ba'i gzungs,* Kangyur D 142, vol. 57 (*mdo sde, pa*) 1b1–6b1.

Bhāvanākrama. Kamalaśīla. Tibetan translation: *Bsgom pa'i rim pa,* Tengyur D 3916, vol. 110 (*dbu ma, ki*) 42a1–55b5.

Bodhicittavivarana. Nāgārjuna. Tibetan translation: *Byang chub sems 'grel gyi rnam par bshad pa,* Tengyur D 4556, (*jo bo'i chos chung, pho*) 185b4–189b6.

Cittavajrastava. Nāgārjuna. Tibetan translation: *Sems kyi rdo rje'i bstod pa,* Tengyur D 1121 (*bstod tshogs, ka*) 69b5–70a2.

Dharmasaṃgīti. Tibetan translation: *Chos yang dag par sdud pa,* Kangyur D 238, vol. 65, 1b1–99b7.

Dohākoṣahṛdayārthagītiṭīkā (DKHṬ). Avadhūtīpa.Tibetan translation: *Do ha mdzod kyi snying po don gyi glu'i 'grel pa zhes bya ba,* Tengyur D 2268 (*rgyud, zhi*) 65b7–106b4.

Hevajratantra, Tibetan translation: *Kye'i rdo rje zhes bya ba rgyud kyi rgyal po,* Kangyur H 378 (*rgyud, ka*) 334b7–353b3. Kangyur D 417 (*rgyud, nga*) 1b1–13b5.

Kāśyapaparivartasūtra. Tibetan translation: *'Od srung gi le'u zhes bya ba theg pa chen po'i mdo,* Kangyur H 87, vol. 40 (*dkon brtsegs, cha*) 211a6–260b5. Kangyur D 87 (*dkon brtsegs, cha*) 119b1–151b7.

Kramaprāveśikabhāvanārtha. Vimalamitra. Tibetan translation: *Rim gyis 'jug pa'i sgom don,* Tengyur D, 3938 (*dbu ma, ki*) 340b7–358a7.

Lalitavistarasūtra. Tibetan translation: *Rgya cher rol pa'i mdo,* Kangyur D 95, vol. 46 (*mdo sde, kha*) 1b1–216b7.

Laṅkāvatārasūtra. Tibetan translation: *Lang kar gshegs pa'i mdo,* Kangyur H 110, vol. 51 (*mdo sde, ca*) 87b7–307a4. Kangyur D 107, vol. 49 (*mdo sde, ca*) 56a1–191b7. Kangyur Q 775, vol. 29 (*mdo sna tshogs, ngu*) 60b7–208b2.

Madhyamakopadeśa. Atiśa. Tibetan translation: *Dbu ma'i man ngag,* Tengyur D 3929, vol. 110 (*dbu ma, ki*) 95b1–96a7.

Mahāparinirvāṇasūtra. Tibetan translation: *Yongs su mya ngan las 'das pa chen poi mdo,* Kangyur D 119, vol. 52–53 (*mdo sde, nya*) 1b1–343a6; (*ta*)1b1–339a7.

Mahāyānottaratantra / Ratnagotravibhāga. Maitreya/Asaṅga. Tibetan translation:
Theg pa chen po rgyud bla ma, Tengyur D 4024, vol. 123 (*sems tsam, phi*)
54b1–73a7.

Mahāyānottaratantraśāstravyākhyā. Maitreya/Asaṅga.Tibetan translation: *Theg
pa chen po rgyud bla ma'i bstan bcos rnam par bshad pa,* Kangyur D 4025
(*sems tsam, phi*) 74b1–129a7.

Mahāyānasūtrālaṃkāra. Maitreya/Asaṅga. Tibetan translation: *Theg pa chen po
mdo sde'i rgyan,* Tengyur D 4020, vol. 123 (*sems tsam, phi*) 1b1–39a4.

*Mahāvyutpatti. A Critical Edition of the sGra sbyor bam po gnyis pa: An old and ba-
sic commentary on the Mahāvyutpatti,* Ishikawa, Mie. 1990. Studia Tibetica no. 18, The Toyo Bunko. Tr. with references to other Śāstras by the
same author in Studia Tibetica no. 28, 1993.

Mañjughoṣastotra. Dignāga. Tibetan translation: *'Jam pa'i dbyangs kyi bstod pa,*
Tengyur D 2712, vol. 73 (*rgyud, nu*) 79a3–79b7.

Munimatālaṃkāra. Abhayākaragupta. Tibetan translation: *Thub pa Dgongs rgyan,*
Tengyur D 3903 (*dbu ma, a*) 73b1–293a7.

Padārthaprakāśikā–śrīsambaramūlatantraṭīkā. Tibetan translation: *Dpal bde mchog
gi rgya cher bshad pa tshig don rab tu gsal ba,* Tengyur D 1412, vol. 17
(*rgyud, ma*) 353b1–450a7.

Prajñāpāramitāhṛdaya. Tibetan translation: *Shes rab kyi pha rol tu phyin pa'i snying po*), Kangyur H 499, vol. 88, (*rgyud, tha*) 45a2–47a2. Kangyur D 21,
vol. 34 (*shes rab sna tshogs, ka*) 144b6–146a3.

Prajñāpāramitāhṛdayaṭīkā. Tibetan translation: *Shes rab kyi pha rol tu phyin
pa'i snying po'i rgya cher bshad pa.* Tengyur D 3818 (*shes phyin, ma*)
267b1–280b7.

Ratnameghasūtra. Tibetan translation: *Dkon mchog sprin po'i mdo,* Kangyur D 231,
vol. 64, 1b1–112b7.

Ratnolkādhāraṇīsūtra. Tibetan translation: *Dkon mchog ta la la'i gzungs zhes bya ba
'i mdo,* D 145, vol. 57 (*mdo sde, pa*) 34a4–82a3.

Samādhirājanāma-Mahāyānasūtra. Tibetan translation: *Ting nge 'dzin gyi rgyal po
zhes bya ba theg pa chen po'i mdo.* Kangyur D 127, vol. 55 (*mdo sde, da*)
1b1–170b7, Kangyur Q 795, vol 31 (*mdo sna tshogs, thu*) 1a1–185a8,
Kangyur H 129, vol. 55 (*mdo sde, ta*) 1b1–269b4.

Samādhirājanāma-Mahāyānasūtraṭīkākīrtimālā. Mañjuśrīkīrti. Tibetan translation: *Ting nge 'dzin kyi rgyal po zhes bya ba theg pa chen po'i mdo'i 'grel pa grags pa'i phreng ba,* Tengyur D 4010 (*mdo 'grel, nyi*) 1b1–163b4. Tengyur Q 5511, vol. 105 (*mdo tshogs 'grel pa, nyi*) 1a1–189b6.

Saṃdhinirmocanasūtra. Tibetan translation: *Dgongs pa nges par 'grel pa'i mdo,* Kangyur H 109, vol. 51 (*mdo sde, ca*) 1b1–87b7. Kangyur D 106, vol. 49 (*mdo sde, ca*) 1b1–55b7.

Saptaśatikāprajñāpāramitāṭīkā. Vimalamitra. Tibetan translation: *Shes rab kyi pha rol tu phyin pa bdun brgya pa'i rgya cher 'grel pa,* Tengyur D 3814, vol. 95 (*shes phyin, ma*) 6b1–89a7.

Śrīmālādevīsiṃhanādasūtra. Tibetan translation: *Lha mo dpal phreng gi seng ge'i sgra zhes bya ba theg pa chen po'i mdo,* Kangyur H 92, vol. 40 (*dkon brtsegs, cha*) 418a6–454a4. Kangyur D 92, vol. 44 (*dkon brtsegs, cha*) 255a1–277b7.

Tathāgataguṇajñānācintyaviṣayāvatāranirdeśasūtra. Tibetan translation: *Ye shes bsam gyis mi khyab pa'i yul la 'jug pa bstan pa zhes bya ba theg pa chen po'i mdo,* Kangyur D 47, vol. 39 (*dkon brtsegs, ka*) 100a1–203a7.

Tattvadaśaka. Advayavajra (Maitrīpa?). Tibetan translation: *De kho na nyid bcu pa,* Tengyur D 2236 (*rgyud, wi*) 112b7–113a6.

Tattvadaśakaṭīkā. Sahajavajra. Tibetan translation: *De kho na nyid bcu pa'i rgya cher 'grel pa.* Tengyur D 2254, vol. 51 (*rgyud, wi*) 160b7–177a7.

Yogabhāvanāvatāra. Kamalaśīla. Tibetan translation: *Rnam 'byor bsgom pa la 'jug pa,* Tengyur D 3918, vol. 110 (*dbu ma, ki*) 68b7–70b4.

Yuktiṣaṣṭikākārikā. Nāgārjuna. Tibetan translation: *Rigs pa drug cu pa'i tshig le'ur byas pa,* Tengyur D 3825 (*dbu ma, tsa*) 20b1–22b6.

Tibetan writings

'Jigs med gling pa Mkhyen brtse 'od zer

— *Rdzogs pa chen po klong chen snying thig gi gdod ma'i mgon po'i lam gyi rim pa'i khrid yig ye shes bla ma.* In: *The Collected Works of Kun-mkhyen 'Jigs-med-gling-pa.* 9 vols. (sde dge par ma) ed. Pema Thinley for Dodrupchen Rinpoche. Gangtok, India, 1985, vol. 8, 519–618.

'Gos Lo tsā ba Gzhon nu dpal

— *'Gos Lo tsā ba gzhon nu dpal's Commentary on the Ratnagotravibhāgavyākyā.* (*Theg pa chen po rgyud bla ma'i 'grel pa de kho na nyid rab tu gsal ba'i me long*). Critically edited by Klaus-Dieter Mathes. Nepal Research Centre Publications, 24. Stuttgart: Franz Steiner Verlag, 2003.

— *Deb ther sngon po.* Varanasi: Vajra Vidya Institute, 2003.

Gtsug lag phreng ba (Second Pawo)

— *Byang chub sems dpa'i spyod pa la 'jug pa'i rnam par bshad pa.* Full title: *Byang chub sems dpa'i spyod pa la 'jug pa'i rnam par bshad pa theg chen chos kyi rgya mtsho Zab rgyas mtha' yas pa'i snying po.* Rumtek: Dharma Chakra Centre, 1975.

— *Mkhas pa'i dga' ston.* Full title: *Dam pa'i chos kyi 'khor lo bsgyur ba rnams kyi byung ba gsal bar byed pa mkhas pa'i dga' ston.* 2 vols. Pe cin: Mi rigs dpe skrun khang, 1986.

Karma pa Mi bskyod rdo rje (Eighth Karmapa)

— *Collected Works of Mi bskyod rdo rje. Mi bskyod rdo rje gsung 'bum,* in 26 vols. Full title: *Dpal rgyal ba karma pa sku 'phreng brgyad pa mi bskyod rdo rje gsung 'bum.* Lhasa: 2004.

— *Dgongs gcig gi gsung bzhi bcu pa'i 'grel pa.* In: *Collected Works of Mi bskyod rdo rje,* vol. 6, 728–939.

— *Dwags brgyud grub pa'i shing rta.* Full title: *Dbu ma la 'jug pa'i rnam bshad dpal ldan dus gsum mkhyen pa'i zhal lung Dwags brgyud grub pa'i shing rta.* Reprod. From a Dpal spungs edition of Zhwa dmar Chos kyi blo gros. Gangtok: Rumtek Monastery 1974. Also: *Dwags brgyud grub pa'i shing rta.* Seattle: Nitartha International Publications, 1996.

— *Sku gsum ngo sprod rnam bshad,* 3 vols. Full title: *Sku gsum ngo sprod kyi rnam par bshad pa mdo rgyud bstan pa mtha' dag gi e vaṃ phyag rgya.* Varanasi: Vajra Vidya Institute Library, 2013.

Karma pa Rang byung rdo rje (Third Karmapa)

— *Collected Works of Rangjung Dorje. Karma pa Rang byung rdo rje gsung 'bum,* in 16 vols. Ziling: mTshur phu mkhan po lo yag bkra shis, 2006.

— *De bzhin gshegs pa'i snying po bstan pa.* In: *Collected Works of Rangjung Dorje,* vol. 7, 282–290. Also in: *Dbu ma gzhan stong skor bstan bcos phyogs bsdus deb dang po*, Rumtek 1990, 55–62.

— *Nges don phyag rgya chen po'i smon lam.* In: *Collected Works of Rangjung Dorje*, vol. 11, 617–622.

— *Zab mo nang don gyi rnam bshad snying por gsal bar byed pa'i nyin byed.* In: *Collected Works of Rangjung Dorje*, vol. 14, 1–554.

Karma phrin las Phyogs las rnam rgyal (First Karma Trinle)

— *Dohā skor gsum gyi tshig don gyi rnam bshad sems kyi rnam thar gsal bar stong pa'i me long*, Varanasi: Vajra Vidya Institute Library, 2009.

— *The Songs of Esoteric Practice (Mgur) and Replies to Doctrinal Questions (Dris-lan) of Karma-'phrin-las-pa.* New Delhi: Ngawang Topgay, 1975, Reproduced from Prints of the 1539 Rin-chen-ri-bo Blocks.

— *Zab mo nang don rnam bshad snying po.* Full title: *Zab mo nang don rnam bshad snying po gsal bar byed pa'i nyin byed 'od kyi phreng ba.* Karma 'phrin las pa. In: *Karma pa Rang byung rdo rje gsung 'bum.* 16 vols. Ziling: mTshur phu mkhan po lo yag bkra shis, 2006. vol. 14, 1–553.

Kong sprul Blo gros mtha' yas

— *Gdams ngag mdzod. The treasury of precious instructions. A collection of essential contemplative teachings of the eight main lineages of tibetan buddhism,* 18 vols., Shechen Publications, Delhi 1999.

— *Rgyal ba yang dgon pa'i khyad chos ri chos yon tan kun 'byung gi snying po ma drug gi gdams zab.* In: *Gdams ngag mdzod*, vol. 10, 243–295.

— *Shes bya kun khyab mdzod.* Full title: *Theg pa'i sgo kun las bdus pa gsung rab rin po che'i mdzod bslab pa gsum leg par ston pa'i bstan bcos shes bya kun khyab*, 3 vols., Beijing: Mi rigs spe skrun khang, 1982.

Red mda' ba gzhon nu blo gros

— *Theg pa chen po gzhi lam 'bras gsal bar byed pa phyag rgya chen po'i rdo rje'i glu.* In: The Collected Works of Rendawa, (vol. 4, 81–97), *Rje btsun chen po red mda' ba'i gsung 'bum thor bu ba las tshigs bcad kyis tshogs*, 89_6–90_2, Bouddha, Kathmandu: Sa skya rgyal yongs gsung rab slob gnyer khang, 1999.

Sakya Paṇḍita

— *Sdom gsum rab dbye.* See below Sakya Paṇḍita 2002.

Sgam po pa

— *Collected Works of Gampopa. Gsung 'bum Sgam po pa Bsod nams rin chen,* in 4 vols. Full title: *Khams gsum chos kyi rgyal po mnyam med sgam po pa 'gro mgon bsod nams rin chen mchog gi gsung 'bum yid bzhin nor bu.* Published by Khenpo Shedrup Tenzin and Lama Thinley Namgyal, Kathmandu: Sherab Gyaltsen, 2000.

— *Chos kyi rje dpal ldan sgam po pa chen po'i rnam par thar pa yid bszhin gyi nor bu rin po che kun khyab snyan pa'i ba dan thar pa rin po che'i rgyan gyi mchog.* In: *Collected Works of Gampopa,* vol. 1, 47–288.

— *Phyag rgya chen po lnga lda.* In: *Collected Works of Gampopa,* vol. 3, 508–513.

— *Rje dwags po rin po che'i tshogs chos chen po.* In: *Collected Works of Gampopa,* vol. 2, 1-68.

— *Snying po don gyi gdams pa phyag rgya chen po'i 'bum thig.* In: *Collected Works of Gampopa,* vol. 3, 89–126.

— *Tshogs chos yon tan phun tshogs.* In: *Collected Works of Gampopa,* vol. 1, 505–75.

— *Tshogs chos legs mdzes ma.* In: *Collected Works of Gampopa,* vol. 1, 484_2–485_3.

Zhwa dmar Mkha' spyod dbang po (Second Shamarpa)

— *Collected Works of Khachö Wangpo, Zhwa dmar pa mkha' spyod dbang po'i gsung 'bum,* in 4 vols. Gonpo Tseten (ed.). Gangtok, 1978, vol. 2, 585–595.

— *Rnal 'byor sgom pa'i rim pa.* In: *Collected Works of Khachö Wangpo,* vol. 2, 585–595.

— *Sgom don mdor bsdus pa.* In: *Collected Works of Khachö Wangpo,* vol. 4, 56–59.

Zhwa dmar Chos grags ye shes (Fourth Shamarpa)

— *Collected Works of Chödrag Yeshe. Chos grags ye shes gsung 'bum.* 6 Vols. Ful title: *Thams cad mkhyen pa zhwa dmar bzhi pa spyan snga chos kyi grags pa'i gsum 'bum bzhugs so.* Beijing: Krung go'i bod rig pa dpe skrun khang, 2009

— *Byang chub sems 'grel gyi rnam par bshad pa*. In: *Collected Works of Chödrag Yeshe*, vol. 4, 651–688.

— *Phyag rgya chen po drug bcu pa. Phyag rgya chen po mtshon par byed pa'i gtam mdor bsdus pa bka' brgyud kyi dgongs pa gsal ba*. In: *Collected Works of Chödrag Yeshe*, vol. 6, 320–324.

— *Rnam par rtog pa chos sku'i sgrub tshul dri med gsung rab gter mdzod*. In: *Collected Works of Chödrag Yeshe*, vol. 3, 21–24.

— *Snyan brgyud rdo rje zam pa'i khrid yig skal bzang mig 'byed,* In: *Rdzogs pa chen po klong sde'i snyan brgyud rin po che rdo rje zab pa'i sgom khrid kyi lag len*. In: *Gdams ngag mdzod*, vol. 1, 417–439.

Zhwa dmar Mi pham chos kyi blo gros (14th Shamarpa)

— *Nges don phyag rgya chen po'i khrid mdzod*, 13 vols. Published by the 14th Shamar Rinpoche. New Delhi: Rnam par rgyal ba dpal zhwa dmar pa'i chos sde, 1997.

— *Phyag rgya chen po'i sngon 'gro'i nyams len rgyun 'khyer tshogs gnyis zung 'jug.* 1996. With German translation, Vienna: Bodhi 1999.

— *Rnam rtog chos sku'i dogs sel sgam po'i dgongs rgyan*. Kalimpong: Shri Diwakar Publications, 2011.

— *Skyabs mgon zhwa dmar sku phreng bcu bzhi pa mi pham chos kyi blo gros mchog gi bla ma'i rnal 'byor yin rlabs grub pa'i dga' ston.* 1966. With English and German translation, Vienna: Bodhi, 2015.

— *Thub dbang mchod pa'i cho ga mdor bsdus bde gshegs lam bstan.* 1980. With German translation, Vienna: Bodhi 2005.

— *Thugs rje chen po rgyal po lugs kyi rgyun khyer snying po'i bcud 'dus.* Ca. 1996. With German translation, Vienna: Bodhi 1996.

Secondary References and Translations from Tibetan into English

Brunnhölzl, Karl. 2007. *Straight from the Heart. Buddhist Pith Instruction.* Ithaca, New York: Snow Lion.

_____ 2014. *When the Clouds Part. The* Uttaratantra *and Its Meditative Tradition as a Bridge between Sūtra and Tantra*. Boston & London: Snow Lion.

Dagpo Tashi Namgyal. 1986. *Mahāmudrā, the Quintessence of Mind and Meditation.* Transl. by Lhalungpa, Lobsang P. Boston: Wisdom Publications. Reprint edition 2001. Motilal Barnasidass, Delhi.

—— 2019. *Moonbeams of Mahāmudrā.* Transl. by Callahan, Elizabeth M. Boulder: Snow Lion.

Draszczyk, Martina. 2015. *Die Anwendung der Tathāgatagarbha-Lehre in Kong spruls Anleitung zur Gzhan stong-Sichtweise.* Wiener Studien zur Tibetologie und Buddhismuskunde, Heft 87. Wien: Arbeitskreis für Tibetische und Buddhistische Studien Universität Wien.

—— 2016. Co-authered with Higgins, David. *Mahāmudrā and the Middle Way. Post-Classical Kagyü Discourses on Mind, Emptiness and Buddha Nature.* For details see below "Higgins".

—— 2019. Co-authered with Higgins, David. *Buddha Nature Reconsidered. The Eighth Karma pa's Middle Path.* For details see below "Higgins".

—— 2020. "Mahāmudrā as the Key-Point of the Third Dharmacakra according to the Sixty Verses on Mahāmudrā by Zhwa dmar Chos grags ye shes." In: *Mahāmudrā in India and Tibet,* ed. by Roger R. Jackson and Klaus-Dieter Mathes, Leiden, Bosten: Brill, pp. 204–236.

Gampopa. 1959. *The Jewel Ornament of Liberation.* Transl. by Guenther, Herbert V. Boston: Shambhala Publications.

—— 1998. *The Jewel Ornament of Liberation. The Wish-fulfilling Gem of the Noble Teachings.* Transl. by Konchog Gyaltsen, Khenpo Rinpoche. Ithaca, New York: Snow Lion Publications.

'Gos Lo tsā ba Gzhon nu dpal. 1979. *The Blue Annals.* Transl. by Roerich, Georges. Delhi: Motilal Banarsidass.

Gyatrul Rinpoche Sherpa, Trungram. 2004. *Gampopa, the Monk and the Yogi: His Life and Teachings.* Unpublished PhD thesis, Cambridge MS: Harvard University.

Gruber, Joel. 2016. "The Sudden and Gradual Sutric (and Tantric?) Approaches of the *Rim gyis 'jug pa'i sgom rim* and the *Cig car 'jug pa rnam par mi rtog pa'i sgom don.*" In: JIABS (*Journal of the International Association of Buddhist Studies*) Vol. 39, 2016, pp. 402–427.

Higgins, David. 2016. Co-authered with Martina Draszczyk. *Mahāmudrā and the Middle Way. Post-Classical Kagyü Discourses on Mind, Emptiness and Buddha Nature.* Wiener Studien zur Tibetologie und Buddhismuskunde, Heft 90.1–2. Wien: Arbeitskreis für Tibetische und Buddhistische Studien Universität Wien.

_____ 2019. Co-authered with Martina Draszczyk. *Buddha Nature Reconsidered. The Eighth Karma pa's Middle Path.* Wiener Studien zur Tibetologie und Buddhismuskunde, Heft 95.1–2. Wien: Arbeitskreis für Tibetische und Buddhistische Studien Universität Wien.

Kongtrul, Jamgön. 2007. *The Treasury of Knowledge. Esoteric Instructions.* Book 8, part 4. Transl. by Sarah Harding. Ithaka, New York: Snow Lion Publications.

_____ 2000 repr. *The Torch of Certainty.* Transl. by Judith Hansan. Boston and London: Shambala.

Lhalungpa, Lobsang P. 1977 (tr.). *The Life of Milarepa.* London: Paladin Books.

Mathes, Klaus-Dieter. 2006. "Blending the Sūtras with the Tantras: The Influence of Maitrīpa and His Circle on the Formation of *Sūtra Mahāmudrā* in the Kagyu Schools." In: *Tibetan Buddhist Literature and Practice: Studies in its Formative Period 900–1400, Tibetan Studies: Proceedings of the Tenth Seminar of the International Association of Tibetan Studies,* Oxford 2006, vol. 10/4. Ed. Ronald M. Davidson and Christian K. Wedemeyer. Leiden: Brill, 201–27.

_____ 2008. *A Direct Path to the Buddha Within, Gö Lotsawa's Mahāmudrā Interpretation of the Ratnagotravibhāga.* Boston: Wisdom Publications.

_____ 2009. Maitrīpa's *Amanasikārādhāra* ("A Justification of Becoming Mentally Disengaged"). In: *Journal of the Nepal Research Centre,* vol. 13, 5–32.

_____ 2016. "bKa' brgyud *Mahāmudrā:* 'Chinese *rDzogs chen*' or the Teachings of the Siddhas?" In: ZAS 45 (2016), 309–340.

McClintock, Sara. 2014. "Kamalaśīla on the Nature of Phenomenal Content (ākāra) in Cognition: A Close Reading of TSP ad TS 3626 and Related Passages." In: *Journal of Indian Philosophy,* 6/2014, vol. 42 (2-3), 327–337.

Patrul Rinpoche. 1994. *The Words of My Perfect Teacher*. Translated by the Padmakara Translation Group. San Francisco: HarperCollinsPublisher.

Sakya Paṇḍita. 2002. *A Clear Differentiation of the Three Codes* Transl. by Rhoton. Albany: State University of New York.

Śāntideva. 1995. *Bodhicaryāvatāra, Śāntideva*. Transl. by Kate Crosby and Andrew Skilton. Oxford: World's Classics 1995.

Shamar Rinpoche. 1993. *On the Meaning of Samaya*. 1993. Transl. by Tina Draszczyk. New Delhi: Dorje and Bell Publications.

―――― 2011. *The King of Prayers: A Commentary on the Noble King of Prayers of Excellent Conduct*. Edited by Lara Braitstein, Thea Howard, Julia Stenzel. Translation of the prayer: Pamela G. While. Kathamandu: Shanti Path Publications.

―――― 2012. *A Golden Swan in Turbulent Waters: The Life and Times of the Tenth Karmapa Choying Dorje*. Lexington, Virginia: Bird of Paradies Press.

―――― 2013. *The Path to Awakening: How Buddhism's Seven Points of Mind Training Can Lead You to a Life of Enlightenment and Happiness*. Edited by Lara Braitstein. Lexington, Virginia: Bird of Paradise Press.

―――― 2013. (repr.) *Boundless Awakening: The Heart of Buddhist Meditation*. Edited by Tina Draszczyk et.al. Lexington, Virginia: Bird of Paradise Press.

―――― 2018. *Boundless Wisdom: A Mahāmudrā Practice Manual*. Edited by Tina Draszczyk and Lara Braitstein. Lexington: Bird of Paradise Press.

―――― 2019. *Buddha Nature. Our Potential for Wisdom, Compassion, and Happiness*. Transl. and introduced by Tina Draszczyk. Lexington: Bird of Paradise Press.

―――― 2020. *Bringing Mind Training to Life: Exploring a Concise Lojong Manual by the 5th Shamarpa*. Transl. by Pamela Gayle White. La Remuée: Rabsel Éditions.

―――― 2020. *A Path of Practice. The Bodhi Path Program*. Edited by Tina Draszczyk. La Remuée: Rabsel Éditions.

Takasaki, Jikido. 1966. *A Study on the Ratnagotravibhāga (Uttaratantra) Being a Treatise on the Tathāgatagarbha Theory of Mahāyāna Buddhism*. Serie Oriental Roma XXXIII. Roma: Istituto Italiano per il Medio ed Estremo

Oriente.

Tauscher, Helmut. 1995. *Die Lehre von den zwei Wirklichkeiten in Tsoṅ kha pas Madhyamaka Werken*. Wiener Studien zur Tibetologie und Buddhismuskunde, Heft 36. Wien: Arbeitskreis für Tibetische und Buddhistische Studien Universität Wien.

Thu'u bkwan, Chos kyi nyi ma. 2009. *The Crystal Mirror of Philosophical Systems*. Transl. by Geshé Lhundub Sopa and edited by Roger R. Jackson. Somerville: Wisdom Publications.

Westerhof, Jan. 2018. *The Golden Age of Indian Buddhist Philosophy*. Oxford: Oxford University Press.

Endnotes

1   Tib. transliteration: *rnam rtog chos sku.*

2   Tib. transliteration: *dwags po bka' brgyud.*

3   Extract from teachings in Vienna on Sept. 26th, 1993.

4   The Karma Kagyü (also called Kamtsang Kagyü) tradition is one among the precious Buddhist transmission lineages that were significantly shaped by Gampopa (1079–1153), the Healer from Dagpo, an area in the south of Tibet. It is in reference to him that these Kagyü traditions are often referred to as Dagpo Kagyü.

5   The translation "Practice of the Connate" (Tib. transliteration: *lhan cig skyes sbyor*; Tib. phonetics: *lencig kejor*) is based on a quotation from Pagmo Drupa (1110–1170), one of Gampopa's direct students, which the Eighth Karmapa, Mikyö Dorje (1507–1554) uses to define this term. See in his *Explanation of the Direct Introduction to the Three Embodiments* (*Sku gsum ngo sprod rnam bshad*), 2013, vol. 1, 122$_{1-5}$: "With respect to these key instructions, which are referred to as the tradition which merges the two streams of Ka[dampa] and [Mahā]mudrā transmitted to Gampopa, the glorious Pagmo Drupa composed *The Practice of the Connate* exactly according to Gampopa's teachings. Therein [Pagmo Drupa] says: 'The three, mind, concepts, and dharmakāya, are connate from the beginning. Thus, because through instructions one integrates [this] in [one's] mind, it is called the "practice of the connate".'" *rje sgam po pa la brgyud pa'i bka' phyag chu bo gnyis 'dres kyi lam srol zhes bya ba'i man ngag 'di la | rje sgam po pa'i gsung ji lta bar dpal phag mo dru pas mdzas pa'i lhan cig skyes sbyor las | sems dang rnam rtog chos sku gsum || dang por lhan cig skyes pa ste || gdams pas sems su sbyor ba'i phyir || lhan cig skyes sbyor zhes su bshad ||.* In the same treatise, Mikyö Dorje refers to a dialogue between Pagmo Drupa and Gampopa in which Pagmo Drupa asks about the difference between Mahāmudrā and the practice of the connate. Gampopa replies: "Mahāmudrā is the primordially spontaneous reality of all phenomena of both saṃsāra and nirvāṇa. It resembles the sky and is timeless wisdom; being nondual and one, it is uninterrupted. The practice of the connate means to unite any thought that arises within the four *kāyas*. Therefore it is not maintained to be timeless and is thus interrupted". *Sku gsum ngo sprod rnam bshad*, 2013, vol. 1, 209$_{12-16}$: *phyag rgya chen po ni*

'khor ba dang mya ngan las 'das pa'i chos thams cad ye nas lhun gyis grub pa chos nyid nam mkha' lta bu dus thams cad pa'i ye shes gnyis med gcig yin te | rgyun chad med pa yin | lhan cig skyes sbyor ni rtog pa gang skyes pa'i sku bzhir sbyor ba yin pas dus thams cad par mi 'dod pas | rgyun chad yod gsung | zhes 'byung ngo ||. See Bibliography: Karma pa Mi bskyod rdo rje.

The Fourteenth Shamar Rinpoche additionally taught in the text translated here (part 2), *The Ornament of Gampopa's Intent. Dispelling Doubts Regarding Concept-Dharmakāya*: (…) [later on, this teaching system] was given the title of a treatise ["Mahāmudrā, the Practice of the Connate"]. Thereby, the name of the result [i.e. Mahāmudrā] was given to the cause [i.e. the Practice of the Connate]. Moreover, I think that at that time people valued [a teaching] more when it involved the terms of the secret mantras. Therefore, this language was used in order to inspire all kinds of trainees to engage in this profound authentic Dharma (…).

Regarding "Mahāmudrā, the Practice of the Connate" and the associated connate/innate/ co-emergent wisdom (Sanskrit: *sahajajñāna*; Tib.: *lhenchik kyépé yeshe*), Shamar Rinpoche explains in his *Boundless Wisdom. A Mahāmudrā Practice Manual*, p. 136: "Innate or coemergent wisdom" refers to the inseparability of the dualistic mind and the wisdom of awakening. *Innate* refers to the intrinsic nature of something. The Tibetan word *lhenchik kyépa* literally means that two different things arise simultaneously and are fundamentally connected. In the case of mind and wisdom, *innate* or, more literally, *co-emergent*, means that both are empty in nature and therefore indivisibly one, even though they have distinguishable features. In other words, mind and wisdom are inseparable here and now, and always have been. Empty in nature, they are beyond the confines of time and space. Innate wisdom can also be examined from the perspective of the ground, path, and fruition. Innate or co-emergent wisdom in the context of the ground pertains to the nature of mind, self-aware and self-illuminating. In other words, the mind and its quality of luminosity are inseparable. Co-emergent wisdom in the context of the path is the increasing insight that arises as you practice on the foundation of study, reflection, and meditation. First, there is a coarse understanding. Then comes a more complete experience, and finally, the realization of that luminosity or wisdom, the view that realizes the inseparability of appearances and emptiness. Co-emergent wisdom in the context of fruition pertains to the stage at which this inseparability has been fully disclosed. The ultimate fruition of innate wisdom shows itself in terms of a two-fold purity: there is the primordially pure nature that was already there at the time of the ground [i.e. also during the state of a samsaric sentient being]; and there is the mind in the state of fruition. In other words, once the mind has been purified of all defilements, its purity fully manifests, is fully revealed. This is innate wisdom in the context of fruition. This presentation accords with the different Mahāyāna and Vajrayāna sources."

6   *Rnam rtog chos sku'i dogs sel sgam po'i dgongs rgyan*. See Bibliography: Zhwa dmar Mi pham chos kyi blo gros.

7   *Rnam par rtog pa chos sku'i sgrub tshul dri med gsung rab gter mdzod*. See Bibliography: Zhwa dmar pa Chos grags ye shes.

8   *Phyag rgya chen po drug bcu pa. Phyag rgya chen po mtshon par byed pa'i gtam mdor bsdus pa bka' brgyud kyi dgongs pa gsal ba*. See Bibliography: Zhwa dmar pa Chos grags ye shes.

9   Tib. transliteration: *gtum mo,* the practice of Powerfulness, often translated as "inner heat" or "heat yoga". It belongs to the so-called Six Dharmas of Nāropa. The others are Illusory Body, Dream Yoga, Luminosity, Intermediate State, and Transference. These Six Dharmas belong to the tantric perfection process with characteristics which means that the meditation is supported by specific methods. In the context of Mahāmudrā this is usually tummo.

10   *Sgom don mdor bsdus pa*. See Bibliography: Zhwa dmar pa Mkha' spyod dbang po.

11   *Rnal 'byor sgom pa'i rim pa*. See Bibliography: Zhwa dmar pa Mkha' spyod dbang po.

12   Tib. *Rim gyis 'jug pa'i sgom don*. See Bibliography: *Kramaprāveśikabhāvanārtha*.

13   Vimalamitra's historical dates and works are not easy to ascertain as both earlier and contemporary Buddhist historians disagree on the dates. For example: according to the *Great History of the Dzogchen Nyingthig (Rdzogs pa chen po snying thig gyi lo rgyus chen mo)* composed by Katog Khenpo Jamyang (Kah thog mkhan po 'Jam dbyang, 1929–1999), Vimalamitra lived in the 5th century A.D. In contrast, Nyang Ral Nyime Öser (Nyang ral nyi ma 'od zer, 1124–1192) claims in his *Copper Temple (Zangs gling ma)* that Vimalamitra was the grandson of the empo-

rer Aśoka (approx. 304–232 B.C.) and born by virginal conception. Some sources again claim that Vimalamitra came to Tibet in the 9th century and, according to Gö Lotsawa ('Gos lo tsa ba, 1392–1481), there were even two different Vimalamitras who travelled to Tibet around the same time, i.e. during the ninth century A.D. See Bibliography: Gö Lotsawa 1979, (tr. by Roerich) *The Blue Annals*, 197, 106–108, 197, 491, 497, 591–592. Various records also differ regarding Vimalamitra's spiritual training; whether this took place mainly in India or in China, an issue which is directly linked with the question of his presenting a gradual approach in meditation practice and / or an approach where enlightenment is attained spontaneously, often referred to as the "sudden approach". Likewise, the authorship of various texts attributed to him has been questioned. For more details on this, see Bibliography: Gruber, Joel. 2016.

14   Zhwa dmar pa Mi pham Chos kyi blo gros.

15   Karma pa Rang byung rig pa'i rdo rje.

16   *A Change of Expression* (1992). *On the Meaning of Samaya* (1993). *A Path of Practice: The Bodhi Path Program* (2020). *Boundless Wisdom: A Mahāmudrā Practice Manual* (2018).). *Bringing Mind Training to Life: Exploring a Concise Lojong Manual by the 5th Shamarpa* (2020). *Boundless Awakening: The Heart of Buddhist Meditation* (2013). *A Golden Swan in Turbulent Waters: The Life and Times of the Tenth Karmapa Choying Dorje* (2012). *The King of Prayers: A Commentary on the Noble King of Prayers of Excellent Conduct* (2011). *Creating a Transparent Democracy: A New Model* (2011). *The Path to Awakening: How Buddhism's Seven Points of Mind Training Can Lead You to a Life of Enlightenment and Happiness* (2014).

17   *Nges don phyag rgya chen po'i khrid mdzod*. See Bibliography: Zhwa dmar Mi pham chos kyi blo gros.

18   See Bibliography: Zhwa dmar Mi pham chos kyi blo gros.

19   Zhwa dmar pa Chos grags ye shes dpal bzang po, often abbreviated to Shamar Chödrag Yeshe or Chökyi Dragpa. For detailed information about the Fourth Zhwa dmar pa's life we can look forward to Mojzes's current dissertation project at Bonn University, Germany: *The Fourth Zhwa-dmar-pa Incarnate: A Comprehensive Study of the Life and Works of Chos-grags ye-shes dpal bzang-po (1453-1524)*.

20   Karma pa Chos grags rgya mtsho.

21   Ban sgar 'Jam dpal bzang po. He was the Mahāmudrā lineage holder after the 6th Karmapa and composed among others the well-known Mahāmudrā prayer called *Dorje Chang Thungma*, which is frequently recited to this day.

22   Gos Lo tsā ba gzhon nu dpal. He had a large number of teachers from various lineages of Tibetan Buddhism. When the Indian Paṇḍita Vanaratna (known in Tibet as Paṇchen Nakyi Rinchen, 1384–1468) came to Tibet, he acted as his interpreter. Gö Lotsawa is famous for his historical work called the *Blue Annals* (*Deb ther sngon po*), but he also wrote a number of extensive treatises. The 14th Shamar Rinpoche considered his detailed commentary on the *Ultimate Continuum* (*Mahāyānottaratantraśāstra* often abbreviated to *Uttaratantra* or *Gyü Lama* and also known as *Ratnagotravibhāga*) to reflect the intent of Dagpo Mahāmudrā. See Bibliography: 'Gos Lo tsā ba Gzhon nu dpal and Gö Lotsawa.

23   Spyan snga Chos kyi grags pa.

24   Lhun grub chos sde and Yangs pa can.

25   *Zhwa dmar bzhi pa spyan snga chos kyi grags pa'i gsung 'bum*, (*Collected Works*) 6 vols. See Bibliography: Zhwa dmar pa Chos grags ye shes. This digitized print was done on the basis of the complete manuscript version of his *Collected Works* with its thirteen divisions in six volumes. These writings cover a variety of topics, such as hymns of buddhas, bodhisattvas and special places; hagiographies of lamas; extensive expositions on philosophical and tantric treatises; questions and answers; as well as miscellaneous advice and prayers.

26   Dpa' bo gtsug lag phreng ba. Pawo Tsuglag Trengwa was a Karma Kagyü master whose activities had a lasting impact on this tradition. Among his teachers were the Eighth Karmapa, Mikyö Dorje (1507–1554), among his students were the Ninth Karmapa, Wangchuk Dorje (Dbang phyug rdo rje, 1556–1603), and the Fifth Shamarpa, Könchog Yenlag (Dkon mchog yan lag,

27   1525–1583). He wrote a substantial collection of hagiographies called *The Feast of the Wise* (*Mkhas pa'i dga' ston*) as well as a comprehensive commentary on the *Introduction to the Bodhi-sattva's Way of Life* (*Bodhicaryāvatāra*). See Bibliography: Gtsug lag phreng ba.

27   Karma phrin las Phyogs las rnam rgyal. Karma Trinle was also a very active master of the Karma Kagyü tradition. Among his teachers were the Seventh Karmapa, Chödrag Gyamtso (1454–1506), the Fourth Shamarpa and the Sakya master Shākya Chogden (Shākya Mchog ldan, 1428–1507). Among his disciples were the Eighth Karmapa, Mikyö Dorje, and the Second Pawo Tsuglag Trengwa. Karma Trinle authored among others an extensive commentary on the *Profound Inner Meaning* (*Zab mo nang don*), an important text for the Karma Kagyü tradition by the Third Karmapa, a collection of writings called *Songs of Esoteric Practice and Replies to Doctri-nal Questions* as well as a commentary on Saraha's *Mahāmudrā Songs*. See Bibliography: Karma phrin las Phyogs las rnam rgyal.

28   Zhwa dmar pa Mkha' spyod dbang po.

29   Karma pa Rol pa'i rdo rje.

30   *Zhwa dmar pa mkha' spyod dbang po'i gsung 'bum.* See Bibliography: Zhwa dmar pa mkha' spyod dbang po'i.

31   Karma pa De bzhin gshegs pa.

32   Tib.: *rnam rtog.*

33   According to Gampopa, the term "concept" refers to all aspects of samsaric perception, i.e. to both consciousness as well as its objects that appear as a seemingly outer world. In his *Excellent Qualities: Teachings to the Assembly* (*Tshogs chos yon tan phun tshogs*), in *Collected Works*, vol. 1, 511_{1-3} he explains: (…) In which way did [the Buddha] teach [about] concepts? By virtue of them being conditioned, he labelled [concepts] skandhas. Their na-ture he labelled dhātus, their capacity he labelled āyatanas (…)." *Tshogs chos yon tan phun tshogs*, in *Collected Works*, vol. 1, 511_{1-3}: *rnam rtog ci ltar bshad na | 'dus pa las phung por btags | rang bzhin la khams su btags | nus pa la skye mched du btags |.*

    At this point it should be mentioned that the five skandhas (Tib. transliteration: *phung po*; Tib. phonetics: *pungpo*), i. e. the five psycho-physical constituents, form, sensation, distinction, compositional factors, and consciousness, encompass all outer and inner phenomena and are therefore not limited to one's own person. The same applies to the dhātus and āyatanas. The eighteen dhātus (tib. transliteration: *khams*; Tib. phonetics: *kham*), i. e. „elements", are: the six sense-consciousnesses, i.e. seeing, hearing, smelling, tasting, touching, and thinking; the six sense faculties, i.e. the eyes, the ears, the nose, the tongue, the body, and the mind; and the six sense-objects, i.e. visual form, sound, odor, taste, touch, and mental phenomena. The twelve āyatanas (Tib. transliteration: *skye mched*; Tib. phonetics: *kyeche*), i. e. "sense fields", are the six consciousnesses along with their particular faculty and the six sense-objects.

34   Tib.: *sems.*

35   Tib.: *sems nyid.*

36   *Tshogs chos legs mdzes ma*, in *Collected Works*, vol 1, 484_2–485_3: *phyi rol dkar dmar gyi snang ba sna tshogs su snang ba dang | nang dran rig gi rtogs pa sna tshogs su 'char ba 'di thams cad kyang 'od gsal chos kyi sku yin | … dran snang gi chos thams cad la yang bde ba dang sdug pa | spang bya dang gnyen po | skyon dang yon tan la sogs pa sna tshogs su snang yang thams cad kyang 'od gsal chos kyi sku'i rang bzhin yin pas | bcas bcos dang | 'phel 'grib dang | dgag sgrub dang spang blang byar med de | rgyud bla ma las kyang | 'di la bsal bya ci yang med | bzhag par bya ba cung zad med | ces gsungs pas so |.*

37   *Dharmacakrapravartanasūtra.*

38   Sanskrit: *pratityasamutpāda.*

39   Nāgārjuna (c. 2nd century) was one of the greatest Buddhist philosophers, the trail-blazer of the Middle Path; he elucidated and systematized the Buddha's teachings on emptiness and depen-dent arising.

40   *Mūlamadhyamakakārikā.*

41 Translation based on the German translation by Tauscher, 1995, p. 3. See Bibliography: Tauscher, Helmut. 1995.

42 See, for example, Shamar Rinpoche's advice in this regard in his *A Path of Practice: The Bodhi Path Program.* See Bibliography: Shamar Rinpoche. 2020.

43 In "Madhyamaka of Unity", "Unity" (Sanskrit: *yuganaddha*; Tib. *zung 'jug*) stands for the inseparability of the two truths, the inseparability of appearances or manifestations, and emptiness. It also implies the unity of emptiness and clarity, of wisdom and compassion etc. For more information on the Madhyamaka of Unity, see the explanations in note 191 on verse four of *The Sixty Verses on Mahāmudrā*, in the context of explanations of the Madhyamaka of Nonabiding (Sanskrit: *apratiṣṭhānamadhyamaka*; Tib. *rab tu mi gnas pa'i dbu ma*).

44 *The Eye-Opener for the Instructions of the Oral Tradition's Vajra Bridge (Snyan brgyud rdo rje zam pa'i khrid yig skal bzang mig 'byed).* In: *Gdams ngag mdzod*, vol. 1, 432$_{1-2}$: *dwags po'i bka' brgyud pa zung 'jug gi dbu ma dang mthun pas | lhan cig skyes pa zhes pa chos gang dang gang gi gshis | stong pa dang gsal ba lhan cig skyes pa yin no ||.* See Bibliography: Zhwa dmar Chos grags ye shes.

45 Natural awareness—Tib. transliteration: *tha mal gyi shes pa.* Tib. phonetics: *tamal gyi shepa.* Natural awareness, a synonym for connate wisdom and/or buddha nature, is one of the key terms in Dagpo Mahāmudrā. The translation as "natural awareness" is based on an explanation given by the Eighth Karmapa, Mikyö Dorje, in one of his commentaries on Jigten Sumgön's *Single Intent (Dgongs gcig)*: "(…) Thus, supreme bliss, buddha nature, is called *prakṛti* ["nature"], and was translated [into Tibetan] among others as 'nature' (*rang bzhin*), 'innate' (*gnyug ma*), 'uncontrived' (*bcos min*), 'connate' (*lhan skyes*), and 'natural' (*tha mal*). Thus, as Koṭali stated, 'Natural awareness awakens in the middle of the heart.' As the precious Bka' brgyud pas say, natural awareness is also called naturally-occuring, *oṃ svāvatara*. Thus, for yogins of the Mantra [path], the innate bodhicitta without beginning or end is [called] "natural being", *ātmabhāva*." (…) *des na | sangs rgyas kyi snying po bde ba chen po ni | pra kṛ ta zhes pa rang bzhin dang gnyug ma dang bcos min dang lhan skyes dang tha mal zhes par yang 'gyur la | des na tog rtse pas | tha mal shes pa snying gi dbus su sad | | ces 'byung bas | bka' brgyud rin po che'i zhal nas | tha mal shes pa rang babs oṃ sva re ba zhes kyang gsungs so | | des na thog mtha' med par gnyug ma byang chub kyi sems la sngags kyi rnal 'byor pas ā tma bha ba (…)* For more information on this term and the context in Dagpo Mahāmudrā see Higgins and Draszczyk 2019, vol. 1, 241–257 and vol. 2, 208 and 239 (for the Tibetan).

Gampopa's discussions of natural awareness are to be found not in his scholastic treatises, such as his famous path summary, the *Precious Ornament of Liberation*, but rather in lectures and conversations recorded by his disciples—which make up the bulk of his *Collected Works*. To gain a better sense of how he understood and used this term, it may be helpful to look at how he defines it. In a collection of Mahāmudrā instructions, Gampopa says: "The connate is natural awareness. It is uncontrived. It is innate. It is the dharmakāya. It is buddhahood. It is to be directly realized. When natural awareness is simply left as is, it remains undisturbed by outer and inner distractions." *Snying po don gyi gdams pa phyag rgya chen po'i 'bum thig*, in his *Collected Works*, vol. 3, 93$_{1-3}$: *lhan cig skyes pa ni tha mal gyi shes pa yin | de ma bcos pa yin | de gnyug ma yin | de chos sku yin | de sangs rgyas yin | de ngo shes par byed pa yin | tha mal gyi shes pa rang gar bzhag pas | phyi nang gi g.yeng bas mi gnod pa yin no ||.*

In other oral teachings, Gampopa credits his teacher Milarepa with describing natural awareness in terms of innate wisdom: "In the words of the revered teacher [Milarepa], who is endowed with experience and realization, connate wisdom (*sa ha zda'i ye shes*) is precisely that which is present right now as natural awareness. *Gnas lugs gnyis kyi man ngag dang go cha gnyis kyi man ngag*, in his *Collected Works*, vol. 3, 493$_5$–494$_1$: *rtogs pa nyams myong dang ldan pa'i bla ma rje btsun gyi zhal nas | sa ha dza'i ye shes ni | da lta tha mal gyi shes pa yod pa 'di nyid yin gsung |.* See Bibliography: Sgam po pa.

46 *Rje dwags po rin po che'i tshogs chos chen po.* In: *Collected Works*, vol. 2, 45$_1$–49$_1$: … *da res 'khor ba las thar bar 'dod na | chos thams cad kyi rtsa ba yin pas tha mal gyi shes pa ngo shes dgos | de yang tha mal gyi shes pa zhes bya ba | rang gi shes pa 'di la chos kyi rnam pa gang gis kyang ma bslad pa | 'jig rten gyi rnam par shes pa gang gis kyang ma rnyogs pa | bying rmugs dang rtog pa gang gis kyang ma gtum par rang sor gzhag pa yin | de ngo shes na rang gi rig pa'i ye shes yin | ma rtogs na lhan cig skyes pa'i ma rig pa yin | rtogs na rig pa zhes bya | ngo bo zhes bya | lhan cig skyes pa'i ye shes shes*

bya | tha mal gyi shes pa shes bya | gnyug ma zhes bya | spros bral zhes bya | 'od gsal zhes bya ... tha mal gyi shes pa ni don dam pa'i bden pa yin | ... don ngos lam du byed pa yin | mngon sum pa yin ... tha mal gyi shes pa ngo shes pa ni shes rab kyi rgyal po yin | ... 'di ye shes thams cad kyi rgyal po yin no | yon tan thams cad kyi rgyal po yin |. See Bibliography: Sgam po pa.

47   Shamar Rinpoche taught partly in Tibetan, partly in English. The Tibetan passages are newly translated; the English passages have been slightly edited.

48   (...) Here, Shamar Rinpoche went into the ways of presenting the Buddha Dharma, which may vary whether it is taught in the West or in a traditional Tibetan environment, as the educational systems are different. He emphasized that, while the *way of presenting* the Dharma should be adapted, the content and the methods as such should not be changed. Changes in this regard and thus teachings of one's own contrivance would cause severe harm for all those who have the karma for and the wish to practice authentic Buddhism as it has been purely and properly transmitted—in terms of both meditation practice and view—throughout the centuries by Buddhist paṇḍitas and meditation masters until the present day.

49   Here, another passage has been omitted. Shamar Rinpoche called on the listeners to be very careful not to misuse the Dharma. He encouraged them to make sure that the pure Buddha Dharma and the "fresh" lineage continue to be transmitted and practiced.

50   Tib. transliteration: *Phyag chen zla ba'i 'od zer.* Tib. phonetics: *Chag chen dawe öser.*

51   Reprint edition 2001. Delhi: Motilal Barnasidass. In 2019, a new translation was published by Callahan, Elizabeth. *Moonbeams of Mahāmudrā.* Ithaka, New York: Snow Lion Publications 2019. It also includes a translation of *Dispelling the Darkness of Ignorance* by the Ninth Karmapa, Wangchug Dorje. Siehe Bibliography: Dagpo Tashi Namgyal.

52   Lobsang P. Lhalungpa (1926–2008) was born in Lhasa, Tibet. From 1940 until 1952, he was a monk-official in the service of the Dalai Lama and the Tibetan government. Having fled to India, he established the first Tibetan-language program of All India Radio and dedicated his life to the promotion and preservation of Tibet's rich spiritual tradition. Lhalungpa also translated *The Life of Milarepa* and authored *Tibet: The Sacred Realm.* For many years he lived in Santa Fe, New Mexico.

53   Dezhung Rinpoche (Tib. Sde gzhung rin po che, 1906–1987) was a Tibetan master of the Sakya school. In 1960 he went to Seattle, Washington, and was one of the first Tibetan lamas to settle and teach in the United States.

54   Mi la ras pa bzhad pa'i rdo rje (1040–1123), Sgam po pa bsod nams rin chen (1079–1153), Phag mo gru pa rdo rje rgyal po (1110–1170), and Karma pa Dus gsum mkhyen pa (1110–1193).

55   Tib. transliteration: *dam tshig* and *sdom pa.* Tib. phonetics: *damtsig* and *dompa.*

56   In the Vajrayāna one distinguishes two processes of meditation: the creation process (Sanskrit: *utpattikrama*; Tib. transliteration: *bskyed rim*; Tib. phonetics: *kyerim*), in which the perception of the world of the sambhogakāya or of the nirmāṇakāya are created; and the perfection process (Sanskrit: *niṣpannakrama*; Tib. transliteration: *rdzogs rim*; Tib. phonetics: *dzogrim*) in which this is dissolved and one abides in the unity of the dharmakāya and the form kāyas, i.e. the sambhogakāya and nirmāṇakāya. Hevajra and Cakrasamvara are among the buddha aspects of the highest tantra class, the so-called niruttaratantras, the practice of which is widespread in the Kagyü tradition.

57   Six Dharmas of Nāropa—Tib. transliteration: *na ro chos drug.* Tib. phonetics: *naro chö drug.*

58   In that order: Tib. transliteration: *gtum mo, sgyu lus, rmi lam, 'od gsal, bar do,* and *'pho ba.* Tib. phonetics: *tummo, gyulü, milam, ösal, bardo,* and *powa.*

59   Perfection process with characteristics—Tib. transliteration: *mtshan bcas.* Tib. phonetics: *tsen ché.* "With characteristics" implies that specific meditative methods, which may also involve physical exercises, are included to accelerate the process of realization.

60   "Break-through" and "leap over"—Tib. transliteration: *khregs chod* and *thod brgal.* Tib. phonetics: *treg chö* and *tö gal. Treg chö* is often translated as "break-through" or "thoroughly cutting through", that is, through resistance, ignorance, and closedness. This practice reveals the view of primordial purity beyond conceptual elaborations. It is considered to be the basis for practic-

ing *Tö gal*, which is often translated as "leap over", "direct crossing", or "the direct approach". *Tö gal* requires stability in the practice of "break-through". It is said to be a swift way of bringing about the dissolution of the practitioner's samsaric perceptions by the realization of "spontaneous presence" and can thereby facilitate the realization of the three kāyas in this lifetime.

61 Practice of the Connate—Tib. transliteration: *lhan cig skyes sbyor.* Tib. phonetics: *lenchig kyé jor.*

62 See note 8.

63 Wisdom of the ground—Tib. transliteration: *gzhi'i ye shes.* Tib. phonetics: *shi'i yeshé.*

64 Mind's mode of abiding—Tib. transliteration: *sems kyi gnas tshul.* Tib. phonetics: *sem kyi netsül.*

65 Concepts—Tib. transliteration: *rnam rtog.* Tib. phonetics: *namtog.* In this teaching, Shamar Rinpoche did not explain more about the precise meaning of thought or "concept" in this context, although a little later in the talk he hints at it. Details are explained in his following texts on concept-dharmakāya. See also the translator's Introduction, part (5) of this book.

66 While Shamar Rinpoche was teaching, there was a lot of noise in the area outside the tent in which the lecture took place. Rinpoche even mentioned at this point that this noise was a good example for these teaching.

67 "Something", that is, the inner representation of an object.

68 Shamar Rinpoche gave detailed instructions on this topic during his last course in Dhagpo Kagyu Ling in France, in May 2014. The course centered on the fourfold presence in mindfulness. These teachings are available from this center in the form of audio and video recordings.

69 Ground of purification—Tib. transliteration: *sbyang gzhi.* Tib. phonetics: *jang shi.*

70 Method of purification—Tib. transliteration: *sbyang thabs.* Tib. phonetics: *jang tab.*

71 Five paths, ten levels—In the Mahāyāna, spiritual development is described by way of the so-called five paths (Sanskrit: *mārga*; Tib. transliteration and phonetics: *lam*) and ten levels (Sanskrit: *bhūmi*; Tib. transliteration and phonetics: *sa*). The five paths are: the path of accumulation, the path of application, the path of seeing, the path of cultivation, and the path of no-more-learning. The third, i.e. the path of seeing, is equivalent to the first so-called bodhisattva bhūmi where a bodhisattva has attained direct insight into reality and is therefore liberated from saṃsāra, in that rebirth is no longer triggered by karma and defilements (Sanskrit: *kleśas*). By virtue of the realization attained, he or she from then on deliberately manifests through the power of compassion and wisdom in samsaric worlds to benefit sentient beings. The fourth path, the path of cultivation, is the entire phase of development from the second to the tenth bodhisattva bhūmi. The fifth path, the path of no-more-learning, is equivalent to buddhahood.

72 At this point another passage from the teaching has been omitted. To illustrate that terms are often unclear when they are used in another culture, Shamar Rinpoche spoke about the word "rinpoche" and "tulku" and described the various misunderstandings that exist with regard to these titles.

73 Madhyamaka, also known as the Middle Path, is a philosophical system within the Mahāyāna based on logical reasoning, in which emptiness is understood as the true nature of every outer and inner phenomenon. The Indian master Nāgārjuna (c. 150–c. 250 CE) was the pioneer of this philosophical school, which is based on the Buddha's sūtras on the perfection of wisdom, the prajñāpāramitāsūtras.

74 For details see Shamar Rinpoche's *A Path of Practice: The Bodhi Path Program* (2020), and *Boundless Wisdom: A Mahāmudrā Practice Manual* (2018).

75 Shamar Rinpoche gave some concluding advice in which he stressed that, in order to be able to benefit from Buddhist teachers giving instructions on the Dharma, practitioners must meditate. Otherwise one does not undergo experiences, and thus no questions arise to form the basis on which a teacher can give further instructions. Finally, Shamar Rinpoche said: "Dharma practitioners should not be extreme. Don't react in extreme ways to what you hear. Otherwise, things can easily go wrong. For example, in Buddhism there is much talk about emptiness, that things do not truly exist. One might then conclude that as nothing really exists, one does not have to do anything. Thinking this way is also extreme. Practice very gently. This also applies to devotion and compassion. Devotion should be practiced in a very gentle and sensible way. This is most important."

76 Zhwa dmar pa Mi pham chos kyi blo gros, *Rnam rtog chos sku'i dogs sel sgam po'i dgongs rgyan.* See Bibliography: Zhwa dmar pa Mi pham chos kyi blo gros.

77 This is the preface written for the Tibetan edition of the Shamarpa's text.

78 The four māras usually refer to the māra of: the evil of death, defilements, the skandhas, and the celestial son or pride; generally speaking, the word *māra* refers to suffering and its causes.

79 Sugata is an epithet for the Buddha. Literally it means "Gone to Bliss".

80 The *Bodhicaryāvatāra* composed by Śāntideva (8th c.), an Indian Buddhist monk and scholar, at the University of Nālandā. This treatise is considered to be one of the most important Mahāyāna treatises. There exist numerous translations into English; see, for example, *Bodhicaryāvatāra*, translated from the Sanskrit by Kate Crosby and Andrew Skilton. See Bibliography: Śāntideva.

81 Degeneration in terms of: (1) the quality and lifespan of one's physical life; (2) the conditions of the time one lives in; the fact that there are, for example, many natural disasters, wars, etc.; (3) the dispositions of human beings; the fact that, for example, despite possessing the potential for it, they do not develop in a positive way, but rather harm each other; (4) wrong views rooted in selfishness and confusion; and (5) being dominated by emotional defilements.

82 The Shri Diwakar Institute is an Institute for higher Buddhist Studies located in Kalimpong, India. It was initiated by the 14th Shamarpa. Associated with the Institute is a publishing house specialized in Tibetan Buddhism which, among other publications, produces this current series of works directly linked with the Karmapas and the Shamarpas.

83 Dagpo Kagyü is the name for all the various Kagyü traditions that refer back to Gampopa, the healer from Dagpo, an area in South Tibet.

84 Mental nonengagement—Sanskrit: *amanasikāra*; Tib. transliteration: *yid la mi byed pa*; Tib. phonetics: *yi la mi jé pa*. This is also one of the key terms of Dagpo Mahāmudrā. According to Maitrīpa, the term *amanasikāra* should be taken to denote an affirming negation, i.e. a correct mental engagement that is a direct experience or realization of emptiness or of nonorigination, on the basis of having become mentally disengaged from holding on to dualistic appearances and characteristic signs, and thus being free from abiding in any extreme views. Maitrīpa reads "nonarising" (*anutpāda*) into the privative "a", taking *amanasikāra* as a compound where the middle word was dropped (*madhyapadalopī samāsaḥ*). Moreover, alluding to the *Hevajratantra*, he interprets the "a" as luminosity and thus as the manner in which emptiness is realized directly. *Amanasikāra* thus stands for cultivating nonconceptual wisdom and is equated with the originally tantric term *svādhiṣṭhāna* or "self-blessing". Generally speaking, Maitrīpa takes *amanasikāra* as nondual continuity that unites emptiness and compassion. See Mathes 2009, 17–29. See also Brunnhölzl 2007, 125–190. See Bibliography: Mathes 2009 and Brunnhölzl 2007.

85 Eight great carriages of practice lineages—Tib. transliteration: *sgrub rgyud shing rta chen po brgyad*; Tib. phonetics: *drubgyü shingta chenpo gyé*; their names along with their most important pioneers are: (1) Nyingma (8th cent.): Śāntarakṣita, Padmasambhava, and Vimalamitra; (2) Kadam (11th cent.): Atiśa and Dromtönpa; (3) Kagyü (11th cent.): Marpa Lotsawa, Milarepa and Gampopa; (4) Sakya (11th cent.): Drogmi Lotsawa and Kön Könchog Gyalpo; (5) Shi Dsche (12th cent.): Padampa Sangye; (6) Shangpa Kagyü (11th cent.): Khedrup Kyungpo Naljor; (7) Jonang (12th cent.): Yumo Mikyö Dorje and Dölpopa; (8) Urgyenpa (13th cent.): Drubtob Urgyenpa.

86 Criticism of Dagpo Mahāmudrā was voiced, for example, by Sakya Paṇḍita (1182–1251) in the latter's famous *Sdom gsum rab dbye*. An English translation, which also includes the Tibetan, has been published by Rhoton with the title *A Clear Differentiation of the Three Codes*. One example of the criticism raised therein is in III.161: "The Mahāmudrā meditation of fools, it is taught, usually becomes a cause of animal birth. If not that, then they are born in the formless realm or else they fall into the śrāvakas' cessation." (Tib. see Rhoton 2002, 303). See Bibliography: Sakya Paṇḍita.

87 This pertains to a structure often used in Buddhist treatises with the following elements: the purpose of the treatise, the concise meaning, the word meaning, objections, etc.

88   Madhyamaka propounding false representations—Sanskrit: Alīkākāravāda Madhyamaka; Tib. transliteration: *rnam brdzun dbu ma*; Tib. *phonetics: namdzün uma*. As far as perception is concerned, certain Buddhist views speak of "false representations" (Sanskrit: *alīkakāra*, Tib.: *rnam rdzun pa*), others of "(actual) representations" (Sanskrit: *kāra*, Tib.: *rnam pa*). This terminology is found in the Buddhist Sautrāntika, Yogācāra and Madhyamaka schools of thought, albeit with slightly different meanings. In the context of Madhyamaka, distinctions in propounders of false representations and propounders of (actual) representations can only pertain to conventional knowledge and its objects, accepted only insofar as no analysis is applied regarding their actual nature. After all, the basic Madhyamaka premise is that any outer and inner phenomenon is without a self-nature, insubstantial, and unreal and therefore does not withstand such analysis. Thus, in terms of ultimate reality there is no ground or foundation to be identified, which makes any superimposition superfluous. In terms of conventional or relative truth, i.e. concerning the ways how inner and outer perception operates, there are slightly different ways of Madhyamaka explanations. Those Mādhyamikas who propound "false representations", "false aspects", or "false images" explain that consciousness, i.e. perception, operates with false representations, lacking any actuality, even though they appear as if they were real, are efficacious, and are experienced by the mind. This is to be understood in contrast to the propounders of "actual representations" who assert that these representations are actual in the sense of them having phenomenal content. It should be added that the Sanskrit term "Alīkākāravāda" is a reconstruction from Tibetan and not found in extant Sanskrit sources. Further terms used in this context for these two views are Sākāravāda and Nirākāravāda (both appear in Sanskrit sources), i.e. those who speak of a consciousness with and those who speak of a consciousness without representations. For more details on this topic see, for example, Ratnākaraśānti's *Instructions of the Perfection of Wisdom* (*Prajñāpāramitopadeśa*) or Śāntarakṣita's *Ornament of the Middle Path* (*Madhyamakālaṃkāra*). See Bibliography: Westerhof 2018 and McClintock 2014.

89   Literally, *lha lam* translates as the "divine path", which in Tibetan poetry pertains to the sky or space.

90   Literally, *mtshan gos* translates as "cloak of darkness", which pertains to the night.

91   "The extreme of peace" alludes to the state of cessation attributed to an arhat.

92   Literally, *dkyil 'khor* translates as "circle" or "maṇḍala", which in Tibetan poetry pertains to the sun.

93   Literally, *thub dbang* translates as "mighty sage", which is an epithet of the Buddha.

94   Nāropa (1016–1100) and Maitrīpa (986–1063) were two of the most important Indian sources of the Tibetan Dagpo Mahāmudrā tradition; Marpa (Mar pa, 1012–1097) and Milarepa (Mi la ras pa, 1040–1123) were the first lineage holders in Tibet.

95   Gampopa (Sgam po pa, 1079–1153) was one of the most important students of Milarepa and the founding father of the Dagpo tradition in Tibet. He united two streams of transmission (*chu bo gnyis 'dres*) of teachings: (1) the monastic Kadam tradition founded on the basis of the Bengali master Atiśa's (982–1054) teaching activities in Tibet and (2) the Mahāmudrā tradition, which Gampopa received from his root guru Milarepa (1040–1123). Gampopa was thus heir to a complex diversity of sutric and tantric Buddhist views and meditative techniques. His great achievement was to integrate these different, and at times seemingly divergent, doctrines and practices into an integrated system of study and meditation. For more information on this see for example Gyatrul Rinpoche 2004. *Gampopa, the Monk and the Yogi: His Life and Teachings.* See Bibliography: Gyatrul Rinpoche.

96   Regarding the meaning of "concept-dharmakāya", see introduction by the translator in parts (5) and (6) of this book.

97   'Jigs med gling pa mkhyen brtse 'od zer (1729/30–1798), an important master of the Nyingma tradition.

98   Dzo is a cross between a yak and domestic cattle. The example is meant to indicate opposites.

99   The third Thu'u bkwan, Chos kyi nyi ma (1737–1802), an important Gelug master and author of the comprehensive work *The Crystal Mirror of Philosophical Systems.* See Bibliography: Thu'u bkwan, Chos kyi nyi ma.

100   Tib. transliteration: *rnam rtog.*

101   Tib. transliteration: *rtog pa.*

102   "Above" pertains to the Cittamātra and Madhyamaka schools of thought. Within Buddhist philosophies, various views are formulated. The Vaibhāṣikas maintain that smallest building blocks of matter exist. Their dynamic interactions are considered to account for the ever-changing flux of material entities in the world. According to this system there is, in fact, a fleeting outer world that exists independently from the perceiving consciousness. The so-called Sautrāntikas also maintain this view. However, in order to explain the fact that sentient beings' minds perceive matter—which is considered to be of a different nature than mind, with the consequence that mind and matter cannot directly interact—the Sautrāntikas, in contrast to the Vaibhāṣikas, speak of mental representations or mental images that are triggered by the presence of the respective external entities that appear in the perceiving consciousness. Thus, what is perceived is not the relevant external entity as such but just a mental image or representation of it. The "above" Mahāyāna schools of thought, i.e. the various Yogācāra (or Cittamātra) and Madhyamaka systems, do not accept a somewhat real external world also in terms of the smallest building blocks; they consider the world to be purely conventional and therefore entirely unreal. Thus, perception is understood to occur nowhere but in the dualistic mind that imagines its world through the influence of deeply ingrained habitual tendencies. Sentient beings with similar habitual tendencies accordingly perceive a similar or even the same world.

103   Tib. transliteration: *rnam pa.*

104   Tib. transliteration: *brda dag sum cu pa.* Tib. phonetics: *badag sum chu pa.*

105   The main function of the second case of Tibetan grammar is similar to the accusative case in English. However, it also has a sub-case function called *de nyid* in Tibetan, which in this context pertains to "identity" with regard to the object of an act and the agent.

106   *Prajñapāramitāsūtras.*

107   *Prajñapāramitāhṛdaya.* Tib. translation: Kangyur H 499, vol. 88, 45–46. Our text is slightly different from the version in the Lhasa Kangyur: instead of of *zag pa med*, i.e. "no contamination", the Lhasa Kangyur (H) (46a$_3$) as well as the Derge Kangyur (D 21, vol. 34, 145$_{b2}$) reads *skrag pa med*, i.e. "no fear". *Zag pa med*, i.e. "no contamination", pertains to conditioned or samsaric states of mind that "contaminate" in that they entail ignorance and emotional defilements and their consequences. See Bibliography: *Prajñapāramitāhṛdaya.*

108   *Samādhirājasūtra.* Tib. translation: Kangyur H 129, vol. 55,135a$_{1-2}$. Here too, there is a small difference to the Lhasa Kangyur (H): instead of the fifth skandha of consciousness, the version of the sūtra in the Lhasa Kangyur speaks about the first of the five skandhas, i.e. form. See Bibliography: *Samādhirājasūtra.* See also a complete translation of this sūtra in the "reading room" of the 84 000 project: https://read.84000.co/translation/toh127.html

109   Constituents—Sanskrit: *skandha*, Tib. transliteration: *phung po*, Tib. phonetics: *pungpo*; refers to the five psycho-physical aggregates that constitute a person, i.e. form, sensations, distinctions, compositional factors, and consciousness, and account for the sense of a constant identity of the individual self and of the world at large even though what is actually at hand is a flux of interdependent changing moments that lack a solid or unchanging self-nature.

110   *Prajñapāramitāhṛdaya.* Tib. translation: Kangyur H 26, vol. 34, 259b$_7$–260a$_1$. See Bibliography: *Prajñapāramitāhṛdaya.*

111   i.e. as two opposite things.

112   The Tibetan term translated as "concrete" is *mtshan ma* (literally: characteristic, mark), which in this context has the connotation that concepts, i.e. thoughts, emotions, ideas, seemingly outer objects, etc. appear in one's perception as if they had an identity. A concept does not appear to be merely something abstract or imagined—a sheer inner representation—, but concrete or clear in the sense that it shapes one's state of mind and may trigger corresponding actions.

113   This quotation occurs for example in his *Chos kyi rje dpal ldan sgam po pa chen po'i rnam par thar pa yid bzhin gyi nor bu rin po che kun khyab snyan pa'i ba dan thar pa rin po che'i rgyan gyi mchog.* In: *Collected Works*, vol. 1, 2051–2. With a slight variation in the first line: *lhan cig skyes pa'i*

rnam shes 'di. In Shamar Rinpoche's Tibetan text translated above, *rnam shes* (consciousness) was replaced with *rnam rtog* (concepts). See Bibliography: Sgam po pa.

114 Genuine (or nonconceptual or nonnominal ultimate (*rnam grangs pa ma yin pa'i don dam*) contrasts with the nominal (or conceptual or figurative) ultimate (*rnam grangs pa'i don dam*). These Tibetan terms appear to go back to Bhāviveka's *Blaze of Reasoning* (*Tarkajvālā*), where he distinguishes between the two; the Sanskrit equivalents are *apāryayaparamārtha* and *paryāyaparamārtha*.

115 The difference between these two is that the Madhyamaka syllogism involves a condition, namely that a concept *ultimately* is the dharmakāya because its nature is free from the four extremes. The yogi or kuśali teaching points directly to the ultimate without involving the condition *ultimately*, thus not making a distinction between the conventional and the ultimate but emphasizing their inseparability.

116 Regarding the translation "[Mahāmudrā,] the Practice of the Connate" see note 5.

117 Sgom chung shes rab byang chub (1130–1173). He was a nephew and direct disciple of Gampopa and the third abbot of the Daklha Gampo Monastery (Dwags lha sgam po) founded by Gampopa. Gomchung was among other known for his extraordinary miraculous abilities as they arise by virtue of deep meditation. It is said that he could ignite fire by simply holding his breath and pointing his finger and that he could make himself invisible.

118 Gampopa himself also gave this instruction frequently, for example, in his *Snying po don gyi gdams pa phyag rgya chen po'i 'bum thig*. In: *Collected Works*, vol. 3, 93$_5$–94$_1$: *rang sems lhan cig skyes pa chos sku dngos || snang ba lhan cig skyes pa chos sku'i 'od || rnam rtog lhan cig skyes pa chos sku'i rlabs || dbyer med lhan cig skyes pa chos sku'i don ||*. See Bibliography: Sgam po pa.

119 Kāyas or „embodiments" of the awakened state: The term dharmakāya denominates the awakened state as such, mind's true nature, full of purpose for oneself. The terms sambhogakāya and nirmāṇakāya pertain to the so-called form embodiments that manifest through the power of mind's compassion for the benefit of sentient beings. Therefore, they are full of purpose for others. The unity of these three kāyas is called svabhāvikakāya.

120 The quotation is contained, for example, in *Rje btsun lho brag pa'i khyad par gyi gdams pa snyan gyi shog dril bzhi'i lo rgyus gzhung lhan thabs dang bcas pa* in *The Treasury of Instructions* (*Gdams ngag mdzod*) vol. nga (8), p. 217$_{2-3}$. See Bibliography: Kong sprul Blo gros mtha' yas.

121 The quotation is contained, for example, in the *Bka' brgyud pa'i phyag chen chos skor*, Karma Leksheyling, Computer Input. Download March 5, 2018.

122 The quotation is contained, for example, in *Dpal mnga' bdag sgra sgyur mar pa lo tsā ba chos kyi blo gros kyi gsung 'bum*, vol. 1. Lhasa: Ser gtsug nang bstan dpe rnying 'tshol bsdu phyogs sgrigs khang, 2009.

123 The quotation is contained, for example, in *Rje btsun mi la ras pa'i rnam thar dang mgur 'bum*, vol. 2, 425$_{4-5}$. Kathmandu: Khenpo Shedup Tenzin and Lama Thinley Namgyal 2006.

124 In: *Chos kyi rje dpal ldan sgam po pa chen po'i rnam par thar pa yid bzhin gyi nor bu rin po che kun khyab snyan pa'i ba dan thar pa rin po che'i rgyan gyi mchog*. In: *Collected Works*, Bd. 1, 205$_{2-3}$. See Bibliography: Sgam po pa.

125 Quotation not identified. It occurs, however, in various collections on Kagyü Mahāmudrā, such as in the *Dharma Cycle of Kagyü Mahāmudrā* (*Bka' brgyud pa'i phyag chen chos skor*), Karma Leksheyling, Computer Input. Download on March 5, 2018. In the two occurrences in this collection, there is an additional line after "These concepts as such are the nature of the expanse" which reads "These two [i.e. concepts and the expanse] primordially are not different" and then continues, as above, with "These two [i.e. concepts and the expanse] are of one flavor."

126 In: *Dpal mnga' bdag sgra sgyur mar pa lo tsā ba chos kyi blo gros kyi gsung 'bum*, vol. 1. Lhasa: Ser gtsug nang bstan dpe rnying 'tshol bsdu phyogs sgrigs khang, 2009.

127 In: *Rje btsun mi la ras pa'i rnam thar dang mgur 'bum*, vol. 2, 425$_5$–426$_1$. Kathmandu: Khenpo Shedup Tenzin and Lama Thinley Namgyal, 2006.

128 See note 118.

129 In: *Praise of Mañjughoṣa* (*Mañjughoṣastotra*). Tib. translation: Tengyur D 2712, VOL. 73, 79B5. See Bibliography: *Mañjughoṣastotra*.

130 In his *Explanation of the Direct Introduction to the Three Embodiments* (*Sku gsum ngo sprod rnam bshad*), vol. 1, 203$_{17-19}$, the Eighth Karmapa, Mikyö Dorje, also explains in this regard: "The Practice of the Connate known in the precious Kagyü is in accordance with the profound path of mantras because, on the mantra path, the fruition, i.e. the four kāyas as such, are made the essence of the cause and path. *bka' brgyud rin po che la grags pa'i lhan cig skyes sbyor 'di nyid zab mo sngags kyi theg pa dang rjes su mthun pa yin te* | *sngags kyi theg pa 'bras bu sku bzhi nyid rgyu lam gyi ngo bor byed pa de'i phyir* |. And, ibid., 192$_{8-11}$: "For the unity of the two—manifold appearances and the primordial nonarising of appearances—which is known as the 'yoga of the unity of *śamatha* and vipaśyanā as luminosity', the Dagpo Kagyüpas use (…) the term 'the fruit has arrived on the ground'." *sna tshogs su snang ba dang snang ba gdod nas skye ba med pa gnyis zung du 'jug par 'od gsal bar zhi lhag zung 'jug gi rnal 'byor zhes bya ste* (…) *'bras bu gzhi thog na phebs pa zhes dpal dwags po bka' brgyud pa dag tha snyad mdzad pa yin* |. See Bibliography: Karma pa Mi bskyod rdo rje.

131 *Ajātaśatrukaukṛtyavinodanānāmamahāyānasūtra*. Tib. translation: Kangyur D 216, vol. 62, *mdo sde, tsha* 211b$_2$–268b$_7$.

132 As pointed out earlier in this treatise by Shamar Rinpoche, the dharmakāya as a synonym for mind's true or ultimate nature is not just understood as emptiness, but also as the embodiment (Sanskrit: *kāya*) of qualities. As Gampopa, for example, puts it in his *Excellent Qualities: Teachings to the Assembly* (*Tshogs chos yon tan phun tshogs*). In: *Collected Works* vol. 1, 511$_{3-4}$: "The truth is the actuality that the nature of mind is *not* nonexistent; connate (*sahaja*) wisdom is the truth. When the mind is realized, the true nature of phenomena (*dharmatā*) is actualized." *bden pa ni sems kyi ngo bo med pa ma yin pa'i don* | *lhan cig skyes pa'i ye shes bden pa yin* | *sems rtogs pa'i dus su chos nyid mngon du grub* |. See Bibliography: Sgam po pa.

133 See note 130.

134 In: *Dpal mnga' bdag sgra sgyur mar pa lo tsā ba chos kyi blo gros kyi gsung 'bum*, vol. 1. Lhasa: Ser gtsug nang bstan dpe rnying 'tshol bsdu phyogs sgrigs khang, 2009.

135 *Mahāyānasūtrālaṃkāra* VI.9: *akalpanājñānabalena dhīmataḥ* | *samānuyātena samantataḥ sadā* | *tadāśrayo gahvaradoṣasaṃcayo* | *mahagadeneva viṣaṃ nirasyate* ||. Tib. translation: Tengyur D 4020, vol. 123, 6b$_6$.

136 *The Root Verses of the Middle Path* (*Mūlamadhyamakakārikā*), XVIII.9: *aparapratyayaṃ śāntaṃ prapañcair aprapañcitam* | *nirvikalpam anānārtham etat tattvasya lakṣaṇam* ||. Tib. translation: Tengyur D 3824, vol. 96, 11a$_{3-4}$.

137 *The Ornament of Clear Realization* (*Abhisamayālaṃkāra*). Tib. translation: Tengyur D 3786, vol. 80, 10a$_3$. Also in: *The Ultimate Continuum* (*Mahāyānottaratantra / Ratnagotravibhāga*), I.157. Tib. translation: Tengyur 4024, vol. 123, 61b$_{5-6}$.

138 In: *Phyag rgya chen po'i rgya gzhung glegs bam gnyis pa*, vol. 2 (Ah).

139 In: Sahajavajra's *Commentary on the Ten Verses on Thatness* (*Tattvadaśakaṭīkā*), a commentary on Maitrīpa's *Ten Verses on Thatness* (*Tattvādaśaka*). Sahajavajra introduces this statement by saying "Maitrīpa said …" [in *Tattvādaśaka* TD 2cd], Tib. translation: Tengyur D 2254, vol. 51, 168b$_5$–168b$_6$.

140 Rendawa Shönnu Lodrö (Tib. *Red mda' ba gzhon nu blo gros*, 1349–1412) was an important author and teacher of the Sakya school and one of the main teachers of Tsongkhapa (1357–1419).

141 In: *Theg pa chen po gzhi lam 'bras gsal bar byed pa phyag rgya chen po'i rdo rje'i glu*. In: *Collected Works* of Rendawa, vol. 4, 89$_6$–90$_2$. See Bibliography: Red mda' ba.

142 For details you can refer to Shamar Rinpoche's *Boundless Wisdom*, pp. 157–164. See Bibliography: Shamar Rinpoche.

143 Subsequent attainment—Tib. transliteration: *rjes thob*, Tib. phonetics: *jé tob*, i.e. how, by virtue of formal meditation and the insight developed thereby, one is able to sustain wisdom and compassion outside of formal meditation.

144 For details you can refer to Shamar Rinpoche's *Boundless Wisdom*, pp. 165–188. See Bibliography: Shamar Rinpoche.

145 Breakthrough—Tib. transliteration: *khregs chod*, Tib. phonetics: *treg chö*. See note 60.

146 Leap-over—Tib. transliteration: *thod brgal*, Tib. phonetics: *tögal.* See note 60.

147 *Ālikāliguhyācintatantra*, not identified in the extant Kangyurs. However, these lines are also quoted in Kongtrul Lodrö Thaye's *Treasury of Knowledge* (*Shes bya kun khyab mdzod*) vol. 3, p. 385. Beijing, 1982), in the section on the Mahāmudrā type of calm abiding and deep insight meditation and the development through the so-called Four Yogas of Mahāmudrā. Fragments of this tantra, but without the above quotation, are contained in the *Dam cos sdug bsgnal zhi byed kyi gzhung bsam gyis mi khyab pa'i rgyud sde'i dum bu rin po che'i snying po* in Kongtrul Lodrö Thaye's *Treasury of Key Instructions* (*Gdams ngag mdzod*, 18 vols.), vol. 13, 1–16. Delhi: Shechen Publication, 1999. Here, Kongtrul aligns the four steps with the Four Yogas of Mahāmudrā. An English translation is found in Jamgön Kongtrul, 2007. *The Treasury of Knowledge. Esoteric Instructions*. Book 8, part 4, pp. 221–222. See Bibliography: Kong sprul Blo gros mtha' yas and Kongtrul Lodrö Thaye.

148 Kong sprul Blo gros mtha' yas (1813–1899), the first Jamgön Kongtrul. He was a lineage holder of the Karma Kagyü school and one of the most important Tibetan Buddhist masters of his time. His writings and compilations play an essential role in the transmission of many Tibetan Buddhist traditions to this day.

149 Nālandā and Vikramaśīla were the great Buddhist sites of learning in the North of India.

150 Empowerment—Sanskrit: *abhiṣeka*; Tib. transliteration: *dbang*; Tib. phonetics: *wang*. In the Vajrayāna *abhiṣeka* or empowerment designates a spiritual process in which a master introduces a disciple into the understanding of mind's nature. The practitioner is introduced into the maṇḍala of a particular yidam or buddha aspect and receives the permission and capacity to engage in the creation and completion processes associated with that yidam.

151 Samayas are the comitments to be upheld by Vajrayāna practitioners. Among others, they are explained in the context of the five types of Buddhas, i.e. Vairocana, Akṣobhya, Amitābha, Ratnasambhava, and Amogasiddhi. Details on this can be found in Shamar Rinpoche's booklet *On the Meaning of Samaya*. See Bibliography: Shamar Rinpoche.

152 *Rdzogs pa chen po klong chen snying thig gi gdod ma'i mgon po'i lam gyi rim pa'i khrid yig ye shes bla ma*. Short titel: *Khrid yig ye shes bla ma mchan can*. An instruction manual for the Longchen Nyingthig by Jigme Lingpa Khyentse Öser (1729–1798; 'Jigs med gling pa mkhyen brtse 'od zer) in which the graduated path of Great Perfection (Mahā Ati) is presented. See Bibliography: 'Jigs med gling pa mkhyen brtse 'od zer.

153 Sanskrit: *phat.*

154 On the path of methods, i.e. the Vajrayāna, one distinguishes into two process of meditation: the process of generation or creation (Sanskrit: *utpattikrama*; Tib. transliteration: *bskyed rim*; Tib. phonetics: *kyerim*), during which one generates the perception of the sambhoga- or the nirmāṇakāya world, and the processes of completion or perfection (Sanskrit: *nispannakrama*; Tib. transliteration: *rdzogs rim*; Tib. phonetics: *dzogrim*), during which these perceptions are dissolved. At this point one abides in the unity of the dharmakāya and the formkāyas, i.e. the sambhoga- and nirmāṇakāya.

155 Atiśa (980–1054).

156 Mental nonengagement (or nonconceptual realization)—Sanskrit: *amanasikāra*; Tib. transliteration: *yid la mi byed pa*; Tib. phonetics: *yi la mi jé pa.* See note 84.

157 *Mahāmudrā, the Practice of the Connate* (*Phyag rgya chen po lhan cig skyes sbyor*). This treatise was written by Pagmo Drupa. See also note 5.

158 The "appropriating consciousness"—Sanskrit.: *adana-vijñana*; Tib. transliteration: *len pa'i rnam par shes pa*; Tib. phonetics: *lenpé nampar shepa*)—comes, just as the term "ground-consciousness"—Sanskrit: ālaya-vijñana; Tib. transliteration: *kun gzhi rnam par shes pa*; Tib. phonetics: *künshi nampar shepa*)—from the Buddhist Yogācāra philosophy that was mainly shaped by Asaṅga and his half brother Vasubandhu (4th c.). The appropriating consciousness labels the

ground consciousness from the perspective that through the power of habitual tendencies or seeds stored therein, a sentient being perceives a body along with the particular environment; consciousness grasps for this and appropriates this perception.

159   See note 45.

160   In: *The Collected Works of Chos grags ye shes*, vol. 3, 21–24. See Bibliography: Zhwa dmar chos grags ye shes.

161   The view of concept-dharmakāya neither implies attributing existence to that which does not have an existence nor denigrates mind's qualities. Therefore, it is perfectly in tune with reality and thus does not constitute any mistaken view with its resulting negativity.

162   The author merely says *bden*, meaning "right." I thank Khenpo Konchog Tenphel for pointing out to me that in modern-day Ladakhi this expression is used to imply "right, this is understandable, but wrong."

163   The Healer from Dagpo—Tib. transliteration: *Dagpo Larje*; Tib. phonetics: *dwags po lha rjes*.

164   For example, in his *Precious Ornament of Liberation*, chapter one. This is taken from a series of reasons that are used to establish that all sentient beings have buddha nature. In this context, buddha nature is equated with the dharmakāya's emptiness. One should keep in mind that according to Gampopa "emptiness" is not a mere negation but a synonym for mind's connate wisdom imbued with qualities.

165   See note 118. In this text by the Fourth Shamarpa, the third verse "That is meditation; only then one understands" was left out.

166   Element—Sanskrit: *dhātu*; Tib. transliteration: *khams*; Tib. phonetics: *kam*. This is a very complex term in Buddhist thought. In the context above it is a synonym for buddha nature. In general, translations of *dhātu* into Tibetan are either *khams* "element", "constituent", or *dbyings* "expanse", "sphere". In the *Compendium of Abhidharma* (*Abhidharmasamuccaya*), for example, *dhātu* is characterized as the "seed of all phenomena" (*sarvadharmabīja*). In the *Ultimate Continuum* (*Mahāyānottaratantra / Ratnagotravibhāga*), the term *dhātu* is used more often than *garbha* in reference to buddha nature. In Karma Kagyü interpretations, *dhātu* is often equated with buddha nature. The first Karma Trinle, for example, defines it as "luminous *dharmadhātu*" (expanse of phenomena), explaining that *dharmadhātu* here signifies the very essence of nonduality.

167   Śrīmālādevīsiṃhanādasūtra. See Bibliography: Śrīmālādevīsiṃhanādasūtra. However, the quotation could not be identified in the Derge Kangyur. Yet, the second part of this quotation (starting with "Therefore, śāriputra, the sentient being's…") appears in Asaṅga's *Commentary on the Ultimate Continuum* (*Mahāyānottaratantra / Ratnagotravibhāga*), the *Mahāyānottaratantraśāstravyākhyā*. Tib. translation: Kangyur D 4025, vol. 123, 97a₁–97a₂. See Bibliography: *Mahāyānottaratantraśāstravyākhyā*.

168   The title *Sūtra of the Inconceivable Mystery* (*Gsang ba bsam gyi mi khyab pa'i mdo*) abbreviates the title *Sūtra Revealing the Entry into the Domaine of Inconceivable Wisdom* (*Ye shes bsam gyis mi khyab pa'i yul la 'jug pa bstan pa zhes bya ba theg pa chen po'i mdo*), the *Tathāgataguṇajñānācintyaviṣayāvatāranirdeśasūtra*. Tib. translation: Kangyur D 47, 128b. See Bibliography: *Tathāgataguṇajñānācintyaviṣayāvatāranirdeśasūtra*.

169   A synonym for buddha nature. "Sugata" literally translates to "gone to bliss." Sanskrit: *sugatagarbha*; Tib. transliteration: *bde bar bshegs pa'i snying po*; Tib. phonetics: *de war shegpé nyingpo*. However, the Sanskrit *sugatagarbha* is not attested in extant Sanskrit sources. It could therefore be simply a re-translation from the Tibetan.

170   *Munimatālaṃkāra*. Tib. translation: Tengyur D 3903,73b₁–293a₇. See Bibliography: *Munimatālaṃkāra*.

171   *Hevajratantra*. See also note 180. Tib. translation: Kangyur H 378b: vol. 79, 366b₄. See Bibliography: *Hevajratantra*.

172   Here, "Heruka" probably refers to *Cakrasamvara*.

173   Quotation not identified.

174 Quotation not identified. However, in Vīryavajra's commentary on *Cakrasamvara*, the *Padārthaprakāśikā-śrisambaramūlatantraṭikā*, this verse is explained. Tib. translation: Tengyur D 1412, vol. 17, 390b₁. See Bibliography.

175 *Dhāraṇirājeśvarasūtra*. The quotation is contained in Asaṅga's *Commentary on the Ultimate Continuum* (*Mahāyānottaratantraśāstravyākhyā*). Tib. translation: Tengyur D 4025, vol. 123, 86a₃₋₄. See also the translation by Brunnhölzl 2014, p. 353. See Bibliography: *Mahāyānottaratantraśāstravyākhyā* und Brunnhölzl 2014.

176 The examples given in these sūtras point to that the innate potential does not reveal itself without effort. Only, when corresponding steps are taken, the potential can be actualized.

177 Quotation not identified.

178 Quotation not identified.

179 *Tathāgatagarbhasūtra*. These similes are also taken up in the *Ultimate Continuum* (*Mahāyānottaratantra*) starting with I.96 and commented on by Asaṅga in his *Commentary on the Ultimate Continuum* (*Mahāyānottaratantraśāstravyākhyā*). Tib. translation: Tengyur D 4025, vol. 123, 106b₂₋₄. See also the translation by Brunnhölzl 2014, pp. 393–394. See Bibliography: *Mahāyānottaratantraśāstravyākhyā* und Brunnhölzl 2014.

180 This line is not contained in our text but was added for the sake of understanding.

181 *Hevajra* II, iv, 69. See Snellgrove 1959, p. 2, (tr.) 107, (Skt.) 70, (Tib.) 71. *sattvā buddhā eva kiṃ tu āgantukamalāvṛtāḥ | tasyāpakarṣaṇāt sattvā buddhā eva na saṃśayaḥ ||*. See Bibliography: *Hevajratantra*.

182 *Mahāyānottaratantra* (or *Ratnagotravibhāga*) RGV I.47 (ed. by Johnston 1950, 40): *aśuddho'śuddhaśuddho'tha suviśuddho yathākramaṃ | sattvadhāturiti prokto bodhisattvastathāgataḥ ||*. However, in this Tibetan version in the Fourth Shamarpa's text, the term "bodhisattva" is replaced by a synonym for it, a "path-abider". See Bibliography: *Mahāyānottaratantra / Ratnagotravibhāga*.

183 The quotation could not be identified in a sūtra. Usually authors attribute it to the so-called *Abhidharmasūtra* which is not extant. In the context of buddha nature treatises it is frequently quoted, for example by the Third Karmapa, Rangjung Dorje, in his *Treatise Revealing Buddha Nature* (*De bzhin gshegs pa'i snying po bsten pa'i bsten bchos*). See Bibliography: Karma pa Rang byung rdo rje.

184 The two form kāyas, i.e. the sambhogakāya and the nirmāṇakāya, embodiments of buddhahood which accomplish the welfare of sentient beings. The sambhogakāya is perceptible by those with a pure mind, the realized bodhisattvas, while the nirmāṇakāya is also perceptible by ordinary sentient beings.

185 Khachö Wangpo (Tib. Mkha' spyod dbang po), the Second Shamarpa (1350–1405).

186 The term "water patterns of fixation" points to an example that is frequently used: patterns on the surface of water dissolve quickly and by themselves. In a similar way will the patterns of fixation dissolve in a practitioner's mind who truly understands these instructions quickly and naturally.

187 In: *The Collected Works of Chos grags ye shes*, vol. 6, 320–324. See Bibliography: Zhwa dmar Chos grags ye shes. Parts of this text were already published in my article "Mahāmudrā as the Key-Point of the Third Dharmacakra according to the *Sixty Verses on Mahāmudrā* by Zhwa dmar Chos grags ye shes." In: *Mahāmudrā in India and Tibet*, ed. by Roger R. Jackson and Klaus-Dieter Mathes, 2020, pp. 204–236. The above translation was partly re-edited for this complete translation of the sixty verses. See Bibliography: Draszczyk 2020.

188 This *śloka* is reminiscent of the famous quotation from the *Ultimate Continuum* (*Ratnagotravibhāga*), the *Ornament for Clear Realisation* (*Abhisamayālaṃkāra*), and a number of additional Mahāyāna treatises: "There is nothing to be removed from it, and nothing to be added. The real should be seen as real, and seeing the real, you become liberated." RGV, I.154: *nāpaneyamataḥ kiṃcidupaneyaṃ na kiṃcana | draṣṭavyaṃ bhūtato bhūtaṃ bhūtadarśī vimucyate ||* (Transl.) Mathes 2008, 8. See also *Abhisamayālaṃkāra* V.21 (with a slight variation in b. *prakṣeptavyaṃ na kiṃcana*) Takasaki 1966, 300 n. 53.
Shamar Chödrag Yeshe thereby indicates that adventitious stains are empty in and of them-

selves while mind's true nature—which is not separate from its qualities—is actualized through yogic direct perception as luminosity free from fabrications.

189   This verse is reminiscent of an explanation by Gampopa that he gave in his short *The Fivefold [Instruction on] Mahāmudrā* (*Phyag rgya chen po lnga ldan*, in his *Collected Works*, vol. 3, 508): "The key instruction of Mahāmudrā is fivefold: realization with the [right] view, meditation with experience, conduct with equanimity, instructions with a lineage, and certainty in [the capacity] to clear flaws." *'dir phyag rgya chen po'i man ngag la rnam pa lnga ste | rtogs pa lta ba dang ldan pa | sgom pa nyam myong dang ldan pa | spyod pa ro snyoms dang ldan pa | gdams ngag brgyud pa dang ldan pa | nges shes skyon bsal ba dang ldan pa'o ||*. In his explanations on each of them he explains regarding the first, i.e. realization with the [right] view, that this concerns the realization that the cycle of existence and the nature of buddhahood are one in the sense of connate mind and that for this reason sentient beings and buddhas have one cause.

190   It appears that the Fourth Shamarpa is alluding to propounders of the so-called Sākāra and Nirākāra systems (both terms are attested in Sanskrit sources). In the first (Tib. *rnam pa dang bcas pa*) it is taught that sensory perception cognizes a "representation", an "aspect", or an "image" of the object and is thus endowed with phenomenal content. In the second, i.e. the Nirākāravāda system (Tib. *rnam pa med pa*), this is not accepted. In the context of Madhyamaka, the distinctions between propounders of representations and non-represenations, i.e. in Sākāravāda und Nirākāravāda, can only pertain to conventional perception and its objects. See also notes 88 and 102. For more details on this topic see for example Westerhof 2018.

191   The term Madhyamaka of Nonabiding [in the sense of] Unity, i.e. the *Yuganaddhāpratiṣṭhānamadhyamaka* (*Zung 'jug rab tu mi gnas pa'i dbu ma*) refers to essencelessness or nonabiding which is considered as connate wisdom or buddha nature naturally endowed with qualities and accessible only to direct yogic perception and with the support of authentic teachers. Unity, i.e. Yuganaddha (Tib.: *zung 'jug*), is thus grounded in the inseparability of the two truths or realities, of manifestation or appearance and emptiness (Tib.: *snang stong dbyer med*). Nonabiding, i.e. Apratiṣṭhāna (Tib.: *rab tu mi gnas pa*), refers to the fact that all outer and inner phenomena, including their most subtle aspects, lack any ontic or epistemic essence or foundation. Madhyamaka, i.e. the Middle Way, refers to being beyond the extremes of existence and nonexistence, eternalism, and nihilism. The term Madhyamaka of Nonabiding or *Apratiṣṭhānamadhyamaka* (*Rab tu mi gnas pa'i dbu ma*), occurs in India, for example, during the time of Maitrīpa and was also known in Tibet. In Avadhūtīpa's *Commentary on the Meaning of the Core of the Treasury of Songs* (*Dohākoṣahṛdayārthagītiṭīkā*, short: DKHṬ), Tib. translation: Tengyur D 2268, 69b$_{2-7}$, we find, for example, a distinction into four types of Madhyamaka of Nonabiding: "In the Highest Yoga, what were termed 'wisdoms' in the Middle Yoga are illusion-like: [1] the indivisibility of mindfulness and mental nonengagement is '*apratiṣṭhāna* in the sense of unity' (Tib.: *zung 'jug rab tu mi gnas pa*); [2] the absence of any mindfulness and mental nonengagement is '*apratiṣṭhāna* in the sense of [a nonconceptual insight into] emptiness' (Tib.: *stong nyid rab tu mi gnas pa*); [3] nonarising and nonobstruction is '*apratiṣṭhāna* in the sense of equanimity'; [4] and, since [this insight] is not intellectually knowable by anyone and inconceivable, it is '*apratiṣṭhāna* in the sense of cessation' (Tib.: *rgyun chad rab tu mi gnas pa*)." *rnal 'byor rab na re | rnal 'byor 'bring pos ye shes su ming du btags pa ni sgyu ma lta bu dran pa dang yid la ma byas pa dbyer mi phyed pa zung 'jug rab tu mi gnas pa tsam yin gyi | gang dran pa med cing yid la bya ba med pa de stong nyid rab tu mi gnas pa dang | skye ba med cing dgag tu med pa de btang snyoms rab tu mi gnas pa | gang gis blos mi rig pa bsam du med pas rgyun chad rab tu mi gnas pa'o ||*. Gampopa is one of the few Tibetan teachers who commented on these Madhyamaka views. Later on, the term was not used much in Tibet. See also Higgins and Draszczyk, *Buddha Nature Reconsidered*, 2019, vol. 1, 30–32 and 30 note 36.

192   This pertains to the so-called third dharmacakra, the "Dharma wheel of precise distinction", which focuses on buddha nature. It was delineated as such in the *Sūtra Unraveling [the Buddha's] Intent* (*Samdhinirmocanasūtra*) and is referred to in most Mahāyāna traditions.

193   The verse is reminiscent of a statement found in Maitrīpa's *Ten Verses on Suchness* (*Tattvādaśaka* TD 2cd), explained in the commentary by his disciple Sahajavajra and cited frequently in Kagyü literature. Sahajavajra explains in his commentary: "[Maitrīpa] said, 'Even the middle [path] (i.e. Madhyamaka) that is not adorned with the words of the guru is only middling,' because it

[only] negates the particular features [of the *sākāra* and *nirākāra* doctrines that separate the latter from Madhyamaka], and what remains [becomes] a postulated object. ...." (Transl.) Mathes 2006, 209, 213. See ed. and tr. of Mathes 2006, 209. See Bibliography: Maitrīpa and Mathes 2006.

194 The perfection vehicle (Sanskrit: *pāramitānaya*) is the sūtric Mahāyāna; the mantra vehicle (Sanskrit: *mantranaya*) is the tantric Mahāyāna or Vajrayāna. The congruence of the pāramitānaya with mantranaya refers back to Maitrīpa's *Ten Verses on Thatness* (*Tattvadaśaka*) and its commentary by his student Sahajavajra. The Eighth Karmapa, Mikyö Dorje, explains in his commentary on Candrakīrti's *Introduction to Madhyamaka* (*Madhyamakāvatāra*), *Dwags brgyud grub pa'i shing rta*, 13₅–14₁: "In the commentary on *The Ten Verses of Suchness* composed by Sahajavajra it is said regarding [the Dagpo Mahāmudrā tradition]: 'There are three features: its nature is pāramitā, it corresponds with the mantras, and it carries the name Mahāmudrā.' In this Dharma tradition of Mahāmudrā, as it is given as experience instructions, secret mantra empowerments are not bestowed. The explicit teaching of this Mahāmudrā is the Madhyamaka of emptiness free from reifications of the sūtra tradition, and implicitly it shows the ultimate profound meaning of the sūtras and tantras, buddha nature in the ordinary and extraordinary [sense]." *De kho na nyid bcu pa'i 'grel pa lhan cig skyes pa'i rdo rje mdzad par yang | ngo bo pha rol tu phyin pa sngags dang rjes su mthun pa | ming phyag rgya chen po zhes khyad par gsum ldan du yang gsungs so | phyag rgya chen po'i chos tshul 'di nang myong khrid 'debs par mdzad pa la gsang sngags kyi dbang bskur ba yang mi dzad la | phyag chen 'di'i dngos bstan mdo lugs kyi spros bral stong pa nyid kyi dbu ma dang shugs las mdo sngags kyi zab don mthar thug bde gshegs snying po thun mongs dang thun mongs min pa ston pa la...*
In his *Explanation of the Direct Introduction to the Three Embodiments* (*Sku gsum ngo sprod rnam bshad*), vol. 1, 203₁₇₋₁₉, Karmapa Mikyö Dorje also explains in this context: "The Practice of the Connate known in the precious Kagyü is in accordance with the profound path of mantras because the mantra path makes the fruition, i.e. the four kāyas as such, the essence of the cause and path. *bka' brgyud rin po che la grags pa'i lhan cig skyes sbyor 'di nyid zab mo sngags kyi theg pa dang rjes su mthun pa yin te | sngags kyi theg pa 'bras bu sku bzhi nyid rgyu lam gyi ngo bor byed pa de'i phyir |.* See Bibliography: Karma pa Mi bskyod rdo rje. The "noble ones of this tradition" presumably refers to the holders of the Dagpo Kagyü lineage.

195 Among the mistaken views the Fourth Shamarpa addresses, the first seems to allude to the so-called Chinese Heshang Mahāyāna which in Tibet was correctly or incorrectly accused of neglecting conventional reality by rejecting the importance of accumulating virtue and overcoming non-virtue. The Fourth Shamarpa warns of the extremely negative karmic results that can accrue from such an attitude.

196 Another mistaken view concerns the notion that the perfection of insight alone can bring about the realization of emptiness and that therefore the methods of the other perfections, i.e. giving, ethics, acceptance, perseverance, and meditation, were not required. Thus, according to the Fourth Shamarpa, development on this path is not possible in the absence of these other pāramitās.

197 Here, the Fourth Shamarpa seems to be alluding to the Prāsaṅgika-Mādhyamikas and their frequent statements that they are free of any standpoint. In this regard, the Fourth Shamarpa warns of the danger of conceptually grasping at freedom from proliferation and thereby disguising the uncertainty in one's view, instead of actually being free from proliferations.

198 The text actually reads "sugatagarbha", which is a synonm for buddha nature.

199 Here, the author critizes the view usually maintained in the Jonang tradition by which buddha nature is considered an ultimate, permanent reality in contradistinction to conventional reality considered as nonexistent and fictitious. While the Fourth Shamarpa certainly is in favor of considering buddha nature as being endowed with the qualities of awakening, he rejects notions of taking it to be a truly existing entity. See in this regard, for example, his statement in his commentary on Nāgārjuna's *Explanations on Bodhicitta* (*Bodhicittavivarana*), 669₅₋₉: "You followers of Mind Only [take as] an entity what is called "perfect [nature]" [or] "self-awareness", because you claim [this entity] to be, in view of its existence, the defining characteristic of the ultimate. This is to cling to the extreme of [taking] the nonconceptual [state] to be something possessing

mental fabrications. Where a fabricated concept has appeared, how can there be a realization of the ultimate, [that is,] nonconceptual emptiness, when such a nonconceptual [state] is freedom from mental fabrication, [that is,] emptiness?" (Transl.) Mathes 2009, 9. *sems tsam pa khyed kyis yongs grub dang so so rang gi rig pa zhes brjod pa de nyid dngos po zhes bya ste | yod pas don dam pa'i mtshan nyid du 'dod pas so || de ni rnam par mi rtog pa spros pa dang bcas pa'i mthar 'dzin pa yin la | de 'dra'i rnam rtog med pa spros bral stong pa nyid yin pa'i tshe | gang du spros pa'i rnam rtog snang bar gyur pa der ni don dam pa rnam par mi rtog pa'i stong nyid rtogs pa ga la yod |.* See Bibliography: Zhwa dmar Chos grags ye shes.

200   Here, the Fourth Shamarpa voices his concern regarding a purely intellectual approach by which essencelessness is repeatedly analyzed and where one stagnates in a philosophical negation, a conceptual limitation born of intellectual assumptions and analytical meditation. Emptiness, the absence of an own-being, remains just an object of inferential knowledge. With this approach one will remain in a domain of understanding where one merely remembers the same concepts all over again, limiting oneself to a mere negation, instead of cultivating the path of direct perception of mind's luminous nature free from elaborations.

201   Mahāmudrā is not accessible to a mere or nonaffirming negation, which takes emptiness as an object and is therefore nothing but a conceptual and dualistic construct about emptiness. Rather, Mahāmudrā is accessible only through a nonconceptual direct yogic perception. As Gampopa, for example, puts it in his *Excellent Qualities: Teachings to the Assembly* (*Tshogs chos yon tan phun tshog*) in *Collected Works*, vol. 1, 511$_{3-4}$: "The truth is the actuality that the nature of mind is not nonexistent; connate (*sahaja*) wisdom is the truth. When the mind is realized, the true nature of phenomena (*dharmatā*) is actualized." *bden pa ni sems kyi ngo bo med pa ma yin pa'i don | lhan cig skyes pa'i ye shes bden pa yin | sems rtogs pa'i dus su chos nyid mngon du grub |.* See Bibliography: Sgam po pa.

202   The so-called direct path (Tib. *mngon sum lam*) is an allusion to a particular type of teaching of Gampopa, the path of direct experience. He taught Mahāmudrā as: (1) sūtra teachings by way of conceptual understanding, (2) a path of blessing in the context of tantric practices, and (3) a path of direct experience. More details are to be found in, for example, Shamar Rinpoche's explanations on this in his *Boundless Wisdom*, 2018, pp. 96–101.

203   The instructions are presented in three parts concerning (1) preliminaries, verses 18–22, (2) the actual meditation practice, verses 23–34, and (3) the so-called subsequent attainment, i.e. the way in which by virtue of formal meditation, the practice is sustained in the phases outside of formal meditation, verse 35.

204   In Buddhist treatises one often finds the term "four conditions". Depending on the context, for example if explained in the framework of the teachings on dependent arising or for example in the context of Yogācāra views, they are interpreted in slightly different ways. In *The Levels of Engaging in Practice* (*Yogācārabhūmi*), a Yogācāra treatise attributed to Asaṅga, the first, i.e. the so-called causal condition (Sanskrit: *hetupratyaya*), is explained as that which is necessary so that something can arise at all. The second, i.e. the main condition (Sanskrit: *adhipatipratyaya*), as well as the fourth, i.e. the object condition (Sanskrit: *ālambanapratyaya*), as that which contributes to this arising in an essential way. The fourth, i.e. the immediate condition (Sanskrit: *samananatarapratyaya*), means that the present moment of mind is preceded by another moment which shapes the present moment of mind. In the verses to follow, the author uses this structure, to emphasize that (1) the causal condition is engaging in virtue and avoiding non-virtue (verse 18); the (2) main condition is to rely on an authentic teacher (verse 19); the (3) object condition is to develop certainty in the right view (verses 20-21); and (4) the immediate condition is to always be free from expectations and fears, also in formal meditation (verse 22).

205   The term "remedies" indicates a synergy of four powers, (1) the power of regretting negative deeds, (2) the power of the resolution to not repeat them, (3) the power of a support which is to recollect the Three Jewels, and (4) the power of an antidote such as absorbing oneself in the Buddha Dharma or meditating.

206   "Permanence" signifies the philosophical view of a permanent existence. "Extinction" signifies the conviction that at the time of death everything comes to an end and that therefore actions performed in this life do not have any longterm effects.

207   In these two lines, the Fourth Shamarpa refers to the view of the Buddhist Vaibhāṣikas, where it is maintained that while phenomena as a whole are impermanent and fleeting, their indivisible particles of matter truly exist and that the respective sense-consciousness is in direct contact with its respective sense-object. See also note 102.

208   This line refers to the Sautrāntika and Yogācāra tenets where self-awareness and self-clarity play an important role.

209   Here, the author is probably referring to views within the Yogācāra school of thought. The view of inner representations is, as mentioned earlier, maintained by both the Sautrāntikas and the Yogācāras as well as partly in the Madhyamaka system. While the Sautrāntikas maintain that there are, in fact, external objects which are grasped by consciousness through their reflections or representations, the Yogācāra system denies an external existence of objects. Yet, in terms of perception, they both consider inner representations as that of which the process consists. Moreover, there are further subschools that respectively speak of real or false representations. While those who propound real representations assert that these representations are really present in consciousness in that they are the mind, those who propound false representations maintain that these inner representations are nothing but the workings of delusion. See for more details and the Sanskrit terms notes 88 and 102.

210   Here, the Fourth Shamarpa refers to different views found within the Madhyamaka system. For details see note 88.

211   The Fourth Shamarpa lists two weaknesses in meditative absorption, i.e. excitement (*rgod pa*) and drowsiness (*bying ba*). Other weaknesses are desire, anger, pride, doubts, etc. Moreover, the Second Shamarpa, for example in his text *Stages of a Meditation Practice of Unity*, speaks of six types of weaknesses for meditative absorption that are to be counteracted by eight particular types of mental formations: (1) laziness is to be counteracted by the four remedies of confidence, aspiration, making an effort, and pliancy; (2) losing one's focus is to be counteracted by the remedy of mindfulness; (3) drowsiness and (4) agitation are to be counteracted by the remedy of clear knowing; and (5) lack of effort and (6) over-exertion are to be counteracted by the two remedies of intention and equanimity. See also the translation of this text in part 6 of this book.

212   The connate pertains to mind being the unity of emptiness and clarity, the dharmakāya's luminosity. This realization reveals itself to a meditator who is able to abide in mind's true nature on the basis of understanding that there is nothing to abide in, no ground that would establish any outer or inner phenomenon, and thereby refrains from any superimposition.

213   These six, literally translated "accumulations", pertain to seeing, hearing, smelling, tasting, feeling, and thinking, i.e. the six senses. They operate through the complex interaction of the various factors involved, that is, the six sense faculties, the six sense consciousnesses, and the six respective sense objects.

214   The "clearing of contamination of water" points to that muddy water will become clear by itself provided that the conditions which stirred up the mud come to an end. Likewise, the mind which is usually stirred up by thoughts, emotions, and ideas regarding meditation, its processes and the desired effects etc. will become calm and clear by itself provided a meditator lets go of these agitating conditions.

215   This might either indicate a vision that the author had of Mañjuśrī or he might be referring to either a sūtra of the Bodhisattva Mañjuśrī or to the so-called legendary Dharmarāja Mañjuśrīkīrti who plays an important role in the context of the Kālacakra-Tradition. As there is no commentary by the author himself, one can only guess what he might have meant. If the reference is to Mañjuśrīkirti, it could relate to the latter's commentary on the *King of Samādhi Sūtra* (*Samādhirājasūtra*), the *Samādhirājanāma-Mahāyānasūtraṭīkākīrtimālā*, Tib. translation: Kangyur D 4010, Kangyur Q 5511, because the *Samādhirājasūtra* is considered a most important source for Dagpo Mahāmudrā as attested by Gampopa himself. See also Bibliography: *Samādhirājasūtra*.

216   See also the statement by Sahajavajra in his *Commentary on the Ten Verses on Suchness* (*Tattvadaśakaṭīkā*) with the example of the vase: Tib. translation: Tengyur D 2254, 190b$_{1-2}$: "Here, 'mental nonengagement' is not like closing one's eyes and then not seeing anything at all like

for example a vase or a woolen cloth. Mental nonengagement rather is [the realization of] the absence of reference of phenomena [which is attained] by virtue of precise inquiry or the key instructions of a teacher." *'dir mig btsums pa ltar bum pa dang snam bu la sogs pa ci yang mi mthong ba ni yid la byed pa ni med do || yang ni rnam par dpyad pa'am bla ma'i man ngag gis dngos po mi dmigs pa nyid ni yid la mi byed pa'o |.* In verse 35, the author refers directly to Maitrīpa and Sahajavajra. See Bibliography: *Tattvadaśakaṭīkā.* Regarding the term mental nonengagement see also note 84.

217   With this line, the Fourth Shamarpa alludes to a view ascribed to a Chinese master referred to as Heshang. He is said to have argued that any type of concept, good or bad, should be abandoned. He is usually seen as the opponent of the Indian Buddhist master Kamalaśīla during the legendary debate at Samye with discussions on view and meditation. Kamalaśīla with his gradual approach is said to have been the winner.

218   Regarding the term "mental nonengagement", i.e. *amanasikāra*, see note 84.

219   In: Maitrīpa's *Ten Verses on Thatness* (*Tattvadaśaka*). Tib. translation. Tengyur D 2236 and Sahajavajra's *Commentary on the Ten Verses on Thatness* (*Tattvadaśakaṭīkā*). Tib. translation. Tengyur D 2254.

220   The "subsequent attainment" pertain to the practice in periods outside of formal meditation sessions.

221   Indicating that one is not perturbed or disturbed by any negative emotion and not threatened by anything.

222   According to the 14th Shamarpa Mipham Chökyi Lodrö (verbal communication), the Mahāmudrā path can be, but does not have to be, supplemented with tantric practices to accelerate progress. If they are practiced, the focus would be on tummo (Tib. *gtum mo*) or powerfulness (often translated as heat-yoga) in its different stages. Practitioners can also proceed on their path without engaging in these tantric practices, carrying on with a particular type of vipaśyanā meditation. For details on this approach, see Shamar Rinpoche's book *Boundless Wisdom: A Mahāmudrā Practice Manual*, 2018.

223   Secret mantra [path]—Sanskrit: *guhyamantra*; Tib. transliteration: *gsang sngags lam*; Tib. phonetics: *sang ngag lam*. A synonym for the Buddhist tantras or the Vajrayāna.

224   With internally directed awareness in the sense of direct non-conceptual perception, the all-ground, i.e. the mind, is seen directly. Because of this, it is through the capacity of inferential knowledge that the practitioner can distinguish between the obscured all-ground, i.e. consciousness or saṃsāra, and the nonobscured all-ground, which is wisdom or nirvāṇa.

225   The author may be alluding to the so-called *Mahāmudrā Prayer* by the Third Karmapa, Rangjung Dorje in his *Collected Works*, vol. 11, *Nges don phyag rgya chen po'i smon lam*, verse 13: "When this is not realized, one wanders in the ocean of saṃsāra. When this is realized, buddhahood is nothing else. Any 'it is this', 'it is not this' are gone. May [I] become aware of the deep meaning of the all-ground, the true nature of reality!" *'di nyid ma rtogs 'khor ba'i rgya mtshor 'khor || 'di nyid rtogs na sangs rgyas gzhan na med || thams cad 'di yin 'di min gang yang med || chos nyid kun gzhi'i mtshang ni rig par shog ||.* See Bibliography: Karma pa Rang byung rdo rje.

226   The Third Karmapa, Rangjung Dorje, quotes in his auto-commentary on his *Profound Inner Meaning* (Tib. *Zab mo nang don gyi rnam bshad snying por gsal bar byed pa'i nyin byed*) the *Garland of Jewels* (*Ratnavāli*) by Nāgārjuna saying "The *Ratnavāli* says: '(...) even if doubts arise regarding [these teachings], samsaric existence will be torn to shreds'." *rin chen phreng ba las | (...) 'di la the tshom skyes pas kyang || srid pa hrul por byed par 'gyur || zhes so |.* See Bibliography: Karma pa Rang byung rdo rje. The teachings referred to are those on emptiness and mind's true nature being naturally luminous.

227   That is, a tantric consort.

228   Indrabhūti is considered as a highly accomplished tantric Indian master and as one of the 84 mahāsiddhas.

229   Commenting on exactly this issue and also referring to Indrabhūti as a source, the Eighth Karmapa, Mikyö Dorje, explains in one of his commentaries on Jigten Sumgön's *Single Intent* (*Dgongs*

gcig gi gsung bzhi bcu pa'i 'grel pa), 227$_{3-5}$: "It is said that even though something like a kar-mamudrā that triggers the becoming manifest of great bliss that exists in one's mind-stream is not entirely forbidden, the sensation of the [sexual] organs that are karmic results are the all-pervading suffering [of conditioned existence] and therefore not the great bliss of nirvāṇa." *bde chen rgyud la yod pa mngon du 'dren ched kyi las rgya lta bu gtan bkag pa min kyang rnam smin gyi dbang po'i tshor bde ni khyab pa 'du byed kyi sdug bsngal yin pas myang 'das kyi bde chen ma yin no zhes |.* In the same text, 227$_5$, he continues to quote Indrabhūti as follows: "As for the state-ment of unfortunate people who say 'the very bliss that occurs through the two [sexual] organs is precisely that [great bliss of enlightenment]'—the supreme victor did not say that this is the great bliss." *indra bhu ti | dbang po gnyis skyes bde de nyid || de nyid yin zhes skye ngan smra'i || de ni bde ba che yin zhes || rgyal ba mchog gis ma gsungs so ||.* See Bibliography: Karma pa Mi bskyod rdo rje.

230 The term "present-day Mahāmudrā" is an allusion to the term used among others by Sakya Paṇḍita to designate the Dagpo Mahāmudrā-Tradition shaped by Gampopa. note 230.

231 Here, the author alludes to Sakya Paṇḍita's *A Clear Differentiation of the Three Codes* (*Sdom gsum rab dbye*), transl. by Rhoton 2002. One of the criticisms of Dagpo Mahāmudrā was that it is a mere approximation to a Chinese meditative tradition which was said merely to suppress men-tal activity. See verse III.175: "(…) The present-day Great Seal is virtually [the same as] the Chinese religious system." (Transl.) Rhoton 2002, 119. (…) *da lta'i phyag rgya chen po ni || phal cher rgya nag chos lugs yin ||.* See Rhoton 2002, 304 (Tib.). See Bibliography: Sakya Paṇḍita and Rhoton.

232 *Madhyamakopadeśa.* An English translation of this text by Karl Brunnhölzl is contained in *Straight from the Heart. Buddhist Pith Instructions,* 2007, pp. 90–91.

233 Saraha is considered as one of the great Indian Mahāsiddhas and as an essential source for the teachings of the Dagpo Mahāmudrā tradition. Yet, there is no certainty about Saraha's dates. Modern historians place him around the 9th century CE, an estimate largely based on dating the historical appearance of some of the texts on which he commented. Traditional Tibetan sources place him in a range of several hundred years, anywhere from two generations after the life of the Buddha (as a disciple of the Buddha's son Rāhula) to the second century (as Nāgār-juna's guru). The latter, i.e. Saraha as the teacher of Nāgārjuna, is the usual traditional view in the Kagyu school.

234 Quotation from the *Madhyamakopadeśa.* Tib. translation: Tengyur D 3929, vol. 110, 96a$_2$. See Bibliography: *Madhyamakopadeśa.*

235 "Mind-Only" pertains to the philosophical Mahāyāna-view of the Cittamātra or Yogācāra tradi-tion, where it is maintained that all outer and innere phenomena are nothing but mind and that the mind as such truly exists.

236 i.e. the *Kālacakratantra.*

237 i.e. the *Prajñāpāramitāsūtras.*

238 *Cittavajrastava* by Nāgārjuna. Tib. translation: Tengyur D 1121, vol. *ka,* 69b$_5$–70a$_2$. This text consists of just a few lines and belongs to the so-called *Collection of Praises* (*Stotragana; Bstod tshogs*). In contrast to Nāgārjuna's *Collection of Reasonings* (*Yuktigana; Rigs tshogs*), where he focuses on emptiness or the lack of a self-nature, in his *Collection of Praises* he mainly describes mind's wisdom and its innate qualities. See Bibliography: *Cittavajrastava.*

239 Here, the Fourth Shamarpa again alludes to Sakya Paṇḍita's *A Clear Differentiation of the Three Codes,* verse III.162: "However excellent that meditation may be, it is no more than a Madhya-maka meditation. The latter meditation, while very good in itself, is nevertheless extremely difficult to accomplish." (Transl.) Rhoton 2002, 117. *gal te de ni bsgom legs kyang || dbu ma'i bsgom las lhag pa med || dbu ma'i bsgom de bzang mod kyi || 'on kyang 'grub pa shin tu dka' ||.* See Rhoton 2002, 303 (Tib.).

240 Thus, the difference between these two Madhyamaka approaches will become clear by virtue of a direct yogic perception that is accessible only through a direct experience of mind's natural luminosity and not through inferential, conceptual knowledge.

241 Here, the Fourth Shamarpa again alludes to Sakya Paṇḍita's *A Clear Differentiation of the Three Codes,* verse III.176–177: "The Great Seal that Nāro and Maitrīpa espoused is held to consist precisely of the seals of Action, Dharma, and Pledge, and of the Great Seal as expounded in tantras of the Mantra system." (Transl.) Rhoton 2002: 119. *na ro dang ni me tri ba'i || phyag rgya chen po gang yin pa (176) de ni las dang chos dang ni || dam tshig dang ni phyag rgya che || gsang sngags rgyud nas ji skad du || gsungs pa de nyid khong bzhed do ||.* See Rhoton 2002, 304 (Tib.).
The issue here concerns the emphasis on and the sequence of the four mudrās, i.e. the Action, Dharma, Pledge, and Mahāmudrā, which are considered to be essential aspects of the highest tantras. The view that it is possible to practice and realize Mahāmudrā without the sequence of the other mudrās, or even alone without tantric methods, indirectly means that Mahāmudrā contains in itself all mudrās and therefore everything by means of which it is attained. For more details refer to Mathes 2016, "bKa' brgyud *Mahāmudrā:* 'Chinese *rDzogs chen'* or the Teachings of the Siddhas?". See Bibliography: Mathes.

242 Even though the Fourth Shamarpa does not specify what he means exactly, one can assume that he refers to the requirement of proper mental nonengagement, i.e. of Dagpo Mahāmudrā, as the innermost core of the practice of Mahāmudrā also when applying tantric methods throughout the various steps of mudrās. In this regard, the Eighth Karmapa, Mikyö Dorje, states in his commentary on the *Introduction to the Middle Path* (*Dwags brgyud grub pa'i shing rta*), 12$_{2-3}$: "It is instructed that, even if great experiences of the tantric wisdom of the inseparability of bliss and emptiness has arisen, still, as a remedy to clear out the hidden and destructive tendencies of elaborations, this very view and meditation [of mental nonengagement] are praised as fully requisite. This is because through this, just like the self-sufficient white medicine, all obscurations are totally dispelled." *gsang sngags kyi bde stong dbyer med kyi ye shes sogs kyi nyams myong chos bzang bzang po skyes pa la'ang da dung spros pa'i bag nyal dang gnas ngan len yod pa sel byed kyi gnyen por lta sgom 'di nyid cher dgos par bsngags te | 'di dper na sman dkar po chig thub dang 'dra bar sgrib pa thams cad rmeg nas bsal bar byed pa'i phyir | zhes gdams pa yin no |.* See Bibliography: Karma pa Mi bskyod rdo rje.

243 These verses are a quote from Sakya Paṇḍita's *A Clear Differentiation of the Three Codes,* verse III.161.

244 The four types of stable meditative concentrations (Sanskrit: *dhyāna;* Tib. transliteration: *bsam gtan;* Tib. phonetics: *samten)* achieved as a result of śamatha meditation; they are important as a basis for vipaśyanā practice. However, it is said that when these states of meditative concentrations are accomplished in this life, but not associated with vipaśyanā, the karmic effect will be rebirth in the realm of form or formlessness. For more information see for example Shamar Rinpoche's *Boundless Wisdom,* pp. 225–226.

245 "The rabbit and the splash" refers to a Jātaka story, i.e. a narration of the Buddha concerning his previous lives as a bodhisattva. In this case, the Buddha described that he was living as a lion in a forest. The short version of the story is as follows: A rabbit once slept next to a pond. When a fruit from a nearby tree fell into the pond, the splash of the water woke the rabbit and terrified him. To him, things were crashing down. He jumped up and started to run. When he passed a fox, the latter asked him why he was running away, to which the rabbit said he should run too, as things are crashing down. The fox started running. They passed other animals such as a monkey, a wild pig, a buffalo, an elephant etc., and all of them started running. Finally, an old lion saw them. Hearing the answer, that things are crashing down, he asked where the noise had come from. The other animals did not have an answer. Just the rabbit said that he heard it. The lion then suggested that they investigate the matter, whereupon the animals returned to the pond. The moment they reached the pond, another fruit fell into the water, making the splashing noise, and the lion advised the other animals not to be afraid and first to investigate what was going on. With this intervention, the lion is said to have rescued all the other animals' lifes because in their blindfold escape they were about to rush into the ocean and to drown. See, for example, the dictionary *Smon lam tshig mdzod chen mo,* entry on *ri bong cal* and *The Jataka,* Vol. III, tr. by H.T. Francis and R.A. Nei, [1897], at sacred-texts.com, No. 322. Daddabha-Jataka: https://www.sacred-texts.com/bud/j3/j3023.htm. Download on June 1, 2020.

246 The name of the Fourth Shamarpa. Tib. phonetics: Chos kyi grags pa ye shes dpal bzang po.

247 In: *The Collected Works of Mkha' spyod dbang po*, vol. 4, 56$_2$–59$_1$. See Bibliography: *Zhwa dmar pa mkha' spyod dbang po.*

248 Presumably the author is referring to his teacher, the Fourth Karmapa, Rölpe Dorje (1340–1383).

249 Precise explanations regarding these eighteen freedoms and endowments are found in, for example Kongtrul Lodrö Thaye's explanations on the preliminaries, i.e. *The Torch of Certainty*, in Gampopa's *The Precious Ornament of Liberation* or in Patrul Rinpoche's *The Words of My Perfect Teacher*. See Bibliography: Kongtrul, Gampopa, and Patrul Rinpoche.

250 Shamar Khachö Wangpo addresses his disciple literally with "son". In the translation we decided to use the neutral "child", thereby not limiting the advice to male students only.

251 The power of purification consists of the power of support, of regret, of resolve, and of the antidote. For details see, for example, Kongtrul Lodrö Thaye's *The Torch of Certainty* or in Patrul Rinpoche's *The Words of My Perfect Teacher.*

252 Here, the Second Shamarpa alludes to a method of Mahāmudrā practice as taught by the Indian Mahāsiddha Saraha. The First Karma Trinle explains these steps in detail in his commentary on Saraha's *Dohās*. The sequence he describes is: (1) mindfulness (Sanskrit: *smṛti*; Tib.: *dran pa*) in the sense that by virtue of the instructions, practitioners understand that any perception or appearance is nothing other but a manifestation of the mind; here, the term *smṛti* is used in a very general sense for anything that mind experiences and therefore not necessarily, but possibly in the context of a state of mind that is focused and self-aware. The next step is (2) non-conceptual mindfulness (Sanskrit: *asmṛti*; Tib.: *dran med*), in the sense of the insight that the perceiving mind is empty. This is followed by (3) the insight into non-arising in the sense of the realization that mind's nature is non-arisen, and finally (4) by transcending the intellect in the sense of an effortless, continuous, direct or nondual realization of ultimate reality. The last is identical to the awakened state of a buddha.

253 The Tibetan reads *rdo rus thug*. Literally this translates as "stone meets bone" and implies certainty, firmness, and precision as well as perseverance. The image implied is that a bone can only be crushed if one hits it with a weighty stone at the right angle and with enough strength.

254 The Tibetan reads *sna thag mi la ma shor ba*. Literally this translates as "don't lose the lead rope tied to [your] nose to [other] people."

255 The Tibetan reads *so 'phrang*. Literally, *so* designates the eldest person in a family and *'phrang* the youngest. Therefore, we understood the meaning of this phrase in the sense of "all aspects" or "in each and every respect".

256 Gampopa is also referred to as Candraprabhakumara (Zla 'od gzhon nu) because he is considered the manifestation of the Bodhisattva Candraprabhakumara. This bodhisattva is said to have played a prominent role when the Buddha taught the *King of Meditation Sūtra* (*Samādhirājasūtra*), which, for this reason, is also referred to as the *Moon Lamp Sūtra* (*Candrapradīpasūtra*). Dagpo Mahāmudrā is frequently said to have its source in this sūtra. See Bibliography: *Samādhirājasūtra* and a complete English translation of this Sūtra in the "reading room" of the 84 000 project: https://read.84000.co/translation/toh127.html.

257 In: *The Collected Works of Mkha' spyod dbang po*, vol. 2, 585$_5$–595$_4$. See Bibliography: *Zhwa dmar pa mkha' spyod dbang po*. As the Second Shamarpa specifies in the colophon, this text is a summary of Vimalamitra's *The Meaning of the Gradual Approach in Meditation* (*Kramaprāveśikabhāvanārtha*). Tib. translation: Tengyur D, 3938, 340b7–358a7. For Vimalamitra, see also note 13. The text has also many parallels with Kamalaśīla's *Stages of Meditation* (*Bhāvanākrama*).

258 The ten pāramitās as specified, for example, in the Mahāyāna *Sūtra of the Ten Levels* (*Daśabhūmikasūtra*) are the *pāramitās* or perfections of giving, ethics, acceptance, joyous effort, meditation, insight, method, aspirations, strength, and wisdom. As the teaching is about a bodhisattva's commitment, obviously these are meant here. In the Theravāda context, detailed, for example, in the *Chronicle of the Buddhas* (*Buddhavaṃsa*) another set of ten pāramitās is taught: giving, ethics, renunciation, insight, joyous effort, acceptance, honesty, resolution, loving-kindness, and equanimity.

259 *Saṃdhinirmocanasūtra*. Tib. translation: Kangyur H 109, vol. 51, 53b$_6$–54a$_1$. See Bibliography: *Saṃdhinirmocanasūtra.*

260 *Saṃdhinirmocanasūtra*. Tib. translation: Kangyur H 109, vol. 51, 54a$_{3-5}$.

261 In Vimalamitra's *The Meaning of the Gradual Approach in Meditation* (*Kramaprāveśikabhāvanārtha*; *Rim gyis 'jug pa'i sgom don*) the example with the "echo" is not provided. Instead a slightly more detailed explanation to this last point regarding an incomplete cause is given. The emphasis is that one cause alone is not sufficient. Rather, for the desired effect to manifest a couple of causes must be appropriately assembled.

262 *Dharmasaṃgīti*. Tib. translation: Kangyur D 238, vol. 65, 1b$_1$–99b$_7$. Quotation not identified. It also occurs, however, in Vimalamitra's *The Meaning of the Gradual Approach in Meditation* (*Kramaprāveśikabhāvanārtha*). Tib. translation Tengyur D 3938, vol. 110, 341a$_4$. See Bibliography: *Dharmasaṃgīti*.

263 Existential unease (Sanskrit: *dauṣṭulya*; Tib. transliteration: *gnas ngan len;* Tib. phontecis: *né ngen len*) is translated among others also as "hindrances", "badness", "unwieldiness" (*karmaṇyatā*), "heaviness" (*gurutva*), "stiffness" (*middhakṛtam āśrayajāḍyam*), "incapacitation" (*akṣamatā*), and "misery" (*dauṣṭulya-duḥkha*). The idea here is that unease or dissatisfaction permeates human existence to such an extent that it is felt most fundamentally as a tension, an affliction, suffering, unease, and/or powerlessness. In the context of spiritual practice, it might hinder, physically and mentally, the yogis' abilities to attain their goal. In the *Mahāvyutpatti (Sgra sbyor bam po gnyis)*, the Tibetan rendering of *dauṣṭulya* is *gnas ngan len* (lit. "identifying with (*len*) a situation (*gnas*) of baseness/badness (*ngan*)." See *Mahāvyutpatti*, s.v. *dauṣṭhulya: dauṣṭhulya zhes bya ba du ni smad pa'am ngan pa | ṣṭhā gatinivṛttau zhes bya ste gnas pa la bya | la ni ādāna ste len ba'am 'dzin pa'o || gcig tu na duṣṭu ni nyes pa 'am skyon gyi ming la ni gong du bshad pa dang 'dra ste | spyir na ltung ba dang sgrib pa'i ming ste gnas ngan len du btags |*.

264 The "bondage of characteristics" pertains to dualistic, conceptual perception and the limitations caused thereby.

265 *Saṃdhinirmocanasūtra*. Tib. translation: Kangyur H 109, vol. 51, 14b$_{2-3}$.

266 *Samādhirājasūtra*, IX.43. *Udraka* (Tib. transliteration: *lhag spyod*; Tib. phonetics: *lhag chö*), was a well-known ascetic and one of Siddhartha Gautama's first teachers. Yet, Siddhartha Gautama was nicht satisfied with the answers he received from Udraka and therefore decided to continue his spiritual path on his own. See Bibliography: *Samādhirājasūtra* and a complete English translation of this Sūtra in the "reading room" of the 84 000 project: https://read.84000.co/translation/toh127.html.

267 Literally *tathāgatagotra* which is another term for buddha nature.

268 Quotation not identified. *Mahāparinirvāṇasūtra*. Tib. translation: Kangyur D 119, vol. 52–53, 1b–343a; 1b–339a. See Bibliography: *Mahāparinirvāṇasūtra.* It also occurs, however, in *The Meaning of the Gradual Approach in Meditation* (*Kramaprāveśikabhāvanārtha*), Tib. translation: Tengyur D 3938, vol. 110, 342b$_{1-2}$ attributed to Vimalamitra.

269 In the following section, a number of interlinear notes are inserted into the original text, maybe by the author himself. The English translation puts these notes in braces: {...}.

270 This verse is also quoted in Kamalaśīla's *The Stages of Meditation* (*Bhāvanākrama*). Tib. translation: Tengyur D 3916, vol. 110, 45a$_7$. See Bibliography: *Bhāvanākrama.*

271 The three spheres pertain to the concept and dualistic distinction of subject, object, and interaction.

272 *Ratnakūṭasūtra*, which consists of a series of sūtras. This quotation comes from one of them, the *Sūtra of the Discourse of Kāśyapa (Kāśyapaparivartasūtra)*. Tib. translation: Kangyur H, vol. 40, 252b$_1$. See Bibliography: *Kāśyapaparivartasūtra.*

273 Touching the ground with the hands, the knees, and the forehead.

274 This alludes to the so-called sevenfold practice: (1) homage and prostration, (2) offerings, (3) confessing negative deeds, (4) rejoicing in virtue, (5) requesting dharma teachings, (6) requesting that buddhas and bodhisattvas will not pass into a one-sided nirvāṇa, and (7) dedicating the merit.

275 "Looking in the direction of the tip of the nose" means that the gaze should be lowered and directed parallel to the bridge of the nose.

276   Discernment of reality—Sanskrit: *bhūtapratyavekṣā*; Tib. transliteration: *yang dag par so sor rtog pa*; Tib. phonetics: *yang dag par sosor tog pa.*

277   Calm abiding here means that no analytical analysis is involved. While practitioners have the overall understanding that any phenomenon is insubstantial and thereby illusion-like, the mind is focused one-pointedly, without any conceptual engagement, on the support of attention.

278   Vimalamitra defines the "goal" as the point at which all obscurations are completely relinquished.

279   *Ratnameghasūtra.* Tib. translation: Kangyur D 231, vol. 64, 1b$_1$–112b$_7$. See Bibliography: *Ratnameghasūtra.* The quotation could not be identified in this sūtra; however, Vimalamitra provides a detailed presentation of this topic in his commentary on the *Sūtra of the Perfection of Wisdom in 700 Stanzas* (*Saptaśatikāprajñāpāramitāṭīkā*). Tib. translation: Tengyur D 3814, vol. 95. See Bibliography: *Saptaśatikāprajñāpāramitāṭīkā.*

280   *Samādhirājasūtra*, IV.22. See Bibliography: *Samādhirājasūtra.* See also a complete translation of this sūtra in the "reading room" of the 84 000 project: https://read.84000.co/translation/toh127.html

281   Vimalamitra explains in his *The Meaning of the Gradual Approach in Meditation* (*Kramaprāveśikabhāvanārtha*). Tib. translation: Tengyur D, 3938, 346b$_{3-5}$: "Then one should practice deep insight: Just like the mental image of the tathāgata neither comes nor goes nor abides and is thus inherently empty and is free of "I" and "mine", so all phenomena are inherently empty, like illusory images that neither come nor go. Thus, they are without any essence such as existence. Analyzing in this way, one meditates on suchness with a mind that is focused, without conceptualizing and verbalizing. One abides in that as long as one wishes." *de nas lhag mthong bsgom par bya ste | ji ltar de bzhin gshegs pa'i sku'i gzugs brnyan 'di gang nas kyang ma gshegs gang du yang mi bzhud bzhugs pa bzhin du yang ngo bo nyid kyis stong la | bdag dang bdag gi dang bral ba de bzhin du | chos thams cad ngo bo nyid kyis stong zhing 'ong ba dang 'gro ba dang bral ba gzugs brnyan lta bu ste | yod pa la sogs pa'i ngo bo dang bral ba'o zhes dpyad nas rnam par rtog pa med cing brjod pa med pa dang gcig tu 'gyur ba'i yid kyis de kho na bsgom zhing ji srid 'dod par 'dug par bya'o ||.* See Bibliography: *Kramaprāveśikabhāvanārtha.*

282   Quotation from Vimalamitra's *The Meaning of the Gradual Approach in Meditation* (*Kramaprāveśikabhāvanārtha*). Tib. translation: Tengyur D, 3938, 346b$_{5-6}$.

283   In Vimalamitra's *The Meaning of the Gradual Approach in Meditation* (*Kramaprāveśikabhāvanārtha*). Tib. translation: Tengyur D, 3938, 346b$_6$, this passage reads "(…) one should call to one's mind the appearance of the Buddha which makes one utterly joyful." (…) *mchog tu dga' ba'i ngnos po sangs rgyas kyi sku gzugs ci 'dra ba yid la bya'o |.*

284   This is an allusion to the so-called four seals of Buddhism: Everything conditioned is impermanent. Everything contaminated [by self-clinging, karma and defilements] is suffering. All things are empty and selfless. Nirvāṇa is peace. These four seals are often described in Mahāyāna scriptures and resemble the so-called three marks of samsaric existence used in Theravāda Buddhism: impermanence, suffering, and selflessness.

285   This last sentence is a quotation from Vimalamitra's *The Meaning of the Gradual Approach in Meditation* (*Kramaprāveśikabhāvanārtha*). Tib. translation: Tengyur D, 3938, 347a$_2$.
       Mindfulness—Sanskrit: *smṛti,* Tib. phonetics: *drenpa*; Tib. transliteration: *dran pa.* Mindfulness is the standard English translation for the Sanskrit *smṛti*, the Pāli *sati*, and the Tibetan *dran pa.* The noun *smṛti* derives from the Sanskrit root *smṛ.* In the context of meditation, the most well-known use of *smṛti* occurs in connection with the so-called "four-fold presence of mindfulness" or the "four-fold establishment of mindfulness" (Sanskrit: *smṛtyupasthāna*; Pāli: *satipaṭṭāna*; Tib.: *dran pa nye bar gzhags pa*) regarding the body, sensations, mind, and dharmas. In various Pāli commentaries they are often also referred to as the four foundations of mindfulness. The basic meaning of the presence of mindfulness is that one remembers to maintain one's focus without being distracted, i.e. one is aware of the present moment. Thus, mindfulness counteracts distraction or absent-mindedness; it is simply about being present and not letting the mind stray into thoughts or drowsiness.
       In the context of meditation, mindfulness requires the support of *clear knowing*—Sanskrit:

saṃprajanya; Pāli: *sampajañña*; Tib. phonetics: *shéshin*; Tib. transliteration: *shes bzhin*. So far, no standard English translation has been established for this term. What one finds are translations such as vigilance, alertness, awareness, clear comprehension, or introspection. Literally, the Sanskrit *prajanya* (the present participle of the verb *to know*) or the corresponding Pāli *pajañña* means "knowing". It is preceded by the prefix *sam* which in this case stands for an intensified and accurate form of knowing and thus for a clear knowing. In Tibetan, *samprajanya* or *sampajañña* was rendered as *shes bzhin*. *Shes* translates the verb "to know"; *bzhin* points to this knowing as a continuous process. Clear knowing is thus the ongoing full awareness of what is taking place in one's mind. This means, for example, that while the mind abides with its focus, one knows that it does so. As the mind wanders, one knows that it does so, etc. Clear knowing therefore provides the ground for counteracting any conditioned or automatic reactivity. It enables the meditator to handle whatever occurs in a wholesome way, neither suppressing impulses nor merely reacting to them or being carried away by them.

In modern, partly also secular, presentations of Buddhist meditation, mindfulness alone is often used as the umbrella term for both mindfulness and clear knowing. In fact, in the context of Dagpo Mahāmudrā as well, the term mindfulness is frequently used to sum up both mindfulness and clear knowing. In Dagpo Tashi Namgyal's famous *Moon Beams of Mahāmudrā*, for example, this is stated and explained explicitly. See Dagpo Tashi Namgyal (tr.) Callahan 2019, p. 202–203. See Bibliography: Dagpo Tashi Namgyal.

286   The classical Buddhist template to describe an individual's perception of his or herself, his or her world and interaction with the world. The template is used to explore whether an individual self in the sense of an unchanging and unique identity can be identified. The five skandhas, or more literally the "heaps", i.e. the psycho-physical constituents, are: form, sensation, distinction, compositional factors, and consciousness. The eighteen dhātus (Tib. transliteration: *khams*; Tib. phonetics: *kham*), i. e. „elements", are: the six sense-consciousnesses, i.e. seeing, hearing, smelling, tasting, touching, and thinking; the six sense faculties, i.e. the eyes, the ears, the nose, the tongue, the body, and the mind; and the six sense-objects, i.e. visual form, sound, odor, taste, touch, and mental phenomena. The twelve āyatanas (Tib. transliteration: *skye mched*; Tib. phonetics: *kyeche*), i. e. "sense fields", are the six consciousnesses along with their particular faculty and the six sense-objects.

287   *Laṅkāvatārasūtra*. Tib. translation: Kangyur H 110, vol. 51, 283b$_5$. See Bibliography: *Laṅkāvatārasūtra.*

288   *Daśabhūmikasūtra*. Contained in the *Flower Garland Sūtra (Avataṃsakasūtra)*. Tib. translation: Kangyur D 44. See Bibliography: *Avataṃsakasūtra.*

289   *Laṅkāvatārasūtra*. Vaidya-Sanskrit edition; Tib. translation: Kangyur H 110, vol. 51, 298$_{15}$–299$_1$ (X.256–257): *cittamātraṃ samāruhya bāhyam arthaṃ na kalpayet | tathatālambane sthitvā cittamātram atikramet || cittamātram atikramya nirābhāsam atikramet | nirābhāsasthito yogī mahāyānaṃ sa^a paśyati ||.* ^{a}The Nanjio-Sanskrit edition reads the verse LAS X.257.4 with *na* instead of the *sa*: "(…) A practitioner who is established in a state without appearances does not see the Mahāyāna." Kongtrul Lodrö Thaye, for example, uses this latter reading in his *Instructions on Other-Emptiness (Gzhan stong lta khrid)*, see Draszczyk 2015, 262 and note 803. See Bibliography: *Laṅkāvatārasūtra.*

290   *Ratnameghasūtra*, Kangyur H 232, vol. 64, 145b$_7$–146a$_3$. See Bibliography: *Ratnameghasūtra.*

291   The quotation could not be identified in this sūtra, but it also occurs in Vimalamitra's *The Meaning of the Gradual Approach in Meditation (Kramaprāveśikabhāvanārtha)*. Tib. translation: Tengyur D, 3938, 348b$_4$.

292   *Lalitavistarasūtra*. A hagiography of the Buddha going back to the 2nd century. Tib. translation: Kangyur D 95, vol. 46, 1b–216b. See Bibliography: *Lalitavistarasūtra*. The quotation could not be identified in this sūtra; however, it also appears in Vimalamitra's *Commentary on the Perfection of Wisdom Heart Sūtra (Prajñāpāramitāhṛdayaṭīkā)*. Tib. translation: Tengyur D, D 3818, vol. 95, 273a$_{3-4}$. See Bibliography: *Prajñāpāramitāhṛdayaṭīkā.*

293   *Ratnolkādhāraṇisūtra*. Tib translation: Kangyur D 145, 34a$_4$–82a$_3$. See Bibliography: *Ratnolkādhāraṇisūtra*. The quotation could not be identified in this sūtra; however, it also appears in Vimalamitra's *Commentary on the Perfection of Wisdom Heart Sūtra (Prajñāpāramitāhṛ-*

dayaṭīkā). Tib. translation: Tengyur D 3818, vol. 95, 273a₃. It is also quoted in his *The Meaning of the Gradual Approach in Meditation* (*Kramaprāveśikabhāvanārtha*). Tib. translation: Tengyur D, 3938, 348b6.

294   Nāgārjuna's *Sixty Verses of Reasoning* (*Yuktiṣaṣṭikākārikā*). Tib. translation: Tengyur D 3825, vol. 96, 21a₅. See Bibliography: *Yuktiṣaṣṭikākārikā.*

295   There are many similar statements in the various *Prajñāpāramitāsūtras*. In precisely this wording it could be found, however, only in Vimalamitra's *The Meaning of the Gradual Approach in Meditation* (*Kramaprāveśikabhāvanārtha*). Tib. translation: Tengyur D 3938, vol. 110, 349b₁₋₃ and in his extensive *Commentary on the Heart-Sūtra* (*Prajñāpāramitāhṛdayaṭīkā*). Tib. translation: Tengyur D 3818, vol. 95, 274a₂₋₃. In the latter he attributes it to the *Prajñāpāramitāsūtra in 25,000 Stanzas.* See Bibliography: *Prajñāpāramitāhṛdayaṭīkā.*

296   *Avikalpapraveśadhāraṇī.* Tib. translation: Kangyur D 142, 1b–6b. The quotation could not be identified in this sūtra, but appears in Vimalamitra's *The Meaning of the Gradual Approach in Meditation* (*Kramaprāveśikabhāvanārtha*). Tib. translation: Tengyur D 3938, vol. 110, 350b₆₋₇. See Bibliography: *Avikalpapraveśadhāraṇī.*

297   Cultivating compassion should thus become a natural part of one's meditation practice on emptiness. An authentic realization of emptiness is said to be naturally permeated by compassion. A general explanation in this regard is that practitioners who realize the true nature of phenomena truly understand that ordinary sentient beings are not aware of this even though it is always present; that through the force of unawareness, the mind of sentient beings is clouded by defilements which in turn trigger actions that accrue suffering. Becoming aware of this entire situation, one cannot but feel an unbiased compassion for all sentient beings who, in fact, experience unnecessary illusionlike suffering which is, as everything else, merely the effect of the coming together of ever-changing causes and conditions. The 14th Shamarpa used to refer to this kind of compassion which is embedded in wisdom as "non-emotional compassion".

298   *Tathāgataguhyasūtra.* Tib. translation: Kangyur D 47 in *Dkon brtsegs*, vol. 39, ka 100a₁-203a₇. The quotation could not be identified in this sūtra but is contained in Vimalamitra's *The Meaning of the Gradual Approach in Meditation* (*Kramaprāveśikabhāvanārtha*). Tib. translation: Tengyur D 3938, vol. 110, 351b4–351b5. See Bibliography: *Tathāgataguhyasūtra.*

299   The quotation could not be identified in this sūtra but is contained in Vimalamitra's *The Meaning of the Gradual Approach in Meditation* (*Kramaprāveśikabhāvanārtha*). Tib. translation: Tengyur D 3938, vol. 110, 351b6–351b7.

300   Aspirations—Sanskrit: *praṇidhāna*; Tib. transliteration: *smon lam*; Tib. phonetics: *mönlam*, translated either as aspirations, wishing prayer, or paths of aspirations (the latter is a literal rendering from the Tibetan). The most wellknown wishing prayers are those of the Bodhisattva Samantabhadra, which is a short excerpt from the *Flower Ornament Sūtra* (*Avataṃsaka-Sūtra*), one of the longest Mahāyāna Sūtras and also known as Hua-Yen or Kegon Sūtra. With these wishing prayers practitioners direct their aspirations toward the bodhisattva path aiming at accomplishing the state of complete awakening while simultaneously wishing to support countless sentient beings in attaing temporary and ultimate wellbeing.

301   The 14th Zhwa dmar pa, Mi pham chos kyi blo gros, *Rnam rtog chos sku'i dogs sel sgam po'i dgongs rgyan.* Slightly different versions of this text were printed. This is the one approved by Shamar Rinpoche in 2011. See Bibliography: Zhwa dmar Mi pham chos kyi blo gros.

302   In the Lhasa Kangyur H 499, vol. 88, 46a₃₋₅ and in the Derge Kangyur D 21, vol. 34, 145_{b2} the text reads slightly different: *shes rab kyi pha rol tu phyin pa zab mo la brten cing gnas te | sems la sgrib pa med pas skrag pa med de* | (…)

303   Text: *nyi tshe bas stong nyid kyi*, amended to *nyi tshe ba'i stong nyid kyis.*

304   Text: *gi*, amended to *gis.*

305   Text: *rtogs pa*, amended to *rtog pa.*

306   Text: *rtog*, amended to *rtogs.*

307   Text: *cir*, amended to *ci.*

308   Text: *lgong nga*, amended to *sgong nga.*

309 Text: *mthong*, amended to *thongs*.

310 In: *The Collected Works of Chos grags ye shes, Chos grags ye shes gsung 'bum*, vol. 3, 21–24. See Bibliography: Zhwa dmar Chos grags ye shes.

311 Text: *dka'*, amended to *bka'*.

312 Text: *dags*, amended to *dwags*.

313 Text: *gyi*, amended to *gyis*.

314 Text: *rtog*, amended to *rtogs*.

315 Text: *skur*, amended to *sku*.

316 In: *The Collected Works of Chos grags ye shes, Chos grags ye shes gsung 'bum*, vol. 6, 320–324. See Bibliography: Zhwa dmar Chos grags ye shes.

317 Text: *bcu*, amended to *cu*.

318 Text: *dags*, amended to *dwags*.

319 Text: *skye bo*, amended to *skye ba*.

320 Text: *rtogs par*, amended to *rtogs pa*.

321 Text: *nus par*, amended to *nus pa*.

322 Text: *dags*, amended to *dwags*.

323 Text: *wbu*, amended to *spu*.

324 Text: *phy*, amended to *phyag*.

325 Text: *kun gzhir nga*, amended to *kun gzhi rang*.

326 Text: *dags*, amended to *dwags*.

327 Text: *rtog*, amended to *rtogs*.

328 Text: *thos*, amended to *thob*.

329 Text: *brdzod*, amended to *brjod*.

330 In: *The Collected Works of Mkha' spyod dbang po, Zhwa dmar pa Mkha' spyod dbang po'i gsung 'bum*, vol. 4, 56_2–59_1. See Bibliography: Zhwa dmar Mkha' sbyod dbang po.

331 Text: *rgyud*, amended to *brgyud*.

332 Text: *bsgoms*, amended to *bsgom*.

333 Text: *nye bdun*, amended to *gnyen po*.

334 Text: *mthong*, amended to *thong*.

335 Text: *bsgoms*, amended to *sgoms*.

336 Text: *srangs*, amended to *bsrangs*.

337 Text: *bla ma*, amended to *bla mas*.

338 In: *The Collected Works of Mkha' spyod dbang po, Zhwa dmar pa Mkha' spyod dbang po'i gsung 'bum*, vol. 2, 585_5–595_4. See Bibliography: Zhwa dmar Mkha' sbyod dbang po. As the author specifies in the colophon, this text is a summary of Vimalamitra's *Kramaprāveśikabhāvanārtha* (Tib. *Rim gyis 'jug pa'i sgom don*), i.e. *The Meaning of the Gradual Aproach in Meditation*. Tengyur D, 3938, $340b_7$–$358a_7$.

339 Text: *spal*, amended to *stsal*.

340 Text: *kyis*, amended to *kyi*.

341 Text: *rje*, amended to *rjes*.

342 Text: *mche*, amended to *che*.

343 Text: *bdus* amended to *sdud*.

344 Text: *grol* amended to *'grol*.

345 Text: *'jog* amended to *'jig*.

346 {...} interlinear notes added in *dbu med* in the blockprint maybe by the author himself.

347   Text: *btsams*, amended to *btsums*.

348   Text: *rtogs*, amended to *rtog*.

349   Text: *dkar*, amended to *kar*.

350   Text: *de*, amended to *des*.

351   Text: *pa*, amended to *na*.

352   Text: *de*, amended to *so*.

Publishing finished
in July 2021 by Pulsio
Publisher Number: 4013
Legal Deposit: July 2021
Printed in Bulgaria